How Harvard and Yale Beat the Market

WHAT INDIVIDUAL INVESTORS CAN LEARN FROM UNIVERSITY ENDOWMENTS TO HELP THEM PROSPER IN AN UNCERTAIN MARKET

Matthew Tuttle

WILEY

John Wiley & Sons, Inc.

Published by John Wiley & Sons, Inc., Hoboken, New Jersey.
Published simultaneously in Canada.

For general information on our other products and services or for technical support, please contact our Customer Care Department within the United States at (800) 762-2974, outside the United States at (317) 572-3993 or fax (317) 572-4002.

Wiley also publishes its books in a variety of electronic formats. Some content that appears in print may not be available in electronic books. For more information about Wiley products, visit our web site at www.wiley.com.

Library of Congress Cataloging-in-Publication Data:

Tuttle, Matthew, 1968–
   How Harvard and Yale beat the market : what individual investors can learn from university endowments to help them prosper in an uncertain market/ Matthew Tuttle.
      p. cm.
   Includes bibliographical references and index.
   ISBN 978-0-470-40176-7 (cloth)
      1. Investments—United States.   2. Harvard University—Endowments.
3. Yale University—Endowments.   4. Institutional investments—United States.
5. Portfolio management—United States.   I. Title.
   HG4910.T88 2009
   332.6—dc22

                                                                    2008047056

Printed in the United States of America
10 9 8 7 6 5 4 3 2 1

Contents

Acknowledgments

I want to sincerely thank the following people who made enormous contributions to this book:

- My agent, Carole Jelen McClendon, for making this project a reality
- My mother, Cheryl Tuttle, and Adam Bluestein who helped me edit the book
- Sherry Carnahan who helped with graphics
- All of the mutual fund companies that provided me facts and figures, including Ivy Funds, DWS-Scudder, and Riversource

Most importantly I want to thank my daughter Cameron, and my sons, Jared and Braden, for tolerating the late nights and weekends that I spent working on this book.

Introduction

WHY YOU SHOULD INVEST LIKE AN ENDOWMENT

Why should you read this book instead of the millions of other books out there that teach you how to invest? Because this book is different from the other investment books I have seen. It will not teach you how to find the next great stock. It will not teach you how to tell when we are in a bull or bear market. It will not predict that the Dow Jones Industrial Average is going to 50,000, nor will it predict that it is going down to 5,000. What it will do is teach you the strategies that large college endowments have used to beat the market with less risk. You can choose to apply these strategies to your portfolio as a whole or as a part of your portfolio, whatever makes the most sense for your situation.

2008 was a difficult year for investors, college endowments included. As an investor, you can choose to put your head in the sand and your money under a mattress, or you can learn the lessons of 2008 and choose to adopt an investment strategy that gives you the best possible chance of achieving your goals. What happened in 2008 does not wipe out years and years of outperformance by large endowments. If anything, it stresses the need for abandoning buy and hold, traditional asset allocation, and indexing in favor of the investment strategies that have made the large endowments successful for years.

Regardless of what some might say, there is no right answer when it comes to investing. If there were, then there would only be one book and you wouldn't need financial advisors like me. If you are looking for a strategy that will grow your portfolio by 80% per year, then this book is not for you. If you are looking for a way to invest for absolute returns regardless of the market environment, then read on.

The vast majority of investors have no strategy; they are buying and selling investments based on their emotions. As I will show you later in this book, your emotions cause you to do stupid things with your money. A well-thought-out philosophy will keep you on track and hopefully keep you from making the mistakes that most investors make. The endowment approach is a philosophy that can keep you on track and can help take your emotions out of the equation.

I do warn you. There is no easy way when it comes to investing. If you want great results, you need to put in the work or you have to be willing to hire someone and delegate the work. There are a lot of people who are tempted to take the easy way out and put all of their money in an index fund. As of this writing, index funds that track the Standard & Poor's 500 Index are down 14.26% year to date and have averaged 2.31% per year over the past three years. My guess is that if you believed that putting all your money into an index fund is the smart way to go, then you probably would not be reading this book.

These days, it is more important than ever to make smart choices about your investments. More and more, individuals will be responsible for a larger part of their retirement and financial security. Years ago, companies offered defined benefit pension plans that paid workers a large percent of their salary when they retired. Now, your company has a 401(k) plan into which you put your own money, and if you are lucky, your company will match part of it. Companies also used to offer postretirement health care to their retirees. We do not see that being offered to current workers anymore, and from time to time we hear about companies trying to wriggle out of their responsibilities to retired workers. I am not going to take on the argument of whether Social Security and Medicare should be overhauled in this book, but I do not believe that what I will get when I turn 65 (as of the release date of this book I will be 40) will bear any resemblance to what my grandparents got and what my mother will get. Retirement used to be a three-legged stool. One leg was your employer, one leg was the government, and your savings was the third leg. Now you need to plan on retirement being a unicycle. The only thing you can really count on is your savings. If the government and/or your employer kick in a large chunk, then that's great. You will have more than you need; that's a good problem to have. If they don't, then you need to be prepared.

I have been involved with the markets in one way or another for almost two decades. This is my second book, and I have contributed to a few others. I am a frequent guest on Fox Business News and BusinessWeek TV and have been on CNBC, Fox News, and CNNfn. I am also frequently quoted in the *Wall Street Journal, SmartMoney,*

Kiplinger's, and many other financial publications. I also manage money for individual and institutional investors through my own registered investment advisor, Tuttle Wealth Management, LLC, and through a second registered investment advisor, PCG Wealth Advisory, LLC. I have long been interested in how institutional investors, large college endowments in particular, have always been way ahead of individual investors. They tend to adopt investment strategies years before individual investors do. By the time individuals catch on, the institutions have already found something better. When institutions were embracing multiasset class allocation, individual investors were trying to pick stocks. Years later, individual investors have finally grasped the importance of traditional asset allocation while the large institutions have realized that it doesn't work well and are now on to bigger and better things.

I have also always hated losing money, so I am constantly looking for investment strategies that give me the highest chance possible of preserving money in any market environment. Part of this is self-preservation and the other part is common sense. During the start of the technology bubble in the late 1990s, I worked for a major Wall Street firm. Although I never got involved in recommending Internet stocks to my clients, many of my colleagues did. For a while things were great for them and their clients, until 2000 when they blew their clients up. To "blow a client up" is a Wall Street term that means lose most or all of your client's money in a bad investment. Blowing a client up is obviously not a good thing. If you blow up all your clients, you basically blow up your own practice as well.

Pearls of Stockbrokerage Wisdom

When I started out at my brokerage firm, one of the grizzled veterans came over to talk to me about the wisdom of surviving as a stockbroker. He told me to cold call like crazy to try to get new clients. Once I got a client, I was supposed to make lots of trades in his or her account (this isn't really legal; the industry calls it "churning"). He said I would probably blow up half my clients; of those who I blew up, half would leave and half would stay, until I blew them up again. I would continually be adding new clients and blowing up my existing clients, but he assured me if I followed this formula I was guaranteed to make a six-figure salary (it might even be enough to pay for bail). Now you know why I needed to find a better way.

Not losing money also makes financial sense. First it keeps you invested while other people are selling and putting money under the mattress. Second, if you don't lose a lot when the market goes down, you don't need to gain a lot when it goes up and you can still end up ahead.

The large college endowments have always had to be more innovative than most institutional investors as they have an almost impossible investment mandate. Not only do they need to generate a large enough real return (return after inflation) so the endowment can spend money, but they also are not expected to take a lot of risk and subject the endowment to losses.

Real Returns

In many parts of this book we will refer to real returns. These are the returns you have after inflation. If I put $50 into a mutual fund and at the end of the year it is worth $100, then I have an actual return of 100%. That's great! However, if inflation is so bad that at the end of the year it takes me $100 to buy what I used to pay $50 for, then in real life I didn't make anything. That is why real returns are so important.

If I am the chief investment officer of some institution and my benchmark is down 20% and I am down only 10%, then my boss is happy. If I was the chief investment officer of a large college endowment, then I would be in danger of losing my job.

There is no reason that there needs to be a gap in what institutions and individuals are doing. Endowments and institutional investors don't keep what they are doing a secret. Harvard, Yale, and the other large endowments publish annual reports where they divulge their asset allocation and their investment thinking. Go to the web site of just about any university, and you should be able to find the annual report of their endowment. You can also type *portable alpha* into any search engine, and you will see what the institutional investors are talking about and where the future of investment management is headed (or read my chapter on portable alpha).

Unfortunately, many investment advisors that serve individual clients do not take the time to figure out how these strategies can be adapted to individuals. Most prefer to stay with the tried-and-true strategies even though they are no longer working. When I started out as a stockbroker in the 1990s, I enthusiastically embraced the asset allocation theory that the large institutions were using. I was not afraid to be on the cutting edge. However, most of the old-line stockbrokers still stuck by their traditional stock picking. It took them years (and tons of losses during the technology stock bubble bursting) to embrace a traditional asset allocation approach. Of course, just as they were embracing asset allocation, the endowments and institutions had already moved on as they realized that asset allocation doesn't protect your principal in a big down market like they had hoped it would.

Some of the concepts in this book are more complicated than a traditional asset allocation approach. However, more and more investment products are hitting the market that are geared toward an endowment philosophy of investing. Advisors and individual investors are also coming around to endowment types of investment strategies. Nearly every day I read an article in one of my industry publications about the benefits of adding "alternative investments" to a traditional portfolio to be able to invest like Harvard and Yale. Investment conferences focus more and more on these types of investments and how to integrate them into a portfolio. More and more advisors talk about how they are starting to hear from their clients who are interested in these types of strategies. Hopefully, this book can hasten the development of new ideas and products that allow individual investors to invest like the large endowments. Of course, some of my motives are selfish. In developing these types of portfolios for my clients, I often wish there were more products to choose from. Many of the mutual funds that can fit into an endowment type of portfolio are poor. There aren't a lot of separately managed accounts that fit these types of portfolios. There is no way to replicate the returns of private equity without high minimum investments and long lockups. As these types of strategies become more and more accepted, product sponsors will be forced to develop products to meet the demand, including mine.

How Harvard and Yale Beat the Market will provide you with the tools you need to make sure your savings are there when you need it. This book will tell you why it is important for you to invest like the endowments do and how the current financial environment will actually enable you to make substantial profits. Part I of the book will talk about the mistakes investors make and why large endowments

Author's Note

Throughout this text you will see the terms *fund* or *money manager*. There are a number of ways in which people can invest. They can buy stocks and bonds directly, but that isn't really what this book is about. They can also hire money managers, either through mutual funds, ETFs, separate account managers, hedge funds, hedge fund of funds, private equity, and private equity fund of funds. Since different investment vehicles will be appropriate for different investors, the terms *fund* and *money manager* are used to apply to all of the different options. I have also used a number of mutual funds as examples throughout the text. These are just that—examples. They are in no way recommendations to buy or sell any of the funds mentioned.

outperform. Part II will give an introduction to the different investment vehicles investors can use that will allow you to create an endowment type of investment portfolio. Part III will talk in depth about the different asset classes you may want to consider for your portfolio. Part IV will then take what you have learned and show you how to apply it when designing your own portfolio.

The large endowments like Harvard and Yale have revolutionized the investment landscape. *How Harvard and Yale Beat the Market* will give you the tools you need to create portfolios like the large endowments do.

PART

I

INVESTMENT 101

AN INTRODUCTION TO THE ENDOWMENT PHILOSOPHY OF INVESTING

Before we talk about how individuals can invest like endowments, in Part I we need to discuss the current financial environment and its implications for investors (see Chapter 1). In Chapter 2 we will explore why investors make the mistakes they do and how they can avoid them. Chapter 3 will then start to lay the groundwork for thinking about your portfolio the same way endowments do. In Chapter 4 we will discuss the two types of money managers that endowments use. In Chapter 5 we will introduce you to the endowment portfolio theory, and in Chapter 6 we will show you how endowments outperform the market.

1

The Current Environment and the Need for New Thinking

As I write this chapter 2008 is almost over—good riddance! This year was a game changer for the investment industry as the three main pillars of investing—buy and hold, traditional asset allocation, and indexing—are either broken or teetering. For years, investors have been told to buy and hold solid stocks, companies like Bear Stearns, Lehman Brothers, Fannie Mae, Freddie Mac, Wachovia, GM, etc., might go down but they will never go bankrupt. Because of what happened in 2008 we can never say that again. Traditional asset allocation says that investors should put some money in small stocks, medium-sized stocks, large stocks, and bonds, that way they will have some protection if one area is going down, hopefully another will be going up. In 2008 there were no safe havens, just about everything went down. A diversified portfolio may have provided some protection, but you still would have been down a huge amount. Index fund advocates argue that most active money managers don't beat their index so investors should just buy index funds. During the lows of November 2008 an investor who bought an index fund 10 years ago would have had a negative 10-year return. I used to tell people that I don't know where the market is going to go but since we have only had two negative 10-year year periods in the market since the depression, it should be up in 10 years. I can no longer say that.

What happened?

We all probably remember the 2000–2002 market crash, but since then things were fine in the markets, until the summer of

2007. It all started with signs that there were problems in mortgages made to people with less than stellar credit ratings, the so-called subprime mortgages. Since this was only a small part of the mortgage market, most people thought it would blow over without much carryover to other areas. They were wrong. When a couple of Bear Stearns hedge funds that had been invested in subprime went belly-up, people started to get worried. The Fed, as it always seems to do, came to the rescue and lowered interest rates. This caused a strong rally in the stock market, until October 9, 2007. Since then, and as of this writing, the market is down nearly 20%; Bear Stearns and Lehman Brothers are bankrupt; Fannie Mae, Freddie Mac, and AIG had to be bailed out by the government; and Washington Mutual failed. What happened and is this a small blip or the continuation of something much larger?

What people learned after October 9th is that the subprime mess was much worse than expected. Mortgage companies had gone crazy giving loans to anyone with a pulse and many times with no money down. Real estate investors saw home prices increasing with no end in sight and leveraged up. Financial magazines were full of articles about how people were making tons of money flipping properties, buying them with a subprime mortgage and no money down, and then selling them shortly after for a profit. In the meantime, the banks making these mortgages sold them to Wall Street firms who packaged them into bonds to sell to institutional investors. Somehow, the Wall Street firms got the credit rating agencies to give the bonds high credit ratings (meaning a low chance of default). The combination of high ratings and higher interest rates meant that there was no shortage of buyers. Many Wall Street firms and other investors leveraged up by borrowing money short term and buying tons of this packaged subprime debt. Things were going great until the bottom fell out.

Housing prices couldn't go up forever, and they didn't. They started going down, which put tremendous pressure on subprime debt as more and more people had negative equity on homes and investment properties. It also turned out that making no money down loans to people who had no real way of paying them back probably wasn't the best idea (go figure). Once these cracks started to show, it created a ripple effect. Firms that had borrowed money to buy subprime loans started seeing the value of the debt going down. This caused the banks, many of which were the investors in this stuff, to start calling in loans. With the loans being called, the investors had to sell stuff to pay them back, but there were no takers for subprime debt. So instead of selling the debt, they either went under or started selling what could be sold, things like high-quality stocks. This caused the stock market to go down as many long/short hedge funds were short low-quality stocks and long the same high-quality stocks that people were selling like crazy. These funds were also leveraged, and they were forced to buy back the low-quality stocks and sell the high-quality stocks, making things worse. It turned out that most of the people who ran these long/short hedge funds either used to work for Goldman Sachs or used the same quantitative screens that Goldman Sachs uses. That meant that everyone was long the same stocks and short the same stocks; when one fund got into trouble, every fund got into trouble. Also, most of the banks and brokerage firms were invested up to their ears in subprime debt and they were hurting. This finally resulted in the collapse of Bear Stearns in 2008.

While all this was going on, oil prices started going through the roof. This is never good for the economy as we need oil to drive our cars, and most industries need oil to run their factories and transport their goods. This hurt the consumer and caused prices to go up for just about everything. To counter the subprime mess, the Fed started lowering interest rates, which is their primary policy tool for combating a slowing economy. However, lower interest rates hurt the value of the dollar because global money flows to the countries that have the highest interest rates. Since oil is denominated in dollars, this caused oil prices to go up even more. Then, just when we thought we understood the crisis and thought it couldn't get worse, it did. Commodities, which had been rising, fell through the floor. Since commodities were the only asset class that was doing well, the hedge funds had bought into them heavily, this caused many hedge funds to go under, further roiling the stock market. October and November were horrendous months for the market. It was this final nail in the coffin that really impacted the large college endowments and caused them to suffer large losses.

Bernie Madoff

Just when we thought it couldn't get worse, we got the Bernie Madoff scandal, the largest Ponzi Scheme in history. Mr. Madoff managed $17 billion dollars (or so people thought) and was able to generate consistent returns year after year. In actuality he was using money from new investors to pay returns to old investors, the classic Ponzi Scheme. While Mr. Madoff's fund was not a hedge fund, hedge fund of funds invested heavily into his company. In this book I talk about hedge funds and hedge fund of funds and recommend them for some investors. While the Bernie Madoff scandal and all of the hedge fund bankruptcies don't render this strategy invalid, they do increase the need for proper due diligence. There are some helpful lessons to be learned from what Madoff did. While there were many red flags that sophisticated investors should have picked up on, there were some things that should have given individual investors pause as well. For example, my firm manages money. If I want to buy a stock in a client's account, I call Fidelity Investments who buys the stock and puts it in the client's own account held at Fidelity. Fidelity then sends the client a confirmation that the stock was bought and at the end of the month,, the client gets a confirmation from Fidelity showing how much their account is worth and what is in it. If Bernie Madoff wanted to buy a stock in a client's account he called Bernie Madoff to place the trade. Bernie Madoff would place the trade in the client's account which was held with Bernie Madoff. Bernie Madoff would send the client a confirmation of the trade and at the end of the month the client would get a statement from Bernie Madoff showing the value of his account. If it looks like there are too many Madoffs in this equation, you are correct. There was no independent third party to raise a red flag. Hedge funds and fund of funds are still valid investments, like any type of investment, there are good and bad. If you don't have the level of sophistication to tell one from the other, or don't have an advisor you trust to help you, then stay away.

The Consequences of Our Actions

The question now becomes is what happened in 2007 and 2008 just an isolated incident that will correct itself, and will it then be back to business as usual? Or, is this the continuation of things that have been happening over time that will fundamentally change our markets? Unfortunately, I would argue for the latter. Now I know what you might be thinking. You have heard before how things have changed only to see them eventually go back to normal. During the technology bubble of the late 1990s, you heard how companies didn't have to make money anymore and how Internet firms that had no prospects of making money anytime soon could be worth more than well-established companies. A few years ago, a Greenwich, Connecticut, real estate broker told me that Greenwich real estate would never come down because of the great schools, low taxes, and proximity to New York City. You've heard it before, but this feels different.

For years we have been living with a global imbalance:

- U.S. consumers purchase goods made in Asia and gas from the Middle East.
- U.S. consumers overextend to purchase these things using credit cards and home equity loans.
- These loans are repackaged by Wall Street as bonds and sold to the same Asian and Middle Eastern countries so that they can invest the proceeds from their sales to U.S. consumers.

This all worked great as we sent money overseas, and it came right back to stabilize our markets. However, this is having, and will continue to have, a number of important consequences on world markets:

1. *Inflation.* For years, inflation has been kept in check partly by cheap labor in emerging markets. However, as more and more money flows in, it is creating a new middle class. As the middle class develops, they will want higher wages. Wages will then increase, causing prices of goods made in China and other countries to increase.
2. *Demand for Commodities.* As these economies grow, so will demand for oil and other commodities, further pushing up prices.
3. *Infrastructure.* As these economies grow, they will increasingly need to build modern cities and other infrastructure projects.
4. *Internal Consumption.* As the middle class grows, they will want the same types of goods and services that the U.S. middle class wants. This will cause these economies to shift from primarily export based to more of an import focus. This will result in a decoupling of these economies from the developed economies. For years, when the United States sneezed,

the emerging markets caught a cold, because our demand for their exports went down. As these economies start to shift and they rely less and less on exports, their economies will decouple from ours.

In the past, emerging market countries would invest their surplus funds in U.S. bonds, primarily Treasuries. This would keep the dollar strong and keep our interest rates low. (This is purely supply and demand: If there is a strong demand for dollars to buy Treasury bonds, the price of each will go up; in the case of Treasury bonds, a higher price means a lower interest rate.) Now, as these countries become more sophisticated, they are setting up sovereign wealth funds (SWFs), many of which are implementing endowment types of investment strategies themselves. These SWFs can have a tremendous impact on financial markets going forward and will most likely result in less money invested in Treasury bonds (increasing our interest rates) and dollar-denominated assets (decreasing the value of the dollar).

The bottom line is that we can no longer rely on emerging markets to prop up our economy by reinvesting the money they get from us into our bonds and our currency. We also can no longer rely on cheap labor in emerging market countries to keep labor costs and inflation down. We also need to assume that demand from emerging market countries will continue to push up the prices of commodities. Finally, SWFs and where they invest their money will have a huge impact on investment markets.

The result could be a lot like the phenomenon we saw in the 1970s when we had lower economic growth and higher prices. With the Fed in a bind, this is happening right now. This is commonly referred to as *stagflation*.

How to Make Money Whether in a Bear or Bull Market

Most market prognosticators, me included, are predicting that we are in for a period of mediocre returns. Others might argue that the markets are just being irrational. The famed economist John Maynard Keynes once said, "Markets can remain irrational longer than you can remain solvent." Bear Stearns and a number of hedge funds would probably agree with this statement.

Table 1.1 shows the major bull markets we have had throughout history ending with the bursting of the technology bubble in 2000. A bull market, or upward-trending market, occurs when each successive high point is higher than the previous one.

Table 1.2 shows all the bear markets we have had including this current period. A bear market, or downward-trending market, occurs when a trend does not rise above the previous high. History has shown us that bear markets tend to last for quite some time. If we are in a bear market, and history holds true, then we have a few more years of mediocre or negative returns to go.

The current and perhaps future investment environment begs for new solutions. The large endowments have shown the ability to make money no matter what the market does, while they stumbled in 2008 this does not invalidate their strategy. Individual investors need to learn how to do the same thing. It always amazes me how people panic when the stock market goes down or oil goes up. No matter what is going on in the stock market, there are ways to make money; you just need to think outside the box. The investment

Table 1.1   Bull Markets

Start	End	Months	Years	Annualized Return	Cumulative Return	Annualized Std. Dev.
12/18/96	1/19/06	110	9	10.56%	148.92%	20.45%
7/19/24	8/19/29	63	5	30.44%	294.66%	17.30%
12/19/54	1/19/66	135	11	8.72%	154.29%	11.68%
11/19/82	1/20/00	206	17	15.09%	1003.19%	15.12%

Source: Tuttle Wealth Management, LLC.

Table 1.2   Bear Markets

Start	End	Months	Years	Annualized Return	Cumulative Return	Annualized Std. Dev.
2/19/06	6/19/24	218	18	−0.24%	−4.29%	18.71%
9/19/29	11/19/54	304	25	0.07%	1.69%	24.96%
2/19/66	10/19/82	202	17	0.05%	0.83%	15.25%
2/20/00	12/20/07	96	8	2.46%	21.24%	13.78%

Source: Tuttle Wealth Management, LLC.

world is not blind to what is going on. They are coming out with new products every day to meet the demand for investments that will go up regardless of what our market does. Individual investors need to understand these new products and how they may or may not fit into their portfolios.

During the late 1990s, anyone throwing a dart at a board could make 30% per year. I used to have people from all industries tell me how they felt bad for me as an investment advisor. Who needed an advisor when the market went up with no advice needed? Today things are different. What used to work no longer does. Eventually we will have another great bull market but who knows when that will be. Will you still be around when it comes; will you still be solvent?

The Old Way

The old way that many individual investors allocated their money was based on a misinterpretation of modern portfolio theory. (We will talk more about how to correctly use it later.) The traditional asset allocation approach involves the following seven step:

1. *Gather the asset classes you will use.* Most investors use large-cap growth, large-cap value, mid-cap growth, mid-cap value, small-cap growth, small-cap value, international, and fixed income.
2. *Forecast returns for each of those asset classes.* Most people take the easy way out and use past performance.
3. *Forecast how correlated they will be to each other.* Most people use past correlation.
4. *Forecast how volatile they will be.* Most people use past volatility.
5. *Create a portfolio based on all your forecasts that will provide the best possible risk-adjusted return.* You would use software called an optimizer to figure this out.
6. *Hire money managers.* They should be style pure (stick to their style, like large-cap value or small-cap growth, and never deviate).
7. *Monitor your managers.* Make sure they don't deviate from their style.

On the surface this approach seems valid. For every level of risk there is one mix of assets that would provide you with the best return. Let's say we rank risk from 1 to 10, with 1 being risk free and 10 being extremely risky. You decide that you are a risk level 5. Let's say at risk level 5 there are two possible portfolios: one that we expect to be up 10% and the other we expect to be up 15%. Which would you choose? This is not a trick question. If each portfolio has the same risk, naturally you would take the one that has an expected return of 15%.

This approach has a number of problems, however. First, the asset classes are too narrow and as I will show you later in the book, they are highly correlated, giving you very little diversification benefit. Second, you cannot forecast returns, correlations, and volatility with any real accuracy. If you can, you should not waste your time reading this book. If you know exactly what each asset class is going to do in the future, you can make a killing. I can easily tell you what portfolio would have done the best in the past but my crystal ball doesn't work well enough to tell you what mix will be the best in the future. The best I can do is make an educated guess. Third, if you can't accurately forecast, then your results are suspect. Also, any good optimizer will have constraints. (You don't have to buy or create your own optimizer; if you work with an investment advisor, he or she probably has one or you can find them online.) If the optimizer didn't have constraints, you would find that your results wouldn't make much sense.

In business school we had to create our own optimizers, and the results we got usually didn't make much sense. Our optimizer would fall in love with some asset class that we projected would have low correlation to the others and high returns. We would get optimal portfolios that would look something like 40% high-yield bonds, 20% emerging market stocks, 20% cash, and 20% small-cap value stocks. Maybe this portfolio would turn out to be efficient, but it would be pretty hard to recommend it with a straight face to a client. To fix this we had to put constraints on our output. So we had to limit a number of asset classes. The combination of flawed forecasts and constraints meant that our eventual output was of little value. Don't get me wrong: Optimization is still a fine approach. It's also much better than how most investors invest. The large endowments forecast returns, volatility, and correlation of the asset classes they use and they use optimizers. The main difference is that they don't solely use past returns to forecast future returns. They realize that optimization is part art and part science so they don't blindly follow the optimizer. They also use a number of asset classes that people usually don't use that truly are not correlated to each other. The broader asset classes are really the key. When most people develop optimized portfolios, they are using assets that are either highly correlated or, even worse, become highly correlated when the markets decline.

The other problem with this approach is that the money managers have to stick to their style religiously. If they deviate, even if the results are good, then they get fired. So let's say your large-cap growth money manager decides that small-cap value stocks are cheap and starts buying them. Even if the trades are profitable, he would be fired under the traditional approach for deviating from his style. This is called *style drift* in the industry. Also, you might find a money manager who has generated great returns over the years but doesn't fit neatly into a style box. Using the traditional approach, you could not use this manager. I once had an interesting meeting with a mutual fund wholesaler. Wholesalers are people who work for mutual fund companies who get paid to convince people like me to buy their funds for my clients. His fund had an amazing track record, beat the market handily, and protected on the downside during the 2000–2002 crash. His problem was that the fund didn't fit neatly into a style box so that most of the advisors he spoke to couldn't use it—even though it handily beat any other fund they might be using.

Time for a Change

For years the large college endowments have been way ahead of individual investors and other institutions in their thinking. It's time that individual investors start to catch up and learn what endowments have known for years. That's what this book is all about. Before we get into what the endowments are doing, we need to talk about the mistakes most investors make that keeps them from having investment success.

CHAPTER 2

Common Investment Mistakes

Buy low, sell high. Sounds simple, doesn't it? Then why do most investors do the opposite?

How you invest your money could make the difference between affording a comfortable retirement and outliving your money. Here is an example. Suppose John Doe is 65 and retired. He has $500,000 in his 401(k) and will get $20,000 per year from Social Security. John wants to be able to generate $40,000 per year after taxes, adjusted for inflation, during his retirement years. Inflation is assumed to be 3%. If John earns 6% on his portfolio, then he will run out of money by age 94. If he can earn 8.5%, then at age 94 he still has over $1 million. Earning an extra 2.5% a year may not sound like much, but it can have a huge effect on your retirement and financial goals.

This is why investors need to pay attention to the investment strategies of the most successful endowments, such as Harvard and Yale. Following these types of strategies could make the difference between a comfortable retirement or running out of money.

In my experience, investors often make six big mistakes:

1. Buying what's hot
2. Trying to blindly beat the market
3. Believing some guru can predict the markets
4. Letting their emotions get involved
5. Being chrono-centric
6. Having a short financial memory

Buying What's Hot

Many of you might remember the technology stock bubble that ended in 1999. By the end of 1999 we kept hearing how things were different this time, companies didn't have to make money any more, and so on. Internet stocks were going through the roof with no end in sight. Many investors were buying Internet stock and mutual funds expecting untold riches. Unfortunately, during 2000 to 2002 many of those investors were wiped out.

What about other years? The top-performing fund in 1997 was the American Heritage Fund, with a return of 75%. If you had invested $10,000 in that fund on January 1, 1998, it would have been worth $955 at the end of 2005 (it was also the top-performing fund in 2004).

Just because a money manager, a mutual fund, or a stock had a good year or a good couple of years does not mean it will continue. There is a reason why every mutual fund prospectus and return calculation tells you in large bold letters: **"Past Performance Does Not Predict Future Results."**

Unfortunately, mutual funds are mostly or partly to blame for this mistake. They constantly advertise market-beating performance when they know full well that just because a fund had a great year doesn't mean that it will do the same thing the next year.

You need to realize that most mutual funds consider themselves to be in the money gathering business, not the money management business. Since their fees are based on how much money they gather, not how much they make, their marketing focuses on generating as much sizzle as they can. Unfortunately, individual investors often get sucked into a hot investment right before it turns cold.

Trying to Blindly Beat the Market

Let's say you walked into my office on January 1, 2000, and asked me to invest your life savings of $1 million. Fast-forward to December 31, 2002, and we are sitting down to go over your results. It turns out I have some great news for you: Your $1 million portfolio has declined to $700,000, a loss of 30%. During the same time period, however, the stock market was down approximately 45%; not only did you beat the market, you crushed it. Are you happy? My guess is that you probably are not.

Beating the market is all well and good, but before you embark on any investment strategy you need to understand what that means. An endowment philosophy seeks to beat the market by protecting money on the downside with the trade-off of not making as much on the upside. Endowments also have a spending policy to be able to use a certain percent of the endowment each year and not eat into their principal. That goal drives their investment policy. What are your goals? Beating the market is meaningless at the end of the day if you have not achieved your goals.

Let's say you are 55 and plan to retire in 10 years. Over that 10-year period the market averages 5% per year and your portfolio averages 7% per year; you handily beat the market. At the end of the 10-year period you realize that you still don't have enough to retire, and you will have to work for at least another 10 years. Are you happy you beat the market? Now let's assume that instead of beating the market over the 10-year period, your portfolio averaged 5% per year and the market averaged 7% per year. At the end of the 10-year period you do have enough money to retire. Are you really unhappy that you didn't beat the market as you walk into your boss's office to announce your retirement? Probably not.

Now your goal might actually be to try to beat the market or some other benchmark, and that's okay as long as you have thought it out. Many institutional investors have the same goal. They often use a strategy called portable alpha that I will talk about later in the book.

Believing Some Guru Can Predict the Market

When you think of the top investors of all time, names like Peter Lynch and Warren Buffett invariably come up. Both of these men have often been quoted saying they have no idea of the short-term direction of the stock market.

So if the three brightest investment minds in our country—Peter Lynch, Warren Buffett, and Matthew Tuttle (okay, so maybe I don't deserve to be mentioned in the same sentence with those guys, but you can't blame me for trying)—don't know what the market is going to do, nobody does. You don't have to be able to predict which way the market is going to do well as an investor.

Many people watch *Mad Money* with Jim Cramer and follow his stock picks. *Barron's* magazine actually wrote an article in August 2007 where they argued that investors would be better off selling Cramer's picks short than buying them.

As someone who is on TV, the radio, and in the news constantly, I know how much the media wants to have experts opine on which way the market is going to go. As one of these so called experts I also realize that the best we can provide is an educated guess. I also know that if you have two or more experts on the same show or quoted in the same article, you will probably get two different opinions. One show asked me to be a guest and take a bearish (negative) position on the market because they already had two other guests to take the positive side. Luckily I was already negative so I didn't have the moral dilemma of going on TV and telling people something opposite of what I really thought. Also luckily, I was right. The media often likes to show two sides of the argument. If they have someone on who is positive about the market, they usually have someone on who is negative. How the audience decides which one is right is anyone's guess. I suppose you could flip a coin but that's probably not the best way to manage your investments.

If anyone ever figures out an ironclad way to determine the direction of the market, you can bet that they won't be telling you about it. Whenever anyone tells me about a scheme they heard about that is guaranteed to beat the market, I always wonder why someone would sell the scheme rather than trade it for themselves. The top money managers in the world go to great lengths to keep their methods secret. They know that if people find out what they are doing and mimic their trades, it will reduce their returns. We run a managed futures fund that uses a computer program to decide when to buy and when to sell financial and commodity futures contracts. On our disclosure documents, we tell only what we are required to reveal about our strategies. I don't want to divulge anymore because if people start mimicking what we are doing, it will be harder for us to make money. Whenever anyone comes to you with a sure thing, ask them why they don't trade for themselves.

The Market Genius Scam

An old investment scam that might still be around goes like this: You call (or e-mail) a certain number of investors with a prediction and tell them a certain stock will go up. You call (or e-mail) an equal amount of different investors and tell them the same stock will go down. No matter which direction the stock goes, there will be a certain amount of people who know you got it right. You then split these investors up and do it again. After a while there is a small amount of people to whom you have given three to four correct stock picks who now think you are a genius.

Letting Their Emotions Get Involved

Individual investors lose money because they let their emotions dictate their buy-and-sell decisions. Their emotions cause them to get greedy and buy something they shouldn't buy, and their emotions cause them to panic and sell something they shouldn't sell. They may read the newspapers and see headlines about how the market went down 100 points, and they panic and sell. Or they may read magazines like *BusinessWeek.* Here's what *BusinessWeek* said about the stock market in 1979:

> For better or worse then the U.S. economy probably has to regard the death of equities as a near permanent condition. The old attitude of buying solid stocks as a cornerstone for one's life savings and retirement has simply disappeared.
>
> *BusinessWeek,* "The Death of Equities," August 13, 1979

This is the financial industry's equivalent to Dewey defeats Truman: totally and completely wrong. If you took this advice you would have missed the more than 1,000% return from the market from 1982 to 2000. So don't read the magazines, don't read the newspapers, and don't listen to the talking heads on TV (except me, of course). Or, if you do, take it all with a grain of salt. Read them like you would read the funny pages. Don't use what you see or read to decide your investment strategy.

Think about it. Have you ever felt like you had an investment curse? Right after you buy something, it goes down and right after you sell, it goes up? When I pose this question in my speeches, I get a lot of nodding heads. The squiggly line in Figure 2.1 is why that happens.

No investment I have ever seen goes up or down in a straight line. It usually goes in a squiggly pattern. Now think about how

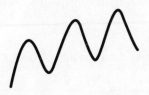

Figure 2.1   Squiggly Line

most investments are sold. You either buy a mutual fund that is advertised in the paper or in a magazine, or you buy a stock recommended by your broker. Have you ever seen a mutual fund advertisement that said this fund was down 25% last year so now is a good time to buy? I doubt it. The advertising firm would probably get fired (too bad you don't see it because that's probably the right time to buy). You usually see an ad saying that a fund was up 25% last year, so it must be a great place to put your money. Does your broker usually call you about a stock that has gone down, or does he call you about a stock that has gone up? Usually, the broker is going to call about a stock that has been appreciating. Therefore, as an individual investor, you are usually buying investments when they are up, and then your emotions cause you to panic, and you sell them when they go down. Wall Street knows that past performance doesn't predict future results, but it does sell mutual funds and stocks. Out of one side of their mouth they tell you that past performance is not predictive, and out the other side they hype the past performance. Most mutual fund firms are large companies; they are not in the business of having great performance, they are in the business of bringing in assets—that's how they get paid. They also know that the way to bring in performance is to tout what's hot. For example, the Oppenheimer Commodity Strategy Fund had a return of –31.35% in 2001, which would have turned off most investors. If investors let their emotions get in the way, they would have missed out on the returns illustrated in Table 2.1.

Money magazine did an interesting study in 1996. They selected five top-performing funds and looked at how the average shareholder did with them. Table 2.2 shows what they found.

So, for example, the Dreyfus Aggressive Growth fund was up 20.7% in 1996, but the average shareholder lost 34.9% that year. How could this be? Was it an accounting scandal? Was it Enron? Think back to the squiggly line in Figure 2.1. The Dreyfus fund didn't go up in a straight line all throughout 1996; it went up and down, up and down. To get a 20.7% return, you would have had to buy the fund

Table 2.1   Oppenheimer Commodity Strategy Performance

Year	2002	2003	2004	2005	2006	2007	As of 5/31/2008
Performance	27.44%	22.63%	19.62%	26.37%	−13.09%	30.23%	30.76%

Table 2.2   Fund Return vs. Shareholder Return

	Fund	Shareholders
Dreyfus Aggressive Growth	20.7	−34.9
Hancock Discovery B	13.1	−3.0
Midas Fund	21.2	−14.5
PBHG Core Growth	32.8	−3.0
Wan Wagoner Emer. Growth	26.9	−20.0

Note: The fund columns show the annualized return reported by the fund. The shareholder column shows the shareholder average return. The difference results because the average investor invests once the fund has risen (near the top) and then gets out when the fund declines. This is not always the case and is merely an example of what occurred in these funds as reported by *Money* magazine during this period.

Source: Money magazine, April 1997. Comparison of fund reported results 12/31/95 to 12/31/96 vs. average investor results (investor results as measured by actual investor accounts in these funds during this period and then averaged). Hancock Discovery B is now Hancock large cap growth B.

on January 1st and hold it until December 31st, but that's not what the average shareholder did. The average shareholder probably saw an ad when the fund started the year well and bought it when it was high. Inevitably during the year the fund must have taken a dip. The average shareholder panicked and sold on the dip. He managed to buy high and sell low all year so that even though he took a fund that was way up, he managed to lose a lot of money.

If we look at every one-year period in the market from 1926 to 2005, we find that 71% of the time the market has been up, and 29% of the time the market has been down. If we look at every five-year period in the market during the same period, we find that 90% of the time the market is up, and 10% of the time the market is down. We have had only two negative 10-year periods in the market, both during the Depression, and we have never had a negative 15-year period in the market. What does that tell you about the market? It tells you that you need to have a long-term time horizon. Whenever anyone asks me what I think the market is going to do, I say that 10 years from now it will be up.

People get confused about the market because the stock market knows nothing about the short term. We see newspaper headlines that scream gloom and doom and then see that the stock market is up that day. Or we see headlines about how great the economy is doing and the market is down that day, and we can't understand it.

I remember one day in 2005 when the market was up 150 points, and the commentators were all saying that it was because of a drop in oil prices. The next day oil prices declined, but the market went down 150 points. If that's not enough to confuse you, I don't know what is.

If you look at it in large chunks of time, it makes perfect sense. Over time, the economy has grown and the market has gone up.

Being Chrono-Centric

Chrono-centricity is the inborn egotism that one's own generation is poised on the cusp of history. It leads investors to believe that what is happening today will define a new era. In actuality, no matter what is going on, and no matter how promising it might seem at the time, we have gone through similar periods over and over again in history. There was the tulip bulb mania in 1636, the stock market collapse in England in 1745, the collapse of the East India Trading Company in 1772, the trust companies in the United States in 1907, the stock market crash of 1929, and the collapse of the technology bubble of 2000, just to name a few. Most of the large crashes can be tied to the development of a new technology that was supposed to change everything. This technology led to panic buying, followed by mania, followed inevitably by a bust.

For instance, in the mid-1990s investors became convinced that the Internet would change everything. This led to panic buying as investors became convinced that the old rules didn't apply anymore. It used to be that companies would need to earn money, or at least have the prospect of earning money very shortly, for stock prices to go up. During the Internet boom, companies that had no prospect of earning money anytime soon had market capitalizations (stock price times stock outstanding) higher than well-established companies. As this went on, the panic buying soon became a mania. All you needed back then was a .com at the end of your name and investors couldn't get enough of your stock. Pretty soon everyone was an expert on Internet stocks, and chances are that at least one of your neighbors quit his job to become a day trader.

The top of the market finally came in March 2000 when my mother called me because she thought she should be buying Internet stocks. She felt like she was missing out on all the action. Did my mother's phone call cause the market crash? Probably not,

Be Careful What the Analysts Tell You

During the Internet boom, analysts at Wall Street firms were touting stocks up until the very end that had no chance of making money during my lifetime. It turns out that these analysts really weren't allowed to do anything but give buy recommendations on these stocks. It all comes down to how analysts get paid. An investment banker generates fees on investment banking deals he brings in. A broker generates commissions on stock trades. How does an analyst add value to a firm? Back in the 1990s the analysts were responsible for also bringing in investment banking business and keeping investment banking clients happy. That meant giving buy recommendations on stocks that were investment banking clients so they didn't get mad at you, and being accommodating to other companies so they would give your firm investment banking business. After the crash, these firms were sued and had to pay a billion-dollar settlement and promise to reform their ways. Have things gotten better with Wall Street research? I still don't see too many sell recommendations (except right after a stock announces it is going bankrupt).

but it was a signal that a top had been reached when very conservative investors finally throw in the towel and decide to get in.

While this might seem like an isolated event that probably won't happen, a study of history will tell you that it happens all the time. Why do investors keep falling for this over and over again? Because we have a shortness of the collective financial memory.

Having a Short Financial Memory

Why do we continually follow the cycle of panic, mania, and then bust? In his book *A Short History of Financial Euphoria* (Viking Penguin, 1993), John Kenneth Galbraith talks about how investors repeat the same destructive patterns over and over again, because about every 20 years or so we completely forget the past history of the markets (unless it was a huge event like the crash of 1929; then it takes a generation to forget). That's why your grandparents are still spending money like they are living in the Depression and you will forget all about the Internet bubble by 2020 and will be suckered in by the next bubble, whatever and whenever it happens to be.

Many investors may think that they have learned something from their experience during the technology bubble of 2000. In fact, I would argue that the most important lesson to be learned is that we are incapable of learning from bubbles. When the next one comes around, we will do the same thing we did the last time because it is in our nature.

In the same book, Galbraith outlines the recurring six-step pattern of market euphoria:

1. New technology
2. Start of real growth
3. Rumors and greed
4. Increased leverage
5. Conspicuous consumption
6. Amateurs enter the market—my mom!

If you look back at financial history from the tulip bulb mania in the 1600s to the technology bubble almost 400 years later, investors have followed this pattern to the letter in every major bubble.

The Solution: A Well-Thought-Out Investment Methodology

You might be unique but most investors follow these mistakes time after time. They buy what's hot and sell what's down, right before it will probably come back up. Their emotions control their investment decisions. They believe that what is happening currently is going to change the world, and they completely forget financial history. You can try to fight it or you can understand that these things are human nature. If you accept that making these mistakes is just part of being human, then the only way to be a successful investor is to have an ironclad, well-thought-out methodology that you can tweak from time to time, but that you will not deviate from.

Trying to figure out what the market will do in the short term is purely guesswork, so stop worrying about it and adopt a well-thought-out investment methodology. Developing a methodology involves having a written plan for how you will invest, what you will invest in, when you will buy, and when you will sell. Your written plan dictates all investment decisions (not your emotions or the headlines), and the plan is only altered if changes in your financial situation necessitate it. Having a well-thought-out methodology is the key to avoiding the most common individual investor mistakes.

In this book, I will argue that a methodology based on endowment investing rules makes the most sense. However, if you never read beyond this chapter (I saw a statistic that most people who buy a book never read beyond the second chapter) and just make the commitment to adopt some methodology, even if it isn't very good, you will be doing yourself a favor and be better off than the vast majority of people who let their emotions dictate their investments.

Don't Make Mistakes

You can recover from mistakes in many areas of your life, but you may not be able to recover from an investment mistake. If you were a few years away from retirement in 2000 and you lost 45% of your money from 2000 to 2002 then you might still be working. Realize that as a human being you are hardwired to make mistakes with your investments and make the commitment to follow a well-thought-out, written investment methodology. Endowments have shown that they are able to beat the markets and protect their portfolios during market downturns; that is the type of methodology you should emulate.

CHAPTER 3

Diversification

THE BEST INVESTMENT STRATEGY

In the previous chapter, I hope I convinced you that you cannot rely on your instincts to guide your investment philosophy. If that's the case, what is an individual investor to do? History has shown us that the only reliable investment approach is diversification.

Diversification is based on Modern Portfolio Theory for which Harry Markowitz won the Nobel Prize. Diversification has been watered down over time to be defined as "Don't put all your eggs in one basket," which is true, but it actually means much more than that. Markowitz proved that you can add a risky asset to a portfolio and improve the risk-adjusted return of that portfolio (and probably also increase the actual return). In English, that means that you can take a portfolio of stocks and bonds, add some asset to it that is very risky, and the overall portfolio will actually be less risky than it was before. It might even have better performance. This philosophy has been around for some time but investors still don't get it. They look at assets in isolation and not on how adding an asset to a portfolio might impact the overall portfolio. Years ago, trustees of trusts had to look at each investment in the trust based on its own merits. If they didn't, they could be sued if an investment lost money, even if the total portfolio gained. The courts finally realized that this made no sense and now the Prudent Investor Act forces trustees to invest as a prudent person would, meaning looking at the portfolio as a whole and diversifying. Failure to diversify a portfolio now subjects trustees to liability. For example, funds that invest in commodities or commodity companies are very risky on their own. If you just look at them in a vacuum you may make the decision that they are too risky for you. However, if you look at how they would impact your portfolio, study after study shows that adding commodities to a portfolio actually reduces risk and increases return. This is a simple concept but it is vitally important.

The most important part of Markowitz's theory for investors is that portfolio performance is enhanced by adding assets with two characteristics:

1. Positive returns
2. Low to negative correlation with the other assets in the portfolio

Our natural psychology gravitates toward positive returns because it feels good. We want to add investments to our portfolio that have had positive returns in the past. That is why investors will continually put money into last year's winners. That is also why many investors thought they had diversified portfolios in 2000. They had some large U.S. stocks, some medium-sized U.S. stocks, some small U.S. stocks, and some international stocks. They had a lot of different funds that all had positive returns but they ignored the second characteristic of low to negative correlation and their portfolios took a beating for it. Most of the investments that people were diversifying into were all very highly correlated because they mostly had technology stocks. When one investment went down, they all did. Most investors and advisors who practice traditional asset allocation ignore the part about low to negative correlation. They have lots of different kinds of stocks—small, large, international, value, growth, and so on—but they are highly correlated, especially during down markets.

A Surefire Way to Turn Your 401(k) into a 201(k)

Most of the investment options in the 401(k) plans we see are lousy. Given a few choices and not much education on how to pick the right funds, many people just put all of their money into the funds with the best recent performance. They figure that if they have a few funds, then they are diversified. Unfortunately, these funds are usually quite similar, which is why they have been going up together, and when things go down they will go down together.

Correlation

Correlation measures how assets move together. (A detailed description of correlation can be found in the Appendix.) A correlation of 1 means that assets will move in the same direction, a correlation of –1 means they move in opposite directions, and a correlation of 0 means there is no real relationship between assets. Table 3.1 is a diversified portfolio of six Vanguard index funds. On the surface the investor may feel diversified because he has six different mutual funds, but on closer review they all have correlations over .5 and most of them are much more highly correlated than that.

A common misconception about correlation is that it measures around 0 whether assets move in the same direction or opposite direction. They believe that if two assets are completely negatively correlated when one is up 10% and the other is down 10%, they cancel each other out. The reason for this misconception is that in real life it works this way: The amount of hours I sleep at night is positively correlated with how rested I feel in the morning. The amount of coffee I drink at night is negatively correlated with how well I sleep, and so on. Actually, correlation, when we are talking about investments, tells us how investments move around their average returns. For example, if two assets are completely negatively correlated, then when one is above its average annual return, the other should be below its average annual return, but not necessarily negative. So, in effect, if we could find two assets that both average 10% compound average annual return, are both volatile, and are completely negatively correlated, and we combine them into a portfolio, we would not average out to 0 as many people might think. In fact, the compound average annual return of this combined

Table 3.1   Correlations from 5/01/05 to 4/30/08

	1	2	3	4	5	6
1. Vanguard 500 Index	1	.77	.81	.91	.53	.87
2. Vanguard Developing Markets	.77	1	.97	.78	.88	.71
3. Vanguard European Stock	.81	.97	1	.76	.71	.73
4. Vanguard Mid Cap	.91	.76	.76	1	.60	.96
5. Vanguard Pacific Stock	.53	.86	.71	.60	1	.53
6. Vanguard Small Cap	.87	.71	.73	.96	.53	1

Source: Prepared by Matthew Tuttle using Morningstar Principia.

Table 3.2 Correlation Example

Monthly Returns	Jan	Feb	Mar	Apr	May	June	July	Aug	Sept	Oct	Nov	Dec
ABC Fund	8%	0%	8%	0%	8%	0%	8%	0%	8%	0%	8%	0%
XYZ Fund	0%	8%	0%	8%	0%	8%	0%	8%	0%	8%	0%	8%
50/50 Blend	**4%**	**4%**	**4%**	**4%**	**4%**	**4%**	**4%**	**4%**	**4%**	**4%**	**4%**	**4%**
Correlation	−1			1								

	Total Return	Standard Deviation
ABC Fund	48%	4.2
XYZ Fund	48%	4.2
50/50 Blend	**48%**	**0**

Table 3.3   Correlation of Vanguard 500 Index and Caldwell & Orkin Market Opportunity

	1	2
1. Caldwell & Orkin	1	−.22
2. Vanguard 500	−.22	1

Table 3.4   Return and Standard Deviation Comparison

Portfolio	Average Annual Return	Standard Deviation
50% Caldwell & Orkin/50% Vanguard	9.16%	5.28
100% Vanguard	8.09%	8.87

portfolio will still be 10%, but with zero volatility. This is the benefit of adding noncorrelated and negatively correlated assets together into a portfolio.

Table 3.2 is a hypothetical example with two funds that are completely negatively correlated. They both returned 48% for the year. (Don't ask me where to find funds these days that return 48% a year; this is just an example.)

In this example both funds had the same return at the end of the year, but when one was up the other was flat for the month. This is negative correlation in action. Each of these funds average 4%/month. When one was up 4% more than its average, the other was down 4% more than its average—but not negative. By combining these into a portfolio, we get the same return we would have had if we used either one, but our volatility (standard deviation) goes to 0! So, in effect, we get the exact same return but with no risk.

Table 3.3 is a real-life example since it is impossible to find assets that have a perfect negative correlation of −1, but rather easy to find assets with negative correlations. It is a chart of the three-year correlation between two funds: the Vanguard 500 Index and the Caldwell & Orkin Market Opportunity.

As you can see from the graph, they have a negative correlation of −.22, not a negative 1%, but still not bad.

Table 3.4 is the performance and risk of a portfolio equally weighted between the two funds versus a portfolio entirely in the Vanguard 500 Index fund for the three-year period ending 4/28/08.

By adding in a negatively correlated asset, we were able to increase the return and lower the risk substantially. The returns of the blended portfolio increased by almost 1% while the risk was almost halved. This is the power of true diversification. Given equal returns, more negative correlation is always better.

Table 3.5 is a chart of the correlations of various asset classes.

It shows us that we can get significant diversification benefits from adding market neutral investments such as TIPS, Gold, Global Real Estate, Commodities, Fixed Income, Emerging Market Debt, and Emerging Market Equity. (More about all of these later.) You will also notice that large-cap equity, small-cap equity, and international equity are all highly correlated to each other. However, most investors stop with those three asset classes when creating a diversified portfolio and they ignore gold, real estate commodities, emerging markets, and so on, because those investments on their own are too risky. However, because they have low correlation to stocks and bonds, adding them to a portfolio can actually reduce the risk of the overall portfolio.

Correlation Rules

1. Look to add assets to your portfolio that have positive returns and low to negative correlation with other portfolio assets.
2. Given equal returns, choose the most negatively correlated asset.

How can you judge correlation if you don't have fancy computer software? If you are well versed in Microsoft Excel, you can use that to calculate correlations. Here's how you do it:

Step 1: Go to a web site that will give you daily price information for mutual funds, for example, finance.yahoo.com.

Step 2: Get the historical prices of the mutual funds you are looking at.

Step 3: Import those prices into Microsoft Excel and put them side by side. This can be done by downloading the spreadsheet or just copying and pasting.

Step 4: Use the Correl function to find the correlation of two or more price streams.

Table 3.5 Correlation Table

Asset Class	Market Neutral	TIPS	Gold	Global Real Estate	Commodities	Emerging Market Debt	Emerging Market Equity	U.S. Small-Cap Equity	Fixed Income	International Equity	Cash	U.S. Large-Cap Equity
Market Neutral	1.00											
TIPS	0.09	1.00										
Gold	0.42	0.30	1.00									
Global Real Estate	0.31	0.06	0.34	1.00								
Commodities	0.11	0.28	0.31	0.06	1.00							
Emerging Market Debt	0.07	0.48	0.20	0.18	−0.08	1.00						
Emerging Market Equity	0.31	0.00	0.41	0.41	0.12	0.35	1.00					
U.S. Small-Cap Equity	0.04	−0.16	0.16	0.27	−0.11	0.23	0.65	1.00				
Fixed Income	0.06	0.87	0.16	0.07	0.07	0.65	−0.03	−0.17	1.00			
International Equity	0.35	−0.05	0.33	0.39	0.00	0.35	0.82	0.73	−0.04	1.00		
Cash	0.21	−0.08	0.07	0.01	−0.15	−0.21	0.01	−0.13	0.1	−0.04	1.00	
U.S. Large-Cap Equity	0.08	−0.21	0.01	0.25	−0.25	0.37	0.66	0.82	−0.14	0.81	−0.05	1.00

Source: Deutsche Asset Management, as of 9/30/07.

Table 3.6   Yearly Returns of Caldwell & Orkin and Vanguard 500 Index

Year	1998	1999	2000	2001	2002	2003	2004	2005	2006	2007
Caldwell & Orkin	22.4%	−3.9%	26.7%	−3.8%	2.9%	−6.6%	−1.0%	−.13%	7.4%	33.1%
Vanguard 500 Index	28.6%	21.1%	−9.1%	−12.0%	−22.2%	28.5%	10.7%	4.8%	15.6%	5.4%

Table 3.7   Yearly Returns of Fidelity Large Cap Stock and Vanguard 500 Index

Year	1998	1999	2000	2001	2002	2003	2004	2005	2006	2007
Fidelity Large Cap Stock	36.5%	30.2%	−14.5%	−17.8%	−23.0%	25.16%	6.37%	7.48%	12.96%	13.09%
Vanguard 500 Index	28.6%	21.1%	−9.1%	−12.0%	−22.2%	28.5%	10.7%	4.8%	15.6%	5.4%

If you are not very computer literate or you can't find a teen-ager to do this for you, then you can just look at the returns of two investments and get a sense of whether they are correlated or not. Table 3.6 shows the year-by-year returns for the Caldwell & Orkin Market Opportunity Fund versus the Vanguard 500 Index Fund.

You don't have to use fancy software to be able to tell that these funds are not correlated. Caldwell & Orkin was down in 1999 while the Vanguard fund was way up. Caldwell & Orkin did very well during 2000–2002 while the Vanguard fund crashed. Caldwell & Orkin suffered during the recovery of 2003–2006 while the Vanguard fund did quite well. Finally, Caldwell & Orkin had a great year in 2007 while the Vanguard fund didn't do nearly as well.

Table 3.7 shows another fund compared to the Vanguard 500 Index. You don't need fancy software to tell that it is highly correlated to the S&P 500 Index. The years when the market was up big, the fund was up big. The years when the market was down, the fund was down. If you do the calculations on Morningstar Principia the 10-year correlation is .94, pretty close to completely correlated. If you want to build a diversified portfolio, it doesn't really help to have both of these funds. They are almost the same.

Put the returns of all of your investments on one page so you can see them together like the tables above. In this way you can get a good feeling about whether they are highly correlated. I am not saying that you don't want to have correlated funds in your portfolio. For each asset class in your portfolio, you want to have more than one money manager. Just in case one is having problems unrelated to their overall asset class, hopefully one of the others is doing okay. The key point here is that having more money managers does not mean that you are diversified. I could have 100 different mutual funds and still not be diversified. It is the correlation that matters.

You want to end up with an overall portfolio with investments that are not highly correlated to each other. One thing to keep in mind is that sometimes things look correlated when they are not, and sometimes things that historically are not correlated can become so in a crisis. During a large market downturn most investments that are related to the stock market will go down. Normally, oil and gold are only moderately correlated, but during the current market crisis they have become highly correlated. This year U.S. financial stocks and Chinese stocks have both gone down, making it appear that U.S. financial stocks and Chinese stocks are highly correlated. However, if you look back over time they actually have a very small correlation.

Another goal of diversification is to develop an overall portfolio that isn't correlated with the market. Imagine your satisfaction at watching the market go down 300 points and seeing that your portfolio actually went up. Most days when the market is down something is up. If you are highly diversified, chances are you are invested in the thing that is up. By combining a bunch of noncorrelated assets, you will end up with a portfolio that is not highly correlated with the market. By diversifying you will hopefully always have at least one area of your portfolio going up regardless of what the market is doing. The flip side, of course, is that when the market is up 300 points you won't be up as much. As of this writing, commodities allocations are holding up our portfolios because commodities have been rising as the market has been falling.

Diversification Is the Key

One of the most important drivers of large endowment investment success is building diversified portfolios. They will normally have a number of different money managers, sometimes 100 or more, with a number of different investment styles. Because of this diversification they are not nearly as affected by such things as the

Asian Currency Crisis of 1998, the bursting of the technology bubble in 2000, and the subprime crisis that we are currently experiencing. Yes, some of the money managers they use get hurt, some quite a bit, but the portfolio is so diversified that the other managers more than pick up the slack. For example, in 2007 Harvard took a $350 million loss when one of its hedge fund investments, Sowood Capital Management, blew up. Harvard was diversified enough that this had little impact on their performance for the year. If you want to have investment results like the endowments, then you need to be diversified much more than you probably are right now. What would happen to your portfolio if one of your investments went down 30%? If you don't like the answer, then you need to be more diversified.

CHAPTER

4

Skill-Based Money Managers versus Style Box-Based Money Managers

During the annual Morningstar Investment Conference in June 2008, many of the fund firms present were talking about coming out with new products to address the changing investment environment. It is obvious that mutual fund firms are moving quickly toward offering new products designed to deliver alpha (absolute returns based on manager skill) instead of their previous focus on beta (tracking or beating an index). (For definitions of alpha and beta, see the Appendix.) Endowments mostly use money managers who focus on absolute returns and generate most of their returns from alpha. For years, individual investors have been investing in mutual funds that either track an index or try to slightly beat an index. The products didn't exist for them to use an endowment methodology even if they wanted to. That is changing. More and more, mutual funds are coming out that focus on absolute returns and alpha. We call these skill-based money managers, and in this chapter we will talk about why they are crucial to building an endowment type of portfolio.

Alpha and Beta

Basically, the return that a money manager or portfolio has is the sum of alpha and beta. *Beta* is simply the return you get for just being in the market. *Alpha* is outperformance and is due to the skill of the money manager. For example, let's say the market was up 10% and a mutual fund that takes as much risk as the market was up 12%. So, 10% of this mutual fund's return is due to beta, just being in the market, whereas 2% is due to alpha. That is how much value added the money manager was able to provide. This can work the other way as well. Suppose that the money manager was up only 8%. Even though 10% still came from beta, this manager detracted from the performance by 2%. Unfortunately, this happens more often than not in the investment business, which is why many people counsel investors to just buy index funds.

Beta is cheap and easy to find. All you have to do is buy an index fund or index exchange-traded funds (ETFs). They have low expense ratios, and rightly so, since all they are giving you is market returns, or beta. Many people would argue that investors should only be concerned about beta and only buy index funds. I disagree; I think alpha can provide extra return and lower the risk in your portfolio. In fact, as of this writing, if I held an index fund based on the S&P 500 on October 9, 2007, then I am down around 20%!

Alpha is much harder to find, and it can be expensive. Many people, my business school professors included, would argue that alpha doesn't exist. They say that the markets are efficient and nobody can beat them. As a money manager and someone who hires money managers, I disagree. I see alpha all the time. I have seen a hedge fund that had only had 8 negative months in

Do People Who Profess That Markets Are Efficient Really Believe It?

My investments professor in business school used to teach us that markets are efficient. Everyone knows everything, and it is all priced into the market. People like Peter Lynch and Warren Buffett are just outliers as would be in any normal statistical distribution. My professor never seemed to have his heart in it when he talked about efficient markets. I always believed that he didn't really buy it, but he had to teach the curriculum. After class one day he told me that he had developed a moving average crossing system for trading currencies that he had sold to a hedge fund. Of course, he didn't mention that this strategy only worked because the markets aren't actually efficient, but I got the point.

11 years, the worst being down 1.1%. All the while it had delivered an average annual performance of 9.8%. I have seen a mutual fund that averaged over 20% a year for the past five years. It also made money in 2002 when the stock market got killed. I could go on and on, but the point is that alpha does exist. There are money managers that have outperformed and continue to outperform their relevant benchmark on a risk-adjusted basis. It is hard to find and it can be expensive, but it is worth it.

Web sites like Morningstar.com calculate alpha for mutual funds so you don't need to do the calculation yourself. Other types of money managers will usually calculate alpha for you. One important note is that Morningstar calculates alpha based on the appropriate index for the fund, not the S&P 500. Which index you calculate alpha against can make a big difference. For example, the Ivy Asset Strategy has a three-year alpha as of 6/31/08 versus the S&P 500 of 17.07. However, if you look at the index that the fund most resembles, the MSCI Emerging Markets, the alpha is only 9.72. This is still very respectable but almost half the alpha versus the S&P 500. When you are comparing funds based on alpha, you want to make sure that the funds are similar and that you are using the appropriate index. Getting the alpha of a bond fund versus the S&P 500 is meaningless because a bond fund has nothing to do with this index. Therefore, comparing the alpha of a stock fund and a bond fund is no help. It only helps you when you are comparing like funds.

For years most investors have invested the old way. They came up with an asset allocation, usually some large-cap growth, large-cap value, small-cap, mid-cap, and international. They then needed style box-based money managers to manage each part of the allocation. The money management field obliged, and most money managers have become closet indexers that seek to closely match the benchmark and get most of their return from beta. From 2000 to 2002, someone with one of these portfolios would have taken a beating. Perhaps not as much as the market overall, but still down quite a bit. Since then, the money management field has been evolving. Before 2002, money managers who sought to get the bulk of their return from alpha didn't have much of a place in traditional portfolios because they could go into whatever style they wanted. One day they may be in large-cap growth stocks, the next they could be in small-cap value. This would play havoc with an asset allocation. Because there was no demand, money management firms didn't spend much time and effort developing alpha-generating products. After 2002, investors started becoming focused on the concept of absolute returns. Traditional money managers focused on relative returns versus their index. If their index was down 10% and they were down 9%, then they did a good job. Absolute return is beating zero, or beating inflation. It is positive return regardless of what the markets are doing. With the 2000–2002 crash fresh in investors' minds, and with the mediocre returns we have been seeing from the stock market lately, investors have been looking for new alternatives. The money management field has again been happy to oblige.

Skill-Based versus Style Box-Based

Many people throw around the term *alternative investments* when they talk about any investment strategy that is not long either stocks or bonds. I think this is a misnomer. There are really only four asset classes: stocks, bonds, cash, and commodities. What makes one money manager different from another is which strategies they use to invest in those four asset classes. Some managers just focus on going long a specific narrow asset class. I call these types of managers *style box-based money managers*. These money managers fit into one of the styles we have been talking about: large-cap growth, large-cap value, small-cap, mid-cap, and so on. Style box-based money managers get most of their performance from beta.

On the other hand, some managers might have much more flexibility to invest across different asset classes, or the ability to go both long and short. I call these types of managers *skill-based money managers*. Skill-based money managers seek to get the bulk of their returns from alpha. These could be mutual funds, separately managed accounts, or hedge funds; it doesn't really matter what vehicle the manager uses. It only matters how much flexibility they have. (I will talk about all of these in later chapters.)

Are Hedge Funds Really Hedged?

The first hedge fund was developed by Alfred Williams. He bought stocks he liked and sold short stocks he didn't, so the fund was hedged, and the term *hedge fund* became part of investment lore. Today's hedge funds don't necessarily need to be hedged, and in fact many are not.

As I mentioned previously, until 2000 most money managers were style box-based. Most investors had rigid portfolios broken down by style that required managers who focused only on a specific style (large-cap growth, large-cap value, small-cap growth, small-cap value, and so on) and never drifted. If a manager deviated from his style, he would probably be removed from the portfolio. I would argue that this was, and still is, a flawed approach. But during most of the 1990s everyone was making money, so no one cared. When the market crashed from 2000 to 2002, investors with style box-based money managers lost tremendous amounts of money. During the 1990s investors were concerned about beating the market. I had one client come to me in the late 1990s to say that he was very conservative and didn't want to lose any money. He would be happy with 30% per year! After 2002 people became more concerned about not losing money; they wanted return *of* their principal versus return *on* their principal.

Recent times have also become more challenging for investors as the baby boomers reach retirement age, and it looks more and more like we are in a period of mediocre returns in the stock market. The challenges have called for new solutions; thus we are seeing more and more skill-based money managers come in the market.

The Changing Investment Environment

Higher volatility in the stock market and low bond yields have made investment success more difficult than ever. From 1995 to 1999 investors could throw darts at a board and make money. Since 2000 that has been far from the case. Add to this the fact that baby boomers are retiring and looking at long life spans and the need to take greater responsibility for their retirement income than past generations. More than ever the consequences for poor investment results are severe.

My crystal ball isn't better than anyone else's but if you look at the market from 1980 to 1999 (Table 4.1), it is hard to fathom how we can see 17.6% average returns over the next 19 years. It is hard to fathom 2.2%, also. Whatever returns end up being my guess, they will not be nearly as high as we were accustomed to in the 1980s and 1990s (until the next stock market bubble, that is).

In the past, international investments provided portfolio diversification by not moving in the same direction at the same time as U.S. investments. Recently, that is no longer the case as they have become more correlated. Table 4.2 shows the correlation of the S&P 500 with international stocks as measured by the MSCI EAFE Index.

Table 4.1   Can We Expect Future Returns to Be Like Past Returns?

	1980–1989	1990–1999	2000–2007
U.S. Stocks Average Return	17.6%	18.2%	2.2%
U.S. Bonds Average Return	12.4%	7.7%	6.3%

Source: Compiled by Matthew Tuttle as of 9/30/07.
Note: U.S. Stocks are represented by the S&P 500 Index; bonds are represented by the Lehman Brothers Aggregate Bond Index.

As mentioned in my previous discussion of correlation, anything nearing 1 is highly correlated. As you can see from Table 4.2, historically international stocks have not been highly correlated with U.S. stocks and therefore have diversification benefits when added to a portfolio. Since 2000 this relationship has changed, and now investors get little diversification benefits from having international stocks. Some might argue that correlations could go back to where they were in the past, but I think that as the economy becomes more global and it becomes harder to tell the difference between a U.S. company and an international company, markets will probably become more correlated. (For example, are McDonalds and Coca-Cola U.S. or international? They get a lot of their sales from overseas.)

Table 4.2   Correlation of S&P 500 to MSCI EAFE

Time Period	Correlation
1980–1989	.47
1990–1999	.54
2000–9/30/2007	.83

Source: Compiled by Matthew Tuttle as of 9/30/07.
Note: MSCI EAFE is an index of international stocks.

Other assets that investors often use for diversification are also highly correlated.

Table 4.3 shows the correlation of value, growth, and small stocks to the S&P 500 Index. Again, investors are not getting much in diversification benefits. Because of this, investors need to look to other places for diversification.

Style Box-Based versus Skill-Based

I had a good friend who was a money manager who invested in small-capitalization growth stocks. Those are stocks of smaller companies

Table 4.3 Correlation of Other Asset Classes to the S&P 500 Index, 9/30/02–9/30/07

Index	Correlation to S&P 500 Index
Russell 1000 Growth	.81
Russell 1000 Value	.96
Russell 2000	.82
Russell 2000 Growth	.82
Russell 2000 Value	.79

Source: Zephyr Analytics.

that are growing or are expected to grow. From 2000 to 2002 these types of stocks took a beating in the market decline. Every day my friend went to work knowing he was probably going to lose money. He couldn't do anything because his fund's mandate was to be close to 100% invested in only those types of stocks. His only hope was that he wouldn't lose as much money as his benchmark so his bosses would still be happy.

Maria Bartiromo Grills a Style Box-Based Money Manager

As I was writing this and listening to CNBC in the background, a style box-based money manager appeared as a guest on Maria Bartiromo's show. He told Maria that he didn't like the stocks in his sector and that he had a large part of his portfolio in cash. Maria replied that he doesn't get paid to be in cash. What she didn't say is that he gets paid to hold his nose and buy the stocks that he thinks aren't as bad as some of the others in his sector and hope he doesn't lose as much as his benchmark.

This is the dilemma that style box-based money managers face. Their mandate forces them to be invested in a certain style only. If their style is in favor, for example, technology from 1995 to 1999, then they will do well. Once their style is out of favor, like technology from 2000 to 2002, then there is nothing they can do. It's usually either feast or famine for the style box-based manager. When

Table 4.4   Skill-Based Money Managers vs. Style Box-Based Managers

	Skill-Based Money Managers	Style Box-Based Money Managers
Performance objective	Absolute return	Relative return
Manager co-investment	Yes	Seldom
Performance-based compensation	Maybe	No
Seek to avoid	Loss	Index underperformance
Market exposure	Variable, opportunity-based	Fully invested

their style is in favor, they get articles in *Barron's* and the *Wall Street Journal* praising their great skill. When it is out of favor, they get articles in the same publications wondering how and why they lost their touch. In actuality, they didn't lose their touch; their style went out of favor and they couldn't create positive returns out of thin air. I see articles all the time now about value managers who have great long-term track records but are currently losing their touch. The writers don't seem to realize that value stocks have had a nice run but that most value investors have a lot of financial stocks and financial stocks have gotten killed lately. When value comes back, which it will (I just can't tell you when), then these managers will come back as well. When their style is out of favor style box-based managers just have to take their losses and try not to lose as much as their benchmark. If they go to cash or invest in a different sector, they will violate their mandate and investors will leave.

Skill-based money managers can move to different sectors, different assets, go long, go short, and so on. Wherever they see potential risk or return, they can skew their portfolio to benefit.

The main differences between skill-based money managers and style box-based money managers are summarized in Table 4.4.

Skill-based managers seek absolute returns, meaning they want to beat zero or inflation every year. Style box-based managers seek relative returns; they want to beat an index and don't mind being negative as long as the index is negative. Skill-based managers tend to have most of their money invested in their funds. Style box-based managers tend not to have much money invested in their funds. (Maybe they read Chapter 3 about diversification and want to have

Table 4.5   Performance of Selected Large-Cap Growth Funds, 2001–2002

Fund	2001 Return	2002 Return
American Funds Growth A	−12.28%	−22.02%
Fidelity Growth Company	−25.31%	−33.45%
Janus Fund	−26.10%	−27.56%
T Rowe Price Growth Stock	−9.79%	−23.00%
Vanguard PRIMECAP	−13.35%	−24.56%

Source: Compiled by Matthew Tuttle using data from mutual fund firm's web sites.

a diversified portfolio as well.) If the skill-based manager is a hedge fund, then they will have performance-based compensation (more about this later). Many investors object to paying their money managers based on performance, but I don't see the problem with it since it just puts the manager even more on the same side of the table as the investor. Skill-based managers look to avoid losses while style box-based managers seek to avoid underperforming their index. Losses are acceptable as long as they are not down more than the index. Finally, skill-based managers tend to have flexible exposure to the market based on where they see opportunity. Style box-based managers tend to be always pretty much fully invested.

Table 4.5 shows the performance of some of the largest large-cap growth funds from 2001 to 2002. These funds invest in large companies that are growing and are expected to grow. As you can see, they all had rough years from 2001 to 2002. Now you may be wondering why these funds didn't change their portfolio when they were losing so much money. Other areas of the market were going up during this time. Why not just change the investments? The reason is that these funds are locked in by prospectus to buying one type of stock and one type of stock only. They do not deviate from their mandate regardless of how much money they are losing or where they think the markets are headed.

Table 4.5 shows the performance of selected large-cap growth funds in 2001 and 2002. These funds, and those like them, are style box-based funds. They only invest in a certain style of stocks regardless of how those stocks are doing or are expected to be doing. There is nothing wrong with style box-based funds. In fact, if you are going to have a traditional portfolio with traditional asset classes, then you will want to use these types of funds.

Table 4.6 Performance of Selected Skill-Based Funds, 2001–2002

Fund	2001 Return	2002 Return
Leuthold Core	−4.81%	−10.06%
Ivy Asset Strategy	−10.98%	3.09%
First Eagle Global	10.21%	10.24%
Boston Partners Long/Short	24.97%	−0.82%
Hussman Strategic Growth	14.67%	14.02%

Source: Compiled by Matthew Tuttle using data from mutual fund firm's web sites.

Table 4.6 shows some skill-based funds that predominantly invest in stocks. These funds have the ability to hedge their bets, go to cash, and/or go to other asset classes if they want. The skill-based funds did a lot better over a tough period than the style box-based funds because they were able to adjust their portfolios to changing times. This is not to be confused with market timing. Skill-based managers aren't going in and out of the market like a day trader. They position themselves in the areas that they think are undervalued or otherwise attractive and avoid the areas they think are overvalued and/or don't provide enough opportunity for the risk. They can also sometimes hedge their portfolios if they are worried about a falling market.

Telling the Difference

How do you tell a style box-based money manager from a skill-based one? Below are some fund descriptions from a few mutual fund web sites that are good examples of each:

- **T. Rowe Price Growth Stock Investment Approach—From the T. Rowe Price web site (www.troweprice.com):**
  Fund Description: The objective is long-term capital growth and, secondarily, increasing dividend income through investments in the common stocks of well-established growth companies.
  Survey Says: This looks like a style box-based fund to me. It buys stocks of well-established growth companies. No mention of hedging, being able to buy value stocks, international, and so on.
- **Fidelity Mid Cap Value Fund Summary—From the Fidelity web site (www.fidelity.com):**
  Fund Description: Normally investing at least 80% of assets in securities of companies with medium market capitalizations

(those companies with market capitalizations similar to companies in the Russell Midcap Index or the Standard & Poor's MidCap 400 Index [S&P MidCap 400]). Investing in securities of companies that Federal Management Regulation (FMR) believes are undervalued in the marketplace in relation to factors such as assets, sales, earnings, growth potential, or cash flow, or in relation to securities of other companies in the same industry (stocks of these companies are often called "value" stocks). Normally investing primarily in common stocks.

Survey Says: The name pretty much gives this one away but even if it didn't, this fund is obviously a style box-based fund.

- **BlackRock Global Allocation—From BlackRock's web site (www.blackrockfunds.com):**

  Fund Description: The Fund seeks to provide high total investment return through a fully managed investment policy utilizing U.S. and foreign equity, debt and money market securities, the combination of which will be varied from time to time both with respect to types of securities and markets in response to changing market and economic trends.

  Survey Says: You can see that this description is much different. The fund can invest in U.S. and foreign stocks, debt, and money market securities (cash), and the combination is varied in response to the market. This is obviously a skill-based fund.

- **Ivy Asset Strategy Investment Approach—From Ivy's web site (www.ivyfunds.com):**

  Fund Description: The Fund may invest in any market that we believe offers a high probability of return or, alternatively, that provides a high degree of safety in uncertain times. Dependent on the outlook for the U.S. and global economies, we make top-down allocations among stocks, bonds, cash, precious metals (for defensive purposes) and currency markets around the globe. After determining allocations, we seek attractive opportunities within each market.

  Survey Says: This is another skill-based fund. It has the ability to go anywhere and do anything.

Ivy Asset Strategy's portfolio during the period from 2000 to 2002, highlighted in Table 4.7, shows how skill-based managers can operate during a market downturn.

Table 4.7   Ivy Asset Strategy's Top Two Asset Classes, 2000–2002

Period	Mar 2000	Sep 2000	Mar 2001	Sep 2001	Mar 2002	Sep 2002
Largest asset class	U.S. Stocks, 74.9%	U.S. Stocks, 57.6%	U.S. Govt Bonds, 51.8%	U.S. Govt Bonds, 59.3%	U.S. Govt Bonds, 65.6%	U.S. Govt Bonds, 59.9%
Second largest asset class	Cash, 9%	Cash, 17.8%	Cash, 22.9%	Gold, Stocks, 21.8%	U.S. Stocks, 12.3%	Gold, Stocks, 11.9%

As you can see, their investments have fluctuated greatly depending on their view of the markets. At the top of the market in March 2000 they had almost 75% of their portfolio in U.S. stocks. As the market started to decline, they shifted toward U.S. government bonds and gold. Because of these shifts, they not only held up during the market decline but they also had a positive return in 2002. When the market was down over 22%, they were up 3.09%. This shows the benefit of a skill-based money manager.

Getting Rid of the Long Only Constraint

Many skill-based managers also have the ability to sell stocks and other assets short. For years mutual funds have only been able to buy stocks; they have not been able to sell them short. That all changed in 1997 when the SEC loosened the restrictions on short selling by mutual funds. Since then we have seen a convergence of the mutual fund world and the hedge fund world. Before that, most mutual funds were long only while most hedge funds were long and short. So many new long/short mutual funds are being offered that both

Is the SEC Going to Get Rid of Short Selling?

As of this writing, the SEC has put in place short selling rules to protect financial stocks from what is called *naked short selling*. This is basically illegal anyway; the SEC's rules simply enforce the law. In a typical short sale the seller needs to borrow the stock from somewhere and then sell it. In a naked short sale, the sellers are selling stock they don't have. With a naked short sale someone could theoretically sell short the entire market cap of a company. With a legal short sale, there is no way anyone could borrow near that amount of stock to sell it short.

Morningstar and Lipper had to create a new mutual fund category. So now that mutual funds can sell stocks short, should they?

Consider the typical style box-based mutual fund. Since it seeks to outperform an index, it will generally overweight stocks it likes versus index weights and underweight stocks it doesn't like. So let's say a fund is trying to beat an index that has a number of stocks in it, including ABC Company, which makes up 5% of the index and XYZ Company that makes up only .01% of the index. The manager will overweight or underweight these stocks based on how he feels they are likely to perform. If the manager wants to overweight ABC, he can have 10% of his portfolio invested in it. If he wants to over-weight XYZ, he can have 1% of his portfolio invested in it. Those are both well above the index weights so it is easy for the money manager to express his positive view on stocks in the index. If he wants to underweight ABC, he can put 2.5% of his portfolio in it. Since ABC is a fairly large part of the index, he can express his negative view. But what happens if he wants to underweight XYZ? He can decide not to buy it at all, but since it is a very small part of the index, that won't have much impact on his portfolio relative to the index. There is no real way for the manager to express his negative view of XYZ. He might be convinced that XYZ is the worst stock since Enron, but there is really no way he can monetize that view.

If we look at an index like the S&P 500, which many money managers use as a benchmark, the largest 10 stocks in the index make up 22% of the index weights. Therefore, it is very hard to underweight a vast majority of the stocks in the S&P 500. SEI Investments Co. did a study of this and looked at four different scenarios: portfolio managers who can underweight or overweight a stock by .25%, .50%, 1%, 1.5%, and 2% versus the S&P 500. So for example, if ABC stock makes up 10% of the index and I can overweight or underweight by .25%, then I would be completely underweight if I have 9.75% of my portfolio in ABC (10% − .25%) and completely overweight if ABC was 10.25% of my portfolio (10% + .25%). If a portfolio manager is only allowed to underweight a stock by .25% versus the index, then any stock in the index that has a weight less than .25% cannot be underweighted. Table 4.8 shows what the study found.

So a manager who can only go long and has a maximum underweight of 1% can only fully underweight 15 stocks in the S&P 500. So, no matter how badly he may feel about the other 485 stocks in the index, he has no real way of expressing or monetizing that view.

Table 4.8   Number of Stocks That Cannot Be Underweighted in the S&P 500

Underweight Limit	No. of Stocks That Can Be Fully Underweighted	Percentage of Stocks That Can Be Fully Underweighted
.25%	88	18%
.50%	45	9%
1.00%	15	3%
1.5%	10	2%
2%	7	1%

Source: SEI and Bloomberg.

Getting rid of the long only constraint can fix this problem. A skill-based manager who has the ability to sell stocks short could short any stock in the S&P 500 getting him further away from the index. This makes his returns less based on beta and more based on alpha. The more short positions he has, the less his performance is going to be based on what the market is doing and the more it is going to be based on whether or not he is good at identifying stocks to short.

The long only manager can translate his positive forecasts for certain stocks into portfolio weightings but has a hard time with his negative forecasts. A manager with no constraints can translate his positive and negative forecasts into portfolio weightings.

Long/Short Advantages

Long/short funds have several advantages over funds that can only go long stocks, including:

- *Better Use of Investment Research.* Most money managers have a system for ranking stocks. Long only managers can make good use of their system in buying stocks they rank highly, but have no use for the research that goes into identifying the lowest-ranking stocks. Managers who have the ability to short can use the full scope of their research by going long the highest-ranked stocks and shorting the lowest-ranked stocks.
- *Enhanced Alpha Potential.* Most long only managers do not want to stray too far from their benchmarks, meaning that their performance will be driven largely by beta. Managers

who have the ability to short are not tracking an index. The leverage inherent in shorting securities also adds potential alpha. When you sell a stock you don't own, you get use of the cash until you decide to buy it back. You can use that cash to buy more stocks you like. Of course, the reverse is also accurate. The long/short structure and leverage can magnify losses as well. If you use the proceeds of short sales to buy stocks that go down in value, then having that leverage hurts your returns.

- *Increased Access to Opportunities.* Long/short managers can pursue opportunities that long only managers would most likely avoid. For example, suppose a money manager liked Microsoft but had a negative view of the technology sector. A long/short manager could buy Microsoft and simultaneously short a technology ETF or weaker technology stocks. A long only manager would probably just avoid Microsoft for fear that a weak technology sector would bring down the stock.
- *Greater Risk Management Potential.* If long only managers see a market decline coming, they can either invest in less risky stocks or go to cash (which is generally not an option as they are expected to stay pretty much fully invested). Long/short managers can increase the short side of their portfolio.

Just because I believe that money managers should be able to sell stocks short does not mean that all of them should do it. There are some disadvantages to selling short:

- *Profit is limited while losses are not.* When I sell a stock short it can only go down to zero but it can keep going up forever. Therefore, my profits are limited but my losses are not.
- *Short sellers sometimes get squeezed.* When a lot of people are short a stock, they can get caught in a short squeeze. In a short squeeze the stock is going up fast, and the short sellers are scrambling to buy shares to cover their short positions. This forced buying causes the stock price to go up further and can magnify losses for the short seller.
- *Short sellers might be right about a stock, but too early.* Smart short sellers might have foreseen the coming technology stock collapse in the late 1990s, but unless they got the timing exactly right, they would probably have had to survive huge losses as tech stocks ran up until they collapsed.

- *Selling short requires a different skill set.* Some money managers are great stock pickers but awful short sellers. It is a skill set that not all money managers possess. Whenever a new long/short fund comes out, I would always wait a while to see how it does.
- *Short selling can dampen returns in an up market.* When the market is going up, even if a stock is bad, a rising tide may lift all boats. Many long/short hedge funds had to endure client complaints during the late 1990s as they underperformed long only money managers, especially those that focused on technology stocks. Of course, they were proven right during the 2000–2002 crash, but many investors didn't stay on to benefit from that.
- *Skill-based money managers have some disadvantages.* Skill-based managers are not the best thing since sliced bread. There are some disadvantages.
- *Skill-based managers don't work well in traditional style box-based portfolios.* If you want to have the typical style box type of portfolio that you had in the 1990s, skill-based managers don't fit well into style boxes. Their short positions and flexibility can cause significant deviations from the indexes. I recently had a meeting with the money manager of an international stock fund who was forced to fire a skill-based advisor because many investment advisors complained that the addition of that manager made the fund deviate from the fund's benchmark.
- *Skill-based managers can create security overlap.* When you have a number of money managers who can invest in whatever they want, you may think you have a diversified portfolio, but what happens if they all decide to invest in the same thing at the same time? When dealing with these managers you need to keep yourself in the loop of what they are doing. Read the annual and semiannual reports and see where they are invested. Also, take a look at their performance versus your other managers to see if they are becoming more correlated.
- *Skill-based managers probably won't beat style box-based managers in market upturns.* During market upturns, style box-based managers will probably do better than skill-based managers. Skill-based managers shine in challenging markets.

- *Skill-based managers have to be better than style box-based managers.* Skill-based managers have to be well versed on the entire world and every asset class. Style box-based managers only need to be familiar with the stocks that fit their style. This makes it harder to find skill-based managers. You need to do your homework to make sure you have the best of the best. Negative returns are also not acceptable for skill-based managers. Style box-based managers can be negative as long as they are not as negative as their index.
- *Skill-based managers will generally charge higher fees.* If you are getting alpha, then I would argue the higher fees are worth it.

Skill-Based Managers Are the Key

Skill-based money managers, those who try to generate most of their returns from alpha, are the key to developing endowment types of portfolios. Style box-based managers have their place but in order to generate absolute types of returns you need managers who add alpha. The investment industry is quickly shifting to this idea as more and more skill-based funds are being introduced. These provide investors with portfolios of any size tools they need to create an endowment type of portfolio.

Introduction to the Endowment Philosophy

The market turmoil of 2000–2002 and 2007–2008 has shaken many investors to the core. Some of the old standby investment strategies are no longer holding up, like buying and holding solid stocks and buying an index fund. It used to be that you could buy and hold solid stocks through thick and thin. They may decline in value, but they would never go bankrupt. It might be hard to remember now, but at one point in time Bear Stearns, Lehman Brothers, Fannie Mae, Freddie Mac, AIG, and Washington Mutual were all considered solid stocks. Buying index funds used to also be a well-thought-of investment strategy. However, as of this writing we are perilously close to the first negative 10-year period in the stock market since the Depression. What is an investor to do in this type of environment? The key is to look at which investors have been doing well now and in the past and see how they are able to do it. If one conducts such a search, it is hard to miss the fact that the endowments of large universities have managed to outperform the market and hold up during the market declines. This chapter will give you an introduction to the investment philosophies of these large endowments and answer the question about how they do so well.

The Large Endowments

Why should you care about what the large college endowments are doing? The Harvard and Yale endowments get a lot of press about

Table 5.1   Large Endowments Outperform—Average Investment Pool Compounded Nominal Rates of Return for Fiscal Years Ending June 30, 2007, for 1, 3, 5, and 10 Years

Investment Pool Assets	1-yr (%)	3-yr (%)	5-yr (%)	10-yr (%)
Greater than $1 billion	21.3	16.4	13.9	11.1
$501 million to $1 billion	19.3	14.2	12.3	9.5
$101 million to $500 million	18.0	13.1	11.5	8.5
$51 million to $100 million	16.7	11.9	10.8	7.9
$26 million to $50 million	15.9	10.7	9.8	7.3
Less than or equal to $25 million	14.1	9.7	8.8	6.7
S&P 500	20.6	11.7	10.7	7.1
Lehman Brothers Aggregate Bond Index	6.1	4.0	4.5	6.0

Source: NACUBO Average Investment Pool Compounded Nominal Rates of Return for FY 2007.

their investment results, and for good reason. They and other large endowments consistently beat the market year in and year out. Most individual investors are convinced that the investment strategies of these multibillion-dollar endowments are out of their reach, but that's not necessarily true. Yes, you probably can't access most of the money managers that these endowments use, at least not at the same fee structure. You also may not be able to access some of the asset classes they use. However, investors with portfolios of any size can use investment vehicles as simple as readily available mutual funds to construct portfolios that have many of the attributes of the portfolios constructed by large endowments.

Why go through all the trouble? Table 5.1 is a chart from the National Association of College and University Business Officers (NACUBO) showing the investment results of large endowments versus smaller endowments, along with the returns from the stock and bond markets.

It is very interesting to note that the large endowments not only beat the markets they also beat the small endowments. Even though they don't publish the money managers that they allocate money to, they do publish the asset classes they use and in what percentage in their annual reports. By reading these reports, investors can get a good idea of what the endowment's overall investment philosophy is.

If we just strip out Harvard and Yale, two of the most successful endowments, they have handily trounced the market over a 1-year

Author's Note

From now on in this book when I talk about endowments, I am talking about large endowments.

and 10-year period. Table 5.2 shows the returns for Harvard and Yale versus the S&P 500.

Large Endowments Invest Differently Than Small Endowments

There are three main reasons why large endowments outperform small endowments: They have more money in hedge funds, less money in bonds, and more money in private equity than do small endowments.

- Large endowments average 20.5% in hedge funds; the smallest endowments average 2.9%.
- Large endowments average 11.2% in fixed income (bonds); the smallest endowments average 27.5%.
- Large endowments average 7.1% in private equity and 3.3% in venture capital; the smallest endowments have virtually no exposure to those asset classes.

Table 5.3 shows the difference in asset allocation between small and large endowments. The difference in the asset allocation of the large versus small endowments is one of the main reasons large endowments do so much better.

Now I know what you are thinking. Hedge funds and private equity are too risky and you have to be ultrarich to invest in them,

Table 5.2   Returns for Fiscal Year Ending June 30, 2007, and 10 Years

	1-yr (%)	10-yr (%)
Yale endowment	28	17.8
Harvard endowment	23	15
S&P 500	20.6	7.1

Source: 2007 Yale Endowment Report and *Harvard University Gazette.*

Table 5.3   Average Asset Class Allocations MW

Investment Pool Assets	Equity (%)	Fixed Income (%)	Real Estate (%)	Cash (%)	Hedge Funds (%)	Private Equity (%)	Venture Capital (%)	Natural Resources (%)	Other (%)
Greater than $1 billion	47	11.2	5	1.6	20.5	7.1	3.3	3.6	0.6
$501 million to $1 billion	50.5	13.3	5.3	2.3	17.7	5.6	2.1	2.4	0.8
$101 million to $500 million	56.6	15.1	3.6	2.8	13.8	2.8	1.1	2.1	2
$51 million to $100 million	60.1	19.2	3.6	3.8	8.7	1.2	0.4	1.3	1.8
$26 million to $50 million	63.2	21.3	3.1	3.1	6.9	0.5	0.1	0.8	1
Less than or equal to $25 million	59.5	27.5	1.8	6.4	2.9	0.4	0.2	0.3	0.9

Source: 2007 NACUBO Endowment Study.

and bonds are the only way to reduce risk in your portfolio. Once you have finished reading this book you might feel differently, but bear with me for now. There is a method to the large endowment's madness.

You may also look at Table 5.3 and think that because they are allocating more money to hedge funds and private equity, that they are taking more risk and should be generating a higher return. This, however, is not the case. In this book I will show you:

- How adding alternative types of assets like hedge funds and private equity can actually reduce the risk of a portfolio
- How any size investor can access these types of strategies
- How bonds could actually be the riskiest investment you own

As shown in Table 5.4, Harvard and Yale have small exposure to fixed income and large exposure to private equity and absolute return (hedge funds).

Yale particularly is not a fan of bonds, as they have only 4% of their portfolio invested in them.

Over the past 10 years across endowments of all sizes, we see that endowments are lowering exposure to fixed income and

Table 5.4   Yale and Harvard Asset Allocation as of June 30, 2007

	Absolute Return (%)	Domestic Equity (%)	Fixed Income (%)	Foreign Equity (%)	Private Equity (%)	Real Assets (%)	Cash (%)
Yale	23.3	11	4	14.1	18.7	27.1	1.9
Harvard	17	12	13	19	13	31	−5

Source: 2007 Yale Endowment Report and Harvard Management Company.

Table 5.5   Average Allocation to Selected Asset Classes FY 1998 and 2007 (All Endowments)

Asset Class	1998 Allocation (%)	2007 Allocation (%)	% Change
Equity	63.5	57.6	−9.3
Fixed income	25.6	18.6	−27.3
Real estate	2.1	3.5	66.7
Cash	4.3	3.5	−18.6
Hedge funds	2.8	10.6	278.6
Private equity	0.4	2.3	475.0
Venture capital	0.7	0.9	28.6
Natural resources	0.2	1.6	700
Other	0.4	1.4	250

Source: NACUBO Press Release and Fact Sheet on 2007 Endowment Study Results (Jan. 24, 2008).

increasing exposure to real estate, hedge funds, private equity, and natural resources. Table 5.5 shows endowment allocations in 1998 versus allocations in 2007. You can see that the main changes are that the average allocation to bonds, stocks, and cash has declined while the average allocation to hedge funds, private equity, and natural resources has more than doubled.

Endowment Investment Rules

Endowments have two key objectives:

1. Don't lose money.
2. Earn a high enough real return (above inflation) so that the university can spend the return only and not have to dip into principal.

Many individual investors have the same objectives, especially those in or near retirement. Individuals don't like to lose money and retirees need to earn a high enough real return so they can withdraw money from their portfolio without outliving their money.

Retirement Investment Myths

Retirees often get advice like once you retire, all of your money should be in bonds and you can live off the interest. Or, they are told to take their age minus 100 and that's how much to invest in stocks; the rest should go into bonds. I don't know how well this advice works. If I live past 100, perhaps then I have to sell stocks short. These rules might have worked when life expectancies were much shorter, but they don't work so well now unless you don't live very long or have a very large surplus in your portfolio.

One of the biggest mistakes individual investors make is that they ignore, or don't understand, the importance of the first rule of the endowments—don't lose any money. Most investors focus too much on how much they can gain. The endowments flip this around and focus first on avoiding large losses. I can't tell you how many investors I talk to whose portfolios are not back to where they were in 1999. If they could have avoided most of the losses they sustained from 2000–2002, they would have much more money now. Instead they had to spend the past six years digging themselves slowly out of that hole. If you learn only one thing from this book, the most important lesson is to invest to avoid large losses and focus on risk. That may seem simple. You may be thinking why did I buy this book just to have this guy tell me to avoid large losses? In actuality though, investors are psychologically wired to gravitate toward investments that will eventually generate the large losses they know they need to avoid. We will talk more about this later.

Returns are out of your control; the market will either go up or it won't. You can make the greatest case for why the market should rally or fall, but unfortunately the market doesn't listen to what you think; it will do whatever it is going to do. Historically, it has gone up more than it has gone down, but if history is any guide, there will be downturns in your future and some of them will be severe.

Trying to figure out what the market is going to do day to day, week to week, month to month, and year to year is an exercise in futility. The only thing you can control in your portfolio is how much risk you take.

As people are retiring earlier, living longer, and having to generate more of their retirement income themselves, many of the old investing rules no longer apply. It used to be that you retired at 65, moved to Florida, put all of your money in bonds or CDs, lived off the interest, and were dead by 75. Now you retire at 55 and could live until 100 or beyond (I once heard a doctor say that a baby born today could live until 130. Imagine getting married at 25 and spending 105 years with your spouse!), and your portfolio has to generate income for you for 45 years! The endowments have an unlimited lifetime but you have a long life expectancy as well. The endowments realize that if they have to spend money every year, they need to earn a high enough return above inflation to be able to spend money and keep the portfolio growing. The same goes for you. The idea of dying broke may sound appealing to you. However, nobody has a crystal ball. If you plan to die broke at 90 and live until 100, then you better hope your kids have enough money to take care of you.

Let me be clear. Individual investors cannot exactly mimic what the largest endowments are doing, for a number of reasons:

1. *There are some asset classes that endowments use that individuals cannot.* For example, some endowments buy actual forests with timber. As an individual you probably don't have the money or the access to invest in timberland. There are ETFs that invest in timber companies, but they do not generate the same return stream as actual timberland.
2. *Endowments do not pay taxes, individuals do.* Endowments can invest without regard to the taxes an investment might generate. As a taxpayer you need to focus on after-tax return because that's what ends up in your pocket.
3. *Endowments have an unlimited lifetime, individuals do not.* Endowments can invest a large part of their portfolio in illiquid assets because they may not plan to access that money for 100 years. Most of your portfolio should probably be liquid.
4. *Endowments can access some money managers that individuals cannot.* There is a large difference between going to a money manager with $1 billion to invest and going to a money manager with

$10,000 to invest. Some of the top money managers in the country are either closed to new investors or have such high minimum investments that you cannot possibly hope to get access to them.

5. *Endowments can access some private equity deals that you can't.* Private equity is unlike any other asset class in that the top players in the market stay on top and the bottom players stay on the bottom. The best deals always go to the best firms, and unless you have millions they don't want to talk to you. I once got a cold call from a private equity firm that wanted me to steer clients to them. Just the fact that they called me out of the blue instead of my having to beg them for access told me everything I needed to know. There are ETFs that invest in publicly traded private equity companies, but just like the timber ETFs, the return streams will be very different than actual private equity. Private equity is the only asset class that I will talk about in this book that many readers simply cannot access. You need to be at least an accredited investor and, even if you are, the minimum investments are usually steep.

6. *Endowments have entire teams of people managing their funds.* These teams have the capability to find and incorporate the best managers; individuals usually don't have these resources.

With that being said, individual investors can still mimic and learn from many of the strategies which the large endowments use for a number of reasons:

1. You can still access most of the asset classes that endowments invest in. Many can be accessed through mutual funds and/ or ETFs.
2. You can still generate attractive after-tax returns. Your 401(k) or IRA is probably where the bulk of your money is anyway, and you don't pay taxes on your gains there.
3. While you won't live forever, you will probably live for a long time.
4. While you can't access every manager, there are still a number of talented money managers that have low minimum investments. There are also funds of funds and mirror funds that can give you access to some of the same managers that the endowments use.

5. Even though private equity can add value to your portfolio, it is not vital.
6. You can always hire your own chief investment officer to help you create an asset allocation, construct a portfolio, and choose the top money managers. That's what my firm, and others like mine, do for a living.

It is critical for investors to learn from these strategies and how they can implement them in their own portfolio.

Creating an Investment Portfolio

There are three activities that go into creating an investment portfolio:

1. *Asset Allocation.* How your assets will be allocated among stocks, bonds, commodities, and cash.
2. *Money Manager Selection and Portfolio Construction.* Money manager selection is which money managers (mutual funds, separate accounts, ETFs, hedge funds, you, etc.) will manage the portfolio. Portfolio construction is how much money you will allocate to each manager.
3. *Security Selection.* Which stocks, bonds, commodities, and cash instruments you will invest in.

Although I will describe these three activities in depth in Chapter 6, it is important to discuss the concept of security selection at this time. Most investors spend an inordinate amount of time on security selection. However, it is asset allocation and money manager selection that provides the most value added. Security selection is the most overvalued activity and is the hardest to get right on a consistent basis. I don't think you would argue with me on this. I would bet that if you could pick stocks that would go up all the time, you wouldn't be reading this book. The large endowments realize this. They decide what asset allocation they want, they hire money managers to manage the money, they decide how much to allocate to each manager, and then they let the managers choose the securities.

Most individual investors spend their time deciding whether they should buy Google or Yahoo, or whether the financial stocks are poised for a comeback. Not only is there the least value added to this approach, it is also time intensive. Would you rather sit at your computer watching quotes all day or doing things you actually enjoy? Instead, you should develop an appropriate asset allocation, find the best money managers, and let them concentrate on what securities to buy.

Success Leaves Clues

In this market environment, more than ever it is important to make smart choices about your money. This is easier than you might think. Investors don't have to reinvent the wheel when it comes to their portfolios. They need to find out who the top investors are and determine what they are doing. The large endowments have consistently beaten the market and protected their portfolios in downturns. Unlike some of the top hedge funds and money managers who strive to keep their philosophies secret, endowments publish their asset allocations every year and talk about their strategies. Figuring out what these endowments are doing is not hard; replicating it in your portfolio is the most difficult part. That is what the rest of this book is about.

6

Why Large Endowments Outperform the Market and How You Can, Too!

In searching for the top investors in the country to emulate, it is not hard to find endowments like Harvard and Yale. These endowments and others like them consistently beat the market and protect their portfolios during market declines. They also do not keep their investment strategies secret. Most endowments publish their Investment Policy Statements (IPSs) every year along with their asset allocation. This makes it relatively easy for individual investors to learn from what they are doing.

In the previous chapter, we focused on what investment classes endowments use and some of the key endowment investment rules. This chapter will go into more detail on the processes that endowments follow and will also discuss how you can adopt the strategies of endowments like Harvard and Yale.

The Formula to Beating the Market

The large endowments outperform because they do a number of things that individual investors don't do:

1. They focus on asset allocation.
2. They focus on money manager selection and portfolio construction and look for the best talent available.

3. They do not focus on security selection.
4. They focus on avoiding large losses.
5. They are willing to think outside the box. In fact, their investment mandate requires that they do so.

Asset Allocation

We have talked a lot in this book about asset allocation and being properly diversified among different and noncorrelated asset classes. Asset allocation is how you will divide your assets among stocks, bonds, cash, and commodities so that you have a diversified portfolio. In a landmark 1986 study, Brinson, Hood, and Beebower showed that over 91% of portfolio returns are due to asset allocation (Gary P. Brinson, L. Randolph Hood, and Gilbert L. Beebower, "Determinants of Portfolio Performance," *The Financial Analysts Journal,* July/August 1986). Although this study has come under attack in recent years, it is hard to argue that asset allocation is not the most important part of portfolio construction.

Consider the asset allocations in Table 6.1 from 2000 to 2002. The investor who had 80% in stocks would have lost 34.35% of their money, while the investor who had 20% in stocks would have gained 6.29%, a difference of over 40% just from the asset allocation decision.

Figure 6.1 shows that just allocating 20% to U.S. stocks, bonds, international stocks, real estate, and commodities would have signif-

Table 6.1   Returns of Different Asset Allocations

Cumulative return after inflation from the bear market of 2000 to 2002	
80% stock/20% bond	−34.35%
70% stock/30% bond	−25.81%
60% stock/40% bond	−19.99%
50% stock/50% bond	−13.87%
40% stock/60% bond	−7.46%
30% stock/70% bond	−0.74%
20% stock/80% bond	+6.29%

Source: Stock return from a Wilshire 5000 Index fund; bond returns from the Lehman Aggregate Index.

icantly beaten simpler portfolio mixes with much less risk. Portfolio 1 is a simple 50% U.S. stocks/50% bond mix. Portfolio 2 adds international stocks and has a slightly higher return with the same amount of risk. Portfolio 3 substitutes real estate for international stocks and has a slightly higher return with less risk. Portfolio 4 substitutes commodities and has about the same return as portfolio 3 with less risk. Portfolio 5 has 20% in each asset class which substantially increases return and lowers risk.

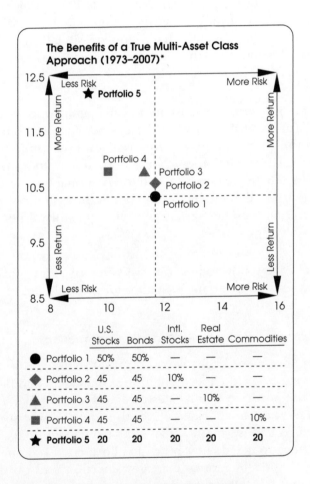

Figure 6.1 Benefits of Multi-Asset Class Portfolios

Source: The Prudential Insurance Company of America—Jennison Dryden.

The large endowments have experienced investment teams who forecast the returns, risk, and correlations for all the asset classes they use. They then put these numbers into a computer program called an optimizer that tells them which portfolio (assuming of course that their assumptions are correct) would produce the best returns for a given level of risk. They also overlay their own judgment on this when deciding how to allocate assets. As an individual investor you don't have access to an experienced investment team and sophisticated investment software (unless you want to spend a ton of money or you have an advisor who has this stuff), but you don't need it. In the chapters that follow we will talk about the asset classes listed below that the endowments use and what you can expect them to do in a portfolio.

1. *Absolute Return.* These are money managers who seek absolute returns regardless of what the market is doing. Endowments use these types of investments as a bond substitute.
2. *Stocks.* These are domestic and international stock investments.
3. *Bonds.* These are domestic and international bond investments.
4. *Real Assets.* This encompasses commodities and real estate.
5. *Private Equity.* These are nonpublic equity investments.

After we have talked about the asset classes, we will talk about risk tolerance and how to use your risk tolerance and goals to determine what your appropriate asset allocation should be.

Money Manager Selection and Portfolio Construction

Once an endowment knows what they want their asset allocation to be, the next step is to choose the money managers and decide how much of the portfolio to allocate to each. For example, let's say an endowment wants to allocate 20% of their portfolio to stocks. They then need to choose money managers to manage that allocation, and they need to decide how much to allocate to each one. I devote an entire chapter to money manager selection and portfolio construction, but basically endowments use the topics we have covered earlier to decide what managers to select and how much to give them. They are looking for managers who are not well correlated to each other and usually look for skill-based managers that have a history of generating alpha, unless they have a specific area that they want to emphasize in the portfolio. They will also tend to use more managers and allocate a small amount to each. That way they can lessen their risks because problems with one manager won't have a huge impact on the portfolio. The flip side of this is that if one manager is having a great year, this won't have a huge impact either, but the endowment is seeking steady returns not one-year home runs.

Security Selection

Deciding which stock to buy or sell is the most overvalued activity an investor can undertake. Most investors spend way too much time on which investments to buy. We have already talked about mistakes that investors make, which is why most investors are not very successful with security selection. The endowments for the most part don't bother with this; they hire the best money managers and leave it up to them.

Avoiding Large Losses

Endowments have an almost impossible mandate; they must generate a return that is high enough for the university to spend money without dipping into principal, while avoiding incurring losses.

The endowments realize that avoiding large losses is much more important than trying to generate large gains. This might seem rather obvious, but individual investor psychology motivates people toward trying to generate a large gain which inevitably leads to large losses. Every day I meet people who tell me they still haven't gotten their portfolio back to where it was in 1999 even though the market was up from 2003 to 2007. That's because they took such a large loss from 2000 to 2002 that it's taking them a long time to dig themselves out of the hole.

Table 6.2 shows the returns for two mutual funds: the Exciting Fund and the Boring Fund. (Don't bother looking in the paper for these funds. I actually made them up.)

The Boring Fund was up 7% a year, every year for five years. The Exciting Fund is much more exciting. It had great returns in years 1 through 3, one bad year in year 4, and another good year in year 5. Which fund would you see profiled on CNBC and in *Money* magazine? Obviously, it would be the Exciting Fund; not

Table 6.2   Boring Fund vs. Exciting Fund

Year	Boring Fund	Exciting Fund
1	7%	10%
2	7%	20%
3	7%	20%
4	7%	−25%
5	7%	10%

many people would care much about the Boring Fund. Without reading the next line, which fund do you think would have made the most money?

The Boring Fund.

If you had invested $100,000 into each, at the end of five years you would have $140,255 in the Boring Fund and $130,680 in the Exciting Fund. The Boring Fund shareholders would have been almost $10,000 richer and would have had a much smoother ride. The reason for this is due to the one year the Exciting Fund had a large loss, which wiped out most of its past performance. To understand this better, you need to understand the math of the markets. Let's say you lose 50% on a stock or mutual fund. How much do you have to earn percentagewise just to break even? The answer is 100%. It's a lot easier to lose 50% than it is to double your money.

As such, one of the golden rules of making money in the market is that, if you can avoid large losses, you don't need large gains. The only reason investors needed to be up 28% in 2003 was to try to recoup some of their losses from 2000 to 2002. It may seem like everyone should know this rule but they don't. If you are constantly chasing hot performance, trying to guess what direction the market is going in, and buying things on hot tips, you will eventually have a large loss.

Tables 6.3 and 6.4 are more examples of the importance of avoiding large losses. Suppose we have two investors: Investor 1 and Investor 2. Investor 1 puts his money into an investment that returns 12% per year. As you can see in Table 6.3, he starts out with $1,000 and at the end of three years he has $1,404 and has achieved a total rate of return (ROR) of 40.49%.

Investor 2 starts out with the same investment as Investor 1 in the first year, but gets bored. His stockbroker gives him a hot tip about a great stock that should double by the end of the year. Instead, it goes down 30%. (Don't you hate it when that happens?)

Table 6.3   Investor 1

	Year 1	Year 2	Year 3	Total ROR
Rate of return	12%	12%	12%	40.49%
Beginning balance	$1,000	$1,120	$1,254	
Growth	$120	$134	$150	
Ending balance	$1,120	$1,254	$1,404	

Table 6.4   Investor 2

	Year 1	Year 2	Year 3	Total ROR
Rate of return	12%	−30%	?	40.49%
Beginning balance	$1,000	$1,120		
Growth	$120	−$336		
Ending balance	$1,120	$784		

(See Table 6.4.) How much does Investor 2 have to earn in year 3 just to equal the return of Investor 1?

Investor 2 has to earn 79.2% in year 3 to equal the return of investor 1!

Table 6.5 is another example. Suppose we have two investments: Investment A and Investment B. The average annual return from each investment is 6.11%. (This is not to be confused with the compounded return; I am just taking a simple average.) But Investment A had a much lower standard deviation than Investment B because it was able to avoid large losses in years when Investment B did not. If we start out each with $100,000, we would have almost $48,000 more in Investment A after nine years!

I know it sounds like I am repeating myself, but the concept of avoiding large losses is vitally important and often missed by individual investors.

Thinking Outside the Box

The endowment investment goals force individual investors to think outside the box. As mentioned in Chapter 5, an endowment manager is told two rules:

1. They are not allowed to lose money.
2. They must also generate a high enough return over inflation so that the endowment can spend money without eating into its principal.

Table 6.5 Investment A vs. Investment B

Starting Value	$100,000	Investment A	$100,000	Investment B
1	10%	$110,000	20%	$120,000
2	−1%	$108,900	−30%	$84,000
3	9%	$118,701	20%	$120,960
4	10%	$130,571	20%	$120,960
5	−1%	$129,265	−30%	$84,672
6	10%	$142,192	30%	$110,074
7	9%	$154,989	30%	$143,096
8	−1%	$153,439	−35%	$93,012
9	10%	$163,783	30%	$120,916
Average annual return	6.11%		6.11%	
Standard deviation	5.35%		28.70%	

You might immediately think that if you are not allowed to lose money you would just invest in bonds and CDs, but at today's interest rates, they provide little if any return over inflation. They can satisfy rule number 1 but not rule number 2. To satisfy both rules, they cannot invest the same way that people traditionally do.

Traditional portfolios tend to have home market myopia (focused on the country that you live in—for example, a U.S. investor has most of his money invested in U.S. stocks and bonds) and tend to only go long (not long term, long as in only buying investments, never selling short). Below is an example of a traditional 70% stock and 30% bond portfolio:

- 55% U.S. equity split up between large-cap, mid-cap, and small-cap stocks and between growth and value stocks
- 15% international stocks split up between developed and emerging markets
- 30% bonds, primarily domestic

The Harvard and Yale portfolios are much different. They have more money in international stocks than U.S. stocks; they own real assets and private equity; they have very little in bonds; and they have large amounts in absolute return investments that have the ability to go long and short.

The large endowments tend to break their investments into five main asset classes:

1. *Absolute Return.* These strategies seek to provide returns regardless of market direction. Most, if not all, of these strategies are invested in hedge funds.
2. *Stocks.* These can be money managers that have stocks of domestic and/or international companies. Most of these managers will be skill-based, and many of them will also be in hedge funds.
3. *Bonds.* Large endowments don't do much with bonds for reasons I will talk about later. How they invest in bonds also differs; some may use money managers while others may run laddered bond portfolios in-house.
4. *Real Assets.* This encompasses commodities and real estate.
5. *Private Equity.* These are buyouts and venture capital investments.

In Part III we devote an entire chapter to each asset class and how you can, and should, invest in it. But for now, I will give you a sneak peak of what the endowment spin on the 70/30 portfolio might look like:

- 10% U.S. equity broken up into long only and long/short
- 30% International equity broken up into developed and emerging market long and long/short
- 10% Event-driven with absolute return and relative return investments
- 10% Global macroeconomic
- 15% Private equity split between U.S. and international
- 15% Real assets split between commodities and domestic and international Real Estate Investment Trusts
- 10% Bonds split up between U.S. and international and including distressed debt

The endowment portfolio is much more diversified, much less focused on bonds, and is not constrained to be long only.

Some Keys to Adopting the Endowment Investment Philosophy

Hopefully, by this point, I have convinced you that you can reap substantial profits by following the investment strategies of large endowments at universities like Harvard and Yale. Now it's time to discuss three of the keys to adopting an endowment methodology.

1. *Put it in writing.* Endowments have an Investment Policy Statement that gets their strategy in writing. You should, too.
2. *Get over the idea of paying too much in fees to have your investments managed.* In most other industries the top people charge more; the same goes with investments.
3. *Get over the idea that active managers can't outperform their index.* Many can't but there are many that do, and active money managers are needed for endowment portfolios.

Investment Policy Statement

Endowments and other institutional investors have an IPS. Most brokerage firms will create an IPS for clients, but they are boilerplate documents that don't really say much when you read through them. Most of them are probably written by attorneys, not investment advisors. A well-thought-out IPS will set out the following:

- What goals you have for your money
- What types of investments you will consider
- Your performance expectations
- What you will benchmark your investments against: S&P 500, Hedge Fund Research Index, Barclay Fund of Funds Index, Lehman Aggregate Bond Index, and so on
- How you will choose money managers, stocks, or bonds
- What has to happen for you to decide to fire a money manager or sell a stock or bond

An IPS states your investment methodology and guides all investment decisions. It is the key to keeping you from making the mistakes that most investors inevitably make. Every investment decision should be weighed against your IPS. When you are thinking about shifting 100% of your portfolio to Internet stocks, look to see what your IPS says about this. Chances are it will not allow it. Following the rules might not be fun and exciting, but it will keep you safe and solvent. We will talk more about how to construct your IPS later on in the book.

Investors make some other mistakes that aren't as dangerous as the ones we already covered, but they should still be corrected: (1) investors who try to buy only low-fee investment products and (2) investors who believe that they should buy only passive index funds.

Fees—They Aren't So Bad

In many parts of this book I will discuss subjects that go against conventional wisdom (in my opinion, conventional wisdom is often neither). My opinion about investment fees is probably one of my most controversial opinions. Many people are cautioned to consider only investments with low fees. Financial columnists focus on fees, Morningstar focuses on fees, Vanguard has built a huge business focusing on low fees, and a lot of the boom in exchange-traded funds (ETFs) is based on low fees. Unfortunately, worrying about fees ignores the reason why we invest—for returns. If I had the choice between a fund that had a fee of 0.5% and a return of 5% and another that had a fee of 10% but a return of 50%, I would take the 50% return every time.

In investment management, just like almost every other industry, the best people charge more. I read somewhere that the hedge fund firm Renaissance Technologies charges a 5% management fee and 44% of profits. That's a huge fee. If I was a believer that you should always look for the lowest-cost provider, I would never invest with Renaissance. (I would never invest with them anyway as their minimum is something like $20 million, and I don't think they take new investors anymore.) However, after fees their returns have been something like 34% per year since 1988. Would you pay someone 5% per year and 44% of profits if you could net 34% a year after fees, or would you rather pay 0.12% for an S&P 500 index fund and earn much, much less? You would expect to pay more for the best attorney, accountant, and doctor, right? Investment managers are no different. If you were convicted of a crime you didn't commit, would you rather have the lowest-cost attorney or the best? If you needed open heart surgery, would you rather have the lowest-cost surgeon or the best? If you are looking to have your money managed, would you rather have the lowest-cost money manager or the best? Solely focusing on fees would cause you to ignore some of the best investment managers and investment vehicles.

That being said, you should still be aware of fees you are paying and as with everything else in your life, you want to make sure you are getting what you are paying for. We will talk a lot more in the book about alpha and beta. Beta is the return from just being in the market. It should be cheap, and is. Alpha is outperformance, and it is hard to come by. Alpha should be, and is, expensive. Look at what you are getting from a portfolio manager. If they are just a closet indexer, meaning they basically mimic their benchmark, then all you are getting is beta and you shouldn't be paying much. If they are beating their benchmark on a risk-adjusted basis then you are getting alpha. When you find a portfolio manager that can consistently generate alpha, you should be willing to pay for it. For example, according to Morningstar, the Putnam Growth Opportunities Fund has returned on average 3.31% a year for the past five years as of July 22, 2008. That trails the S&P 500 by 3.93% a year. Also, according to Morningstar, its alpha versus the S&P 500 over the past three years was −1.07 and its beta was 1.04. All of its return came from beta; its alpha was negative which means that not only did the portfolio manager add no value he actually detracted from the fund. The expense ratio of this fund is 1.32%. Would I pay 1.32% for a fund where all of its return came from beta or would I rather pay much less for an index fund and have better return? (I am not picking on this fund specifically; I just picked it out randomly. There are many funds just like it that may not be worth the fees.) Obviously I would go for the index fund. On the other hand, the Fidelity Contrafund over the same five-year period returned 12.9% a year and had a three-year alpha versus the S&P 500 of 6.63. Its expense ratio is 0.89%. Would I pay 0.89% to get an alpha of 6.63? You bet! Renaissance is another great example. Its fees are huge, but it has obviously generated a ton of alpha for its clients so it can charge them an arm and a leg. They will happily pay it to get the returns.

Active versus Passive

These days investors are inundated with information touting index funds and indexed ETFs. The argument is that actively managed funds can't beat the market and have higher fees (see previous paragraph about fees), so you are better off with a passive index. Passive investors, index funds, and ETFs believe you can't beat the market so they simply buy all of the stocks in a specific index. They think alpha is nearly impossible to get, so you should just focus on beta. Because of the simplicity of the strategy and the fact that a monkey at a computer can run it, the fees tend to be lower. Active investors believe the market is inefficient and that securities become mispriced to the point where there are opportunities that they can capitalize on. They believe they can generate alpha.

Passive investment advocates have three key beliefs:

1. Information about markets is readily available to all market participants.
2. All market participants act on that information.
3. All investors are rational.

While these beliefs may sound plausible, they often fail to hold up in real markets, especially the belief about investors being rational. (We talked about that earlier in the chapter.)

Active investments have the following four advantages over passive investments:

1. In an actively managed portfolio, investors get an expert portfolio manager (assuming they do their homework about the manager—more on this later).
2. An actively managed strategy has the potential to outperform an index either on an absolute basis or on a risk-adjusted basis.
3. Actively managed portfolios can be managed with an eye toward what is going on in the world, the markets, and the economy (more on this later also).
4. Active managers have the ability to mitigate or avoid market losses in a downturn.

In short, active managers have the ability to generate alpha, and at the risk of sounding repetitive, alpha is what you want to have if you want an endowment type of portfolio.

According to research done by SEI Investments, there have been four negative years in large-cap U.S. stocks during the past 20 years (as measured by the Russell 1000 Index). During those years, the average active large-cap manager outperformed the index by 1.33% net of fees. Also, during 2000 the average active manager outperformed the index by 2.86%; in 2001 they outperformed by 0.55%; and in 2002 they outperformed by 0.19%.

Returns from index funds and ETFs are purely from beta, because they are not actively managed. The money managers that endowments use try to get most of their return from alpha and as little as possible from beta. This allows these managers to do well regardless of what the markets are doing. Of course this is easier said than done. Getting beta is easy; just buy an index fund. Alpha is much harder, and you need to do more work to find the best money managers who have been able to consistently deliver alpha and should be able to do so going forward.

Whether to invest passively also depends on what types of money managers you want to use. Many money managers are not much different than the index funds. They are judged on their performance versus an index so they don't deviate much from it. Instead they try to overweight or underweight different stocks in the index to try to increase returns a little bit. Most of the time they don't. These are what I call style box-based money managers. See Chapter 4 for a discussion about them and skill-based money managers.

If you still think index funds are for you but you want to adopt some endowment strategies, Chapter 17 on portable alpha will show you how to do that.

The debate about which strategy is better will never end; both sides can point to periods when their strategy did better. However, creating an endowment type of portfolio necessitates that active money managers play a significant role.

Endowment Investment Success

Now that you have a better idea of how endowments achieve their success and an understanding of how to implement this model, Part II will focus on the different investment vehicles that you can use in your portfolio.

PART II

INVESTMENT VEHICLES

Now that you have an understanding of the most common investor mistakes and the foundation for how endowments invest, Part II will focus on the different types of investment vehicles you can use in your portfolio. In particular, in Chapter 7, I recommend mutual funds, separately managed accounts, exchange-traded funds, and exchange-traded notes. In Chapter 8, I discuss structured products, and in Chapter 9, I provide a lot of information about hedge funds and fund of funds, which many individual investors can take advantage of.

Since every investor is different, not all of these vehicles might be appropriate for your situation. Rest assured that you don't need to have a multimillion-dollar portfolio to be able to invest like an endowment. You can mimic much of what endowments do just by using mutual funds.

CHAPTER 7

Mutual Funds, Separately Managed Accounts, Exchange-Traded Funds, and Exchange-Traded Notes

Endowments can afford to put most of their portfolios in illiquid hedge funds. Individual investors need to be more liquid and may not meet the qualifications to invest in hedge funds. Therefore, for most individual investors your portfolios will be made up mostly of either mutual funds, separately managed accounts, exchange-traded funds, and/or exchange-traded notes. With the proliferation of skill-based products, individual investors can create an endowment type of portfolio just using these products alone. This chapter will give you an overview of each.

Mutual Funds

Mutual funds are investment companies that pool investor assets to invest into a diversified pool of securities. Funds will have a manager or team of managers responsible for buy-and-sell decisions and a board of directors responsible for overseeing the fund and protecting the interests of investors. If you have $500,000 or less to invest, then the bulk, if not all, of your portfolio should probably be in mutual funds. Mutual funds tend to have very low investment minimums, making it easy for just about any size investor to construct a well-diversified portfolio. There are enough skill-based money managers in the mutual fund world to construct a perfectly good endowment type of portfolio entirely with mutual funds.

Mutual funds trade based on their net asset value (NAV), which is calculated at the end of every trading day by dividing total assets of the fund by the shares outstanding. Unlike a stock, an investor can only purchase a mutual fund at its NAV at the end of the day. Mutual fund companies redeem the shares of people who want to sell and issue new shares to people who want to buy.

Why Mutual Funds?

Mutual funds offer investors several advantages that individual securities do not.

1. *Diversification.* Mutual funds may hold hundreds of stocks or bonds. Individuals would need millions of dollars to create a portfolio as diversified as a mutual fund.
2. *Professional Money Management.* Mutual funds are managed by professionals who spend all day researching investments and making buy/sell decisions.
3. *Liquidity and Convenience.* Mutual funds can be liquidated at any time and also generally will allow small investments and reinvestment of dividends and capital gains. To discourage market times, most mutual funds now have small redemption charges if funds are sold within a certain period of time.

Types of Mutual Funds

There are a number of different types of mutual funds. Below are 17 of the most common:

1. *U.S. Stock Funds.* Also known as equity funds. These types of funds invest in common stocks of U.S. companies.
2. *International Stock Funds.* These funds invest in stocks of international companies. These can be diversified or single-country funds.
3. *Emerging Market Stock Funds.* These funds invest in stocks of companies based in emerging markets (Latin America, Asia, Japan, etc.).
4. *Sector Funds.* These funds invest in stocks of companies in specific sectors, for example, technology, financial, and so on.

5. *Long/Short Funds.* These funds have the ability to buy stocks long and sell them short.
6. *Bear Market Funds.* These are short biased funds.
7. *Balanced Funds.* These funds invest a portion in stocks and a portion in bonds.
8. *Allocation Funds.* These can be conservative, moderate, or aggressive. They tend to invest across a number of different asset classes.
9. *Corporate Bond Funds.* These funds invest in bonds issued by companies.
10. *Government Bond Funds.* These funds invest in bonds issued by the government.
11. *High-Yield Bond Funds.* These funds invest in bonds issued by companies that have a lower credit rating and therefore have a higher risk of default.
12. *International Bond Funds.* These funds invest in bonds issued by foreign companies or governments.
13. *Emerging Market Bond Funds.* These funds invest in bonds issued by emerging markets.
14. *Treasury Inflation Protected Security (TIPS) Funds.* These funds invest in TIPS, which are government bonds that tie some of their return to inflation.
15. *Multi-Market Bond Funds.* These funds invest in a mix of different types of bonds.
16. *Municipal Bond Funds.* These funds invest in tax-free bonds issued by states and municipalities.
17. *Money Market Funds.* These funds invest in high-quality, short-term, fixed-income investments.

Open-End Funds versus Closed-End Funds

Open-end funds are just that: open-ended. Fund companies consistently issue new shares when a new investor buys in and redeem existing shares when an investor cashes out. There is no limit to the amount of shares that an open-end fund can issue. Open-end funds are also traded at NAV. Closed-end funds issue a fixed amount of shares and are trading on an exchange. When an investor buys, they buy shares from someone else who is selling; no new shares are issued. Closed-end funds also have a NAV but they can trade at a discount or premium to it.

Fees and Expenses

Mutual funds have two different types of expenses:

1. *Expense Ratio.* This is the fee that goes to the fund company to pay for the fund management. This fee is taken out of the fund's NAV before it is reported, so you don't actually see it but it is there. If a fund returned 20% and had an expense ratio of 1%, then the return to investors would be 19%. The key to the expense ratio is whether you are paying for alpha or beta. If it's beta, then the expense ratio should be low.
2. *12b-1 Fees.* These fees are supposedly for distribution, but they basically pay the broker who sells them. Like the expense ratio, this fee is also taken right out of the NAV.

All of these fees are disclosed in a fund's prospectus.

Share Classes

No-load funds are offered directly through the fund company or on a fund supermarket like Fidelity, Charles Schwab, and TD Waterhouse. Load funds have some sort of sales charge and are sold through brokers. While there are a number of different share classes for load funds, the most common are A shares, B shares, and C shares.

A Shares. These shares generally have a 5% upfront sales charge. So, for example, if you invest $100 in an A share fund, $95 will be invested in the fund and $5 will go to the broker. These shares also have break points where the sales charge declines for larger amounts.

B Shares. These shares have a back end sales charge if the fund is sold during a certain period of time, generally seven years. The back end charge will decrease each year. During this period the fund will charge an extra 1% fee. At the end of the period, the fund will convert to A shares (without a front end sales charge).

C Shares. These shares have a back end sales charge that generally lasts one year and charge an extra 1% per year, every year.

If you are working with commission-based advisors, they will typically like one share class over another. Some might prefer to earn 1% per year while others might like the large upfront payments of A or B shares.

Distributions and Taxes

There are three types of distributions that mutual funds may make to investors each year: dividends, interest, and capital gains. At year end, funds are required to distribute capital gains to shareholders. All of these distributions are taxable unless the fund is in a retirement plan or IRA, even if you reinvest them. One disadvantage of mutual funds is imbedded capital gains. Let's say the XYZ fund bought Microsoft stock a number of years ago for $1 per share. At the beginning of the year they finally decide to sell their stake and have a huge capital gain. You then buy into the fund in October, and it goes down through the remainder of the year, so you are holding it at a loss. The fund is required to pay out its Microsoft gain at year end, and you will be taxed on it even though you are holding the fund at a loss and never experienced the gain.

Separately Managed Accounts

Separately managed accounts (SMAs) are generally managed by the same firms that manage mutual funds. The difference is that you actually own the securities and give the manager discretion to make trades in your account. You see all buys and sells and have complete fee transparency. SMAs also have advantages when it comes to taxes. Once you set up an SMA, the securities are bought for you so there are no imbedded capital gains. SMAs also allow you to sell certain securities that you may have at a loss to generate tax losses that can offset other gains. Finally, SMAs also allow investors to screen for socially responsible stocks or stocks in which they may have large positions in other parts of their portfolio. Many people compare mutual funds to buying a suit off the rack whereas SMAs are like having a suit custom made. I would not go quite that far, but you definitely can have more customization in an SMA than a mutual fund.

The disadvantage with SMAs is that there are very few skill-based managers who manage SMAs, so even if you are an SMA advocate you will still probably need some mutual funds to round out your portfolio. SMAs also have high minimums, usually $100,000,

$250,000, or even more. Because of that, you really need a high six- or seven-figure portfolio for SMAs to play a large role.

In our firm, we don't use SMAs very much because we can't find many good skill-based managers. We think that will change just like the mutual fund industry is changing. We do use SMAs when we get new clients who are coming from an SMA. One benefit to the SMA is that your existing stocks can be sold without a transaction fee. We frequently get clients from other brokerage firms where they had SMAs; they may have an account with hundreds of stocks in it. While our primary custodian only charges $8.95 per stock trade, it can get pretty expensive when we start talking about hundreds of stocks. In these cases sometimes an SMA can save a lot of money on commissions.

Exchange-Traded Funds and Exchange-Traded Notes

As of this writing, some sponsors are coming out with actively managed exchange-traded funds (ETFs), but the vast majority of ETFs essentially track an index. Because of this, the role of an ETF in your portfolio is to get returns from beta. There are some other uses for ETFs that we will talk about in a later chapter. ETFs are also the hottest new investment trend, as they generally have low expenses and some flexibility that mutual funds don't have.

Which Is Better: A Mutual Fund or an SMA?

The argument continues to rage in my industry about which is better: a mutual fund or an SMA. Mutual funds have a number of disadvantages: phantom capital gains (capital gains tax due on gains you never got), selling from other investors impacting the portfolio, no ability to manage taxes, and no transparency or customization. Most SMAs, however, are style box-based managers. All things being equal, we would prefer the SMA because it would allow you to customize the portfolio to an extent, take tax losses, avoid paying capital gains tax on gains you didn't get, and you could see the entire portfolio. However, until the SMA industry embraces an absolute return approach, we will still primarily use mutual funds.

ETF Basics

ETFs are like index mutual funds except that they are traded on the stock exchange like stocks. Unlike a closed-end mutual fund that can trade at a discount or a premium to their underlying portfolio value, ETFs trade at approximately their net asset value. Because they trade like stocks, ETFs can be bought or sold at anytime during the day, where mutual funds can only be bought or sold at the end of the day. Also, unlike mutual funds, ETFs are not redeemed by the issuer. If you want to sell your ETF, it is sold on the exchange to someone who wants to buy it.

Because they trade on the stock exchange, you will also pay a commission to buy an ETF, the size of which will depend on whether you use a full service or discount brokerage firm.

ETF Advantages

- ETFs can be traded intraday, unlike mutual funds which can only be traded at the day end NAV.
- ETFs have low expenses. Since ETFs are index funds, they get their return from beta and therefore have lower expenses than actively managed mutual funds.
- ETFs don't have short-term redemption fees so they are more conducive to active trading than mutual funds (assuming you are using a discount broker to trade them).
- ETFs are tax efficient. Since they are not actively trading, ETFs don't have to sell stocks at a gain very often. Also, since ETFs are not redeemed by the issuing company, they do not have to sell shares to meet redemptions.
- ETFs exist for some areas of the market where mutual funds are nonexistent or scarce. Some examples are frontier markets such as Africa and the Middle East, nuclear energy, and so on.

ETF Disadvantages

- Because they are passive, their return comes from beta, not alpha.
- Because they trade like stocks, there are commissions to buy and sell.

Exchange-Traded Notes

Exchange-traded notes (ETNs) are just like ETFs except that ETNs track an index where ETFs hold actual securities. ETNs are also unsecured debt securities of the issuing company. That means if the company that issued the ETN goes bankrupt, then you could be in trouble. Because of this, ETNs are struggling to get interest from investors who are avoiding them because of worries about default risk. According to the *Wall Street Journal* in an article entitled "ETNs Suffering Growing Pains As Buyers Flee," as of July 18, 2008, there were $575 billion in ETFs versus $7.3 billion in ETNs. Furthermore, there are only 89 listed ETNs, and 64 of them have less than $15 million in assets.

The Future of ETFs and ETNs

The future will most likely see a number of new issues that give exposure to specific sectors and risk factors. We will most likely see the following:

- Specialized global markets, for example a new ETF that has been issued recently provides exposure to frontier markets (Egypt, Morocco, Oman, and so on).
- ETFs backed by commodities that will give investors a pure play on actual commodities, not just stocks of companies involved in commodities.
- More leveraged and inverse ETFs that broaden the trading strategies that investors can use.
- New derivative type ETFs that would give investors access to strategies that were previously only available to institutional investors.
- Specialized risks, for example there are ETFs in registration that provide exposure to medical price inflation.

Active Trading

Because you can buy ETFs intraday and there are no back end sales charges (there are commissions), they are ideally suited to people who are active traders but don't have the time or the wherewithal to trade individual stocks.

We run an internal opportunistic ETF overlay portfolio for some of our clients. We like the fact that we can trade ETFs without restriction, and we have a large number to choose from, both on the long side and the short side. We will talk more about this in a later chapter.

Hedging

One advantage of ETFs is that they allow you to hedge your portfolio. While it is great to talk about having a long-term time horizon and all, you still want to be able to sleep at night and there are times when you might get nervous about a certain market. You probably don't want to change your asset allocation, and selling some investments could have tax consequences. There are a number of short ETFs that give the inverse return of different indexes. If you are nervous short term about a certain market, you could buy one of these ETFs to hedge against a decline, and then sell the ETF when you feel more comfortable. We will talk more about this concept in a later chapter, also.

So Many Different Financial Products

Mutual funds, separately managed accounts, ETFs, and/or ETNs will play a large role for most investors who are constructing an endowment type portfolio. Which one is right for you depends on your situation and what you want to accomplish. In the next chapter we will talk about a more specialized type of investment product for people looking for more protection from losses.

8

Structured Products

Structured products aren't necessarily used by endowments. However, individual investors might use structured products to protect their portfolio from losses.

Structured Products

Structured products are investments created by large investment banks that seek to monetize certain market views or hedge against market risks. As of this writing I have not been using structured products in my clients' portfolios, but I am constantly reviewing them and am certainly open to using them. Because of their unique features, they can fit quite well into an endowment type of portfolio.

Advantages

Some ways that structured products can add value to a portfolio are as follows:

- They can provide enhanced returns on a number of asset classes.
- They can provide access to alternative types of asset classes, such as commodities, currencies, interest rates, yield spreads, and inflation.
- They can provide return profiles that are not available through traditional strategies like mutual funds and ETFs.
- Return formula at expiration is known when you buy the structured product.

- They can usually be bought in denominations of as little as $1,000.

Structured products are getting more popular, according to the Structured Product Association. The issuance of new structured products has increased from $28 billion in 2003 to $100 billion in 2007.

Disadvantages

On the surface, structured products sound too good to be true, but they are not. However, structured products have four disadvantages:

1. There is no liquid secondary market. If you are not going to hold your investment until maturity, there is no guarantee you will get fair value when you sell it. Many of the sponsors have been working hard to develop a more liquid secondary market, and things are better than they used to be, but selling a structured product before maturity is not nearly the same as selling a stock or a mutual fund. Principal protection and stated payouts apply only at maturity.
2. Structured products are backed by the full faith and credit of whatever company is issuing them. You need to be reasonably sure that the company will still be there when your notes mature.
3. These products are much more complex than mutual funds and other investment vehicles which make it hard for investors to understand exactly what they have and how it will perform. They will also be very hard to track; you won't see them listed in the paper and the numbers on your statement may not reflect what they are really worth if you try to sell them.
4. The IRS has issued very little guidance on the taxation of structured notes.

How Structured Products Work

Structured products are issued with a stated maturity, usually one to five years. They include a principal component plus a performance component, the formula of which is stated at purchase. There are a number of different structures for the principal and performance. The principal can either be fully protected (you get back at maturity at least as much as you put in), partially protected, or fully at risk. The performance can either provide leveraged returns, unique returns, or exposure to multiple underlying investments.

The main types of structured products an individual might use are as follows:

- Principal protected notes
- Efficient allocation return notes
- Absolute return barrier notes
- Buffered underlying securities

Principal Protected Notes

Principal protected notes (PPNs) make the most sense for investors who are more risk averse and who want exposure to more volatile asset classes (commodities, emerging markets, etc.) without the risk.

The principal component of these notes will generally be a zero coupon bond. A zero coupon bond is bought at a discount and pays no interest during its life. At maturity it pays full par value. So, for example, if you put $1,000 into a five-year principal protected note, the issuer may invest $785 into a zero coupon bond that will guarantee you $1,000 at the end of five years. That would guarantee that you would get your initial investment back. The remaining $215 would go into various derivative contracts, and pay the fees that the investment bank earns for setting all this up, which would provide the performance component.

The return stream of the note could be calculated using a number of different formulas, as shown in Table 8.1.

Efficient Allocation Return Notes

An efficient allocation return note (EARN) provides 100% of principal at maturity, guaranteed. The returns are based on three underlying indexes: the S&P 500, MSCI Emerging Markets, and the MSCI EAFE. At the end of four years, the investor gets back the greater of 100% of his principal or the principal plus the performance component: 50% of the return of the best performing index + 30% of the return of the second best performing index + 20% of the return of the worst performing index.

Table 8.1   Performance Formulas

Type of Performance	Payoff at Maturity Equals . . .
Point to point	Percent return of an underlying investment from the trade date to the maturity date.
Averaging	The average return of an underlying investment from the trade date to the maturity date; averaging is either monthly or quarterly. (Note: In an up market, averaging can significantly water down returns.)
Range accrual	The payoff is based on the number of days an underlying investment stays within a predetermined range.
Efficient allocation	Performance of a number of different indexes based on how well they perform during the period. The best performing index during the period gets the highest allocation and the worst gets the lowest. This structure allows 20/20 hindsight.

Performance is figured using quarterly averaging. Quarterly averaging adds up each index value at the end of the quarter and divides by the number of quarters. So, for example, if we had a two-quarter note and if the S&P 500 was at 1,000 at the end of the first quarter and 2,000 at the end of the second quarter, then the average would be 1,500 (1,000 + 2,000 ÷ 2). So while the index was up 100%, quarterly averaging would only provide a return of 50%. You may be looking at this and thinking it is too good to be true, but quarterly averaging can significantly water down returns. An investment bank could never offer a note like this with full principal protection and a point-to-point performance.

Here is how the return works at the end of the term. Let's assume that we have the following averaged index returns at the end of four years:

MSCI EAFE	70%
S&P 500	26%
MSCI Emerging Markets	−10%

The returns would be 50% × the top performer (MSCI EAFE) + 30% of the second best (S&P 500) + 20% of the worst (MSCI Emerging Markets) = 40.8%. So the investor who put $1,000 into this note four years ago would get $1,408.

Absolute Return Barrier Notes

Many investors may not be sure whether a market is going up or down, but they are reasonably certain that the market will trade in a range. Absolute return barrier notes (ARBNs) help investors protect their principal and have the potential to offer large returns as long as the underlying investment stays within a predefined range. These products usually have maturities of 12 to 18 months and have 100% principal protection. Their performance is linked to an underlying index, and the return is based on the index staying within a certain range. For example, let's say you buy an ARBN based on the S&P 500 with a range of 20%. That means that as long as the index never trades above or below 20% of the initial level, your return will be your principal plus the absolute return of the return on the index. (*Absolute return* in this context just means if the performance is negative, you remove the minus sign and it becomes positive.) In our example, let's say the S&P 500 ends up down 10% from where it was when you bought the note. Your return would be your principal *plus* 10%. If the index ended up at 10%, your return would be the same. However, if at some point during the term of the note, the index goes up 21% then you will only get your principal back. With an ARBN it doesn't matter whether return is positive or negative, just that it never breaks the barrier. If the index breaks the up or down barrier at any time during the life of the note, then your return will be only what you put in.

The main risk with an ARBN is lost opportunity cost. In our example, if the S&P was up 30% then you would only get your principal back; you would have missed out on the entire 30% move.

If you expect the market to be range bound, in other words, trade around in a small range instead of going way up or way down, then ARBNs are a great way to monetize your market view.

Buffered Underlying Securities

Buffered underlying securities (BUyS) are partially principal protected notes that allow the upside potential with only some of the downside in an underlying investment. The underlying asset in this example is a commodity index and the maturity is three years. This type of note is partially principal protected. In our example, the investor does not participate in the first 20% downside of the index; only 80% of the investment is at risk. If the underlying return is positive, then the investor gets the return times a specified participation percentage. If the index is anywhere from down 20% to flat, then the investor gets just the principal back. If the index goes down more than 20%, then the investor gets 100% of the principal minus the sum of the return of the index plus 20%. Below are some hypothetical return examples:

Example 1: Commodity index is up 20% at maturity and participation rate is 130%

- 20% × 130% = 26%
- If an investor put in $1,000, he would get back $1,260.

Example 2: Commodity index closes somewhere between 0 and negative 20%

- Investor gets back $1,000 principal.

Example 3: Commodity index closes down 35%

- 100% − 35% actual return + 20% buffer = 85%
- Investor gets back $850, so even though the index went down 35% the structured product only went down 15% because of the buffer.

How to Fit Structured Products into an Endowment Type of Portfolio

Structured products are not a replacement for mutual funds, money managers, and so on, but they can enhance them. The first step is figuring out what your asset allocation is going to be: how much in stocks, bonds, cash, and commodities. Once you know your allocation, you need to decide how to allocate to the asset classes. There could be classes you want exposure to, but you also want some principal protection. There could be others that you think are in a trading range; therefore, you could add ARBNs. Endowments don't necessarily need structured products because they can access advanced investment strategies like these through hedge funds. As an individual investor, you may not have access to these types of funds or strategies so adding structured products to your portfolio can reduce the overall risk.

What's Next

The next chapter will focus on the third investment vehicle that you can use in your endowment type of portfolio: hedge funds and fund of funds. Most endowments like Harvard and Yale have the majority of their money in hedge funds, but most individual investors don't understand these products. Chapter 9 will demystify them.

CHAPTER 9

Hedge Funds and Funds of Funds

A hedge fund is an actively managed investment vehicle that is only available to high net worth investors. (Since you may qualify as a high net worth investor even if you think you don't, please read on.) Hedge funds tend to be more flexible than mutual funds and may utilize shorting strategies, options, derivatives, illiquid securities, and leverage. Many funds seek to provide an absolute return (instead of beating a benchmark). Endowments like Harvard and Yale have most of their money invested in hedge funds, so this is an extremely important chapter for you to read and understand.

According to Old Mutual Capital, Inc., based on information from Hedge Fund Research, Inc., from 1990 to 2006 the hedge fund market has done the following:

- Increased from 530 to over 8,000 funds
- Grown from less than $30 billion to over $1.2 trillion in assets
- Shown positive returns in both bull and bear markets
- Posted an average annual return of 14.5% net of fees
- Achieved positive returns in 15 out of 16 years
- Consistently outperformed the S&P 500 Index

Today, the term *hedge fund* is really a misnomer in that there are a wide variety of investment strategies, some hedged and some not hedged. Sometimes you might hear people saying that hedge funds are risky, but that's just like saying mutual funds are risky. Some are and some are not. Just as a mutual fund investor wouldn't want to invest in only one strategy, a hedge fund investor should be diversified as well.

The Founder of Hedge Funds

Alfred W. Jones is credited with creating the first hedge fund in 1949. Jones sold short as many stocks as he bought long. He avoided registration under the Investment Company Act of 1940 by limiting his fund to only 99 investors in a limited partnership. He was compensated solely by taking 20% of profits. All of these components—going long and short, setting up a limited partnership structure, and taking 20% of profits—are mainstays of modern hedge funds. The hedge fund structure became widely known in 1996 when *Fortune* magazine wrote an article about Jones entitled "The Jones Nobody Keeps Up With." Within three years after the article was published, 130 new hedge funds were started including George Soros's Quantum Fund and Michael Steinhardt's Steinhardt Partners.

Table 9.1 shows the returns of different hedge fund strategies along with stocks and bonds from 1998 to 2006. The top-performing hedge fund categories change from year to year; therefore, it is just as important for hedge fund investors to be diversified as it is for mutual fund investors.

Availability

Many investors are convinced that they aren't qualified to invest in hedge funds. Some may be surprised to find out that they actually do qualify as accredited investors. In order for hedge funds to avoid registering with the SEC, they can only be purchased by accredited investors. An accredited investor is:

- An individual with at least a $200,000 annual income or a $1 million net worth. (Since this can include your house, many people are accredited investors and don't realize it.)
- A corporation, partnership, LLC, or trust formed for a purpose other than investing in a hedge fund with at least $5 million in assets.

Some hedge funds are only available to qualified purchasers. A qualified purchaser is:

Table 9.1 Hedge Fund Style Returns

1998	1999	2000	2001	2002	2003	2004	2005	2006
S&P 500 28.58%	Equity Hedge 44.22%	Merger Arbitrage 18.02%	Convertible Arbitrage 13.37%	Lehman Bond Index 10.26%	Russell 2000 45.37%	Distressed 18.89%	Equity Hedge 10.60%	Russell 2000 17.00%
Equity Hedge 15.98%	FOF 26.47%	Convertible Arbitrage 14.50%	Distressed 13.28%	Convertible Arbitrage 9.05%	Distressed 29.56%	Russell 2000 17.00%	Distressed 8.27%	Distressed 15.83%
Statistical Arbitrage 10.14%	Event Driven 24.33%	Relative Value 13.41%	Event Driven 12.18%	Fixed Income Arb 8.78%	S&P 500 28.69%	Event Driven 15.01%	FOF 7.49%	S&P 500 15.80%
Lehman Bond Index 8.67%	S&P 500 21.04%	Lehman Bond Index 11.63%	Relative Value 8.92%	Macro 7.44%	Event Driven 25.33%	S&P 500 10.88%	Event Driven 7.29%	Event Driven 15.32%
Convertible Arbitrage 7.77%	Russell 2000 19.62%	Equity Hedge 9.09%	Lehman Bond Index 8.42%	Relative Value 5.44%	Macro 21.42%	Equity Hedge 7.68%	Macro 6.79%	Merger Arbitrage 14.26%
Merger Arbitrage 7.23%	Macro 17.62%	Statistical Arbitrage 8.89%	Macro 6.87%	Distressed 5.28%	Equity Hedge 20.54%	FOF 6.86%	Merger Arbitrage 6.25%	Statistical Arbitrage 13.60%
Macro 6.19%	Distressed 16.94%	Event Driven 6.74%	Fixed Income Arb 4.81%	FOF 1.02%	FOF 11.61%	Fixed Income Arb 5.99%	Relative Value 6.02%	Relative Value 12.36%

(Continued)

99

Table 9.1 (Continued)

1998	1999	2000	2001	2002	2003	2004	2005	2006
Relative Value 2.81%	Relative Value 14.73%	Fixed Income Arb 4.78%	FOF 2.80%	Merger Arbitrage -0.87%	Convertible Arbitrage 9.93%	Relative Value 5.58%	Fixed Income Arb 5.60%	Convertible Arbitrage 12.15%
Event Driven 1.70%	Convertible Arbitrage 14.41%	FOF 4.07%	Merger Arbitrage 2.76%	Statistical Arbitrage -3.17%	Relative Value 9.72%	Macro 4.63%	Statistical Arbitrage 5.29%	Equity Hedge 11.70%
Russell 2000 -3.45%	Merger Arbitrage 14.34%	Distressed 2.78%	Statistical Arbitrage 1.59%	Event Driven -4.30%	Fixed Income Arb 9.35%	Lehman Bond Index 4.34%	S&P 500 4.91%	FOF 10.43%
Distressed -4.23%	Fixed Income Arb 7.38%	Macro 1.97%	Russell 2000 1.03%	Equity Hedge -4.71%	Merger Arbitrage 7.47%	Merger Arbitrage 4.08%	Russell 2000 3.32%	Macro 8.14%
FOF -5.11%	Statistical Arbitrage -0.17%	Russell 2000 -4.20%	Equity Hedge 0.40%	Russell 2000 -21.58%	Lehman Bond Index 4.11%	Statistical Arbitrage 3.99%	Lehman Bond Index 2.43%	Fixed Income Arb 7.33%
Fixed Income Arb -10.29%	Lehman Bond Index -0.83%	S&P 500 -9.10%	S&P 500 -11.89%	S&P 500 -22.10%	Statistical Arbitrage 3.38%	Convertible Arbitrage 1.18%	Convertible Arbitrage -1.86%	Lehman Bond Index 4.33%

Source: Hedge Fund Research, Inc., as of 3/26/07.

- An individual with investable assets of at least $5 million. (This doesn't include your house.)
- A corporation, partnership, LLC, or trust formed for a purpose other than investing in a hedge fund with at least $25 million in assets.

A hedge fund that complies with Section 3(c)1 of the Investment Company Act of 1940 can have only 100 accredited investors. A fund that complies with Section 3(c)7 can have an unlimited amount of qualified purchasers. In order to comply with these acts, the funds must be private placements and cannot be advertised or marketed to the public. That's the reason you see tons of ads for mutual funds but never for hedge funds.

Hedge Fund Risks and Disadvantages

The main risks and disadvantages of hedge funds are that they are unregulated, they lack transparency, they can use large amounts of leverage, it is very important to select the right manager, they often have lockups, they charge high fees, they are not tax efficient, and they have blowup risk.

Lack of Regulation

Hedge funds are structured as private placements, meaning that as long as they take only accredited and qualified investors they do not have to register with the SEC. The government's logic is that as long as a fund only has sophisticated investors who fully understand the risks they take, then registration is unnecessary. Hedge funds do benefit from this lack of regulation, but it also allows a small percentage of unethical managers to cheat investors, which often makes for interesting headline news.

This lack of regulation means that investors need to spend more time in due diligence of hedge funds than they would with mutual funds. Hedge funds of funds are investment vehicles that invest in different hedge funds. These managers routinely hire private investigators to dig into the personal lives of hedge fund managers before they will consider investing with them.

Some funds do take the extra step of registering under the Investment Company Act of 1940 and must disclose their holdings to investors at least every six months.

Lack of Transparency

Unlike mutual funds where investors get reports twice a year showing fund holdings, hedge fund investors might never know what their fund is invested in. This is good and bad for investors. Full transparency gives the prospective investor the information needed to evaluate the fund. On the other hand, reduced transparency protects the funds' ideas from competitors. This is especially important for hedge funds that sell stocks short. Some investors specialize in trying to drive up the price of a stock that other investors have shorted. This can create a short squeeze where the shorts sell in a panic and drive the price up further.

Funds of funds generally will only invest in a fund if they have full transparency. In this case, they will sign confidentiality agreements with the hedge fund manager.

Leverage

Leverage means using borrowed funds to buy more securities. This can be good and bad as leverage will magnify both gains and losses. Whenever you hear about a hedge fund blowing up, chances are it was partially or completely caused by overleveraging.

Manager Selection Risk

As of this writing there is no investible index fund for hedge funds; therefore, investors must choose active managers. Although Morningstar and other services provide tremendous amounts of objective information about mutual funds, there is no real service as of yet where individual investors can get the same information about hedge funds.

Lockups

Mutual funds can call up their fund any time and generally get their money out in three to seven days. That is not the case with hedge funds. Because managers might be dealing with illiquid securities and complex financial instruments, most funds have lockups that last between 12 and 24 months. Because of this, investors should never invest money in a hedge fund if they might need it back over a short time frame.

Fees

Mutual funds charge an expense ratio. There might also be commissions depending on where the fund was purchased through. Hedge funds typically also charge an asset management fee that is higher than most mutual funds and a performance-based fee that is generally about 20% of profits. Therefore, a hedge fund has to significantly outperform a mutual fund gross of fees so that it can compete once fees are taken out. Some, myself included, would argue that performance fees are actually good for investors as it compensates managers for performance and gives them incentive to have as high a performance as possible.

Hedge fund management fees generally run from 1% to 4% of assets under management; 2% is the most common management fee. Although the typical performance fee is 20% of profits, some higher-profile managers can charge much more. Some funds also have a high watermark. This means that the manager only gets a performance fee if the fund is higher than the highest point that it has achieved. For example, if a fund is worth $100 per share and goes up $20 the first year, then the performance fee will be paid on the entire $20 gain. If the fund goes down $10 to $110 the next year, then no performance fee is due. If the fund goes up $20 the third year to $130, the performance fee will be based on the move from $120 to $130, not $110 to $130. This means that if a fund with a high watermark has a significant loss in any given year, it could be a long time before hedge fund managers can charge their performance fee. Many funds in this situation just close and reopen so they can start from scratch.

Some funds have a hurdle rate where they will not charge their performance fee unless the fund exceeds a risk-free rate such as T-bills or London Interbank Offered Rate (LIBOR).

Tax Implications

Due to the trading strategies of hedge fund managers, most gains will be taxed as ordinary income or short-term capital gains, both of which are subject to the highest income tax rates. For investors who are subject to state income taxes, this often results in gains being taxed as high as 40%. Hedge funds also tend to report tax information to investors after April 15th. If you invest in hedge funds, you will probably need to file an extension on your taxes.

Hedge funds are also problematic if they are included in tax-exempt vehicles such as charitable remainder trusts or foundations. Because most hedge funds are set up as limited partnerships, earnings of the funds typically are classified as unrelated business taxable income (UBTI).

Hedge Fund Blowup Risk

When most people think of hedge funds, they think of great risk because of some of the spectacular hedge fund blowups. Long Term Capital Management, Amaranth, Bayou, and so on are some of the names you might remember from the news. There is a big risk in dealing with hedge funds, which largely comes from their nature as highly leveraged arbitrageurs who focus on reversion to the mean. To explain what I mean, consider the following example.

Let's say that Apples and Oranges always trade at about $1 each. From time to time the prices get out of line, but they always come back to around $1 each. One day I look at my computer and Apples are trading at $.95 per Apple and Oranges are trading at $1.05 per Orange. I assume that just like they always have, Apples will eventually move up to $1 and Oranges will eventually fall to $1, a reversion to the mean. So I decide to buy Apples and sell Oranges short. To magnify my returns (or my losses), I decide to borrow billions of dollars from banks to place into this trade. Most of the time things work as expected, and I am consistently able to make money and show investors an attractive return history. But then one day something happens outside of the Apple and Orange industry that was completely unexpected. It was so unexpected that my risk models never even thought to account for it. This event causes Apples to go down in price even more and Oranges to go up even more; now I am losing money on both sides of my trade. I know that eventually the crisis will subside and things will go back as expected, but my losses are causing the banks to call in their loans. To meet the loan calls, I need to start selling my losing positions in a hurry. This alerts Wall Street to my predicament, making it harder to sell and causing my investors to want out of my fund. Eventually Apples and Oranges go back to trading at $1, but I am not in business to see it and my investors are wiped out.

Often when you hear about a hedge fund blowing up, unless fraud is involved, it tends to be a situation like the one above.

Generally, it is a highly leveraged fund that is making safe bets based on historical price relationships, and then something comes out of left field that throws these relationships out of whack long enough for the fund to lose most, if not all, of its money.

Unfortunately, these once in a lifetime events are happening more frequently. In 1987 we had the stock market crash, in 1998 we had the Asian Currency Crisis, in 2000 we had the bursting of the technology bubble, in 2001 we had 9/11, and in 2007 we had the sub-prime debt crisis.

Famous Hedge Fund Blowups.   Here are a few stories of some of the most famous hedge fund blowups. I do not present these to you to scare you away from hedge funds. Instead, I hope to impress upon you the importance of due diligence when examining individual hedge funds. If investors are not comfortable with this level of diligence, they are better off staying with hedge fund of funds or mutual funds.

> *Long-Term Capital Management (LTCM) 1998:* LTCM was a dream team of Nobel Prize winners and some of the smartest people in finance at the time. It was formed by John Meriwether, the former head of bond trading at Salomon Brothers. The board of directors included Myron Scholes and Robert Merton, who shared the Nobel Prize in economics in 1997. LTCM used massive amounts of leverage to bet mainly on fixed income arbitrage. They developed mathematical models to trade global bonds, betting that similar bonds with different prices would eventually converge. For the first few years, returns were extraordinary. As the fund's asset base grew and other Wall Street firms started to mimic their strategies, it became harder to find convergence trades. This caused LTCM to go outside of their area of expertise. During the Russian debt and Asian currency crisis of 1998, the firm had equity of $4.72 billion and had borrowed over $124.5 billion. When their bets went against them, the leverage caused huge losses that threatened to take down the entire financial system. Crises like these tend to turn Wall Street on its head as relationships that are normally present get inverted. These are the so-called Black Swan events. During 1998 Russia defaulted on its bonds,

causing investors who owned bonds in other countries to sell them for the safe haven of U.S. Treasury bonds. Instead of bond prices converging, which LTCM was betting on, the prices diverged. In his book *The Black Swan,* Nassim Taleb compared LTCM's strategy to "picking up pennies in front of a steamroller"—a likely small gain balanced against a small chance of a large loss. Eventually, Wall Street investment banks got together and bailed the fund out to save the financial system from collapse.

Lessons learned: When evaluating a hedge fund, you need to look at more than just performance and people. LTCM's performance was amazing and they employed geniuses. The strategy however, was hard to scale to larger amounts of capital and the amount of leverage taken exposed the firm to a small risk of a huge loss—which ended up coming to pass.

Amaranth 2006: Amaranth was primarily an energy trading fund that held $9 billion in assets. It collapsed after losing $6 billion in one week in September 2006. The fund used 8:1 leverage to bet on the relative prices of natural gas futures contracts. They believed that the prices of the March 2007 and 2008 futures contracts would increase relative to the prices of the April 2007 and 2008 contracts. Unfortunately for Amaranth, the April contracts went up versus the March contracts. The amount of leverage they were using caused the huge losses.

Lessons learned: Amaranth made one bet that had the potential to cause huge losses. Investors in hedge funds need to be aware of what types of risk controls are in place to limit the chance of these types of bets.

Bayou Hedge Fund Group: The Bayou Hedge Fund was run by Samuel Israel III and had raised $450 million from investors. Unlike the previous stories, Bayou's collapse was not the result of bad trades as much as it was outright fraud. After poor returns in 1998, investors were lied to about the results, and a fake accounting firm was set up to provide fake audits for the fund.

Lessons learned: Bayou's auditor was a sham company run by Bayou's CFO, so in effect an employee from Bayou was auditing and verifying Bayou's fake financial results.

Also, Bayou made its trades through a broker dealer that it owned, racking up commission revenue that was funneled back to Bayou as profits. Investors need to be careful that a hedge fund they are looking at doesn't have these cozy relationships. Auditors must be independent, and trades should be done through independent brokers. If Bayou had done this, investors would have known right away what was really going on.

Hedge Fund Advantages

Some of the hedge fund disadvantages can also be advantages.

- *Lockups.* The ability to lock up client money allows managers to exploit investment opportunities that mutual funds cannot invest in because they need to be liquid. Hedge funds can invest in all sorts of private deals, distressed debt, and other illiquid holdings. These types of investments can offer higher returns than typically available public investments because of an illiquidity premium.
- *Fees.* The large fees in hedge funds often attract the best money managers since they can make much more money running a hedge fund than a mutual fund. You see a lot of hedge fund managers in the Forbes 400 list but not many mutual fund managers. The incentive fees that hedge funds charge, typically around 20% of profits, also completely align the interests of the manager with the investors.
- *Leverage.* The ability to use leverage can also maximize returns if you are dealing with a good hedge fund manager. Leverage also allows hedge funds to use low volatility and low return types of strategies like arbitrage and market neutral, and increases the returns.

Finally, the lack of regulation allows flexibility to pursue a number of different skill-based investment strategies.

Hedge Fund Investing Styles

The term *hedge fund* could mean a number of different strategies. Table 9.2 shows the most common types of hedge funds and how they are categorized.

Table 9.2   Hedge Fund Styles

Opportunistic Equity	Enhanced Fixed Income	Absolute Return	Private Real Estate	Energy and Natural Resources
Long/short equity	Distressed	Market neutral	REIT L/S	L/S commodities
Global macro	Emerging market	Convertible arbitrage	Real estate partnerships	Managed futures
Short biased	L/S debt	Merger arbitrage		Oil and gas partnerships
Equity non-hedge		Fixed income arbitrage		Timber

Descriptions of some of the major hedge fund categories follow.

- *Convertible Arbitrage.* Convertible bonds are bonds that are issued by companies that are convertible into that company's stock. Convertible arbitrage hedge funds invest in convertible bonds of a company while simultaneously selling the stock short. This strategy seeks to take advantage of arbitrage opportunities between convertible bonds and the underlying stock.
- *Short Bias.* Years ago, short sellers were plentiful but the long bull market put many of them out of business. These funds try to maintain net short positions, so they may have 20% of their portfolio long in stocks that they think are going to go up and 80% short in stocks that they think are going to go down.
- *Emerging Markets.* These funds invest in emerging market stocks and/or bonds.
- *Equity Market Neutral.* These funds try to go long and short by equal amounts. For example, a market neutral fund may think that Ford will outperform GM, so it would go long Ford and short an equal amount of GM. These funds use fundamental analysis to make decisions on longs and shorts.
- *Statistical Arbitrage Market Neutral.* Like market neutral funds, these funds try to keep a neutral position in the stock market. However, they use computerized technical analysis and quantitative factors to make buy-and-sell decisions.

- *Relative Value.* These strategies often involve arbitrage techniques that do not depend on the direction of the market. Relative value funds tend to have low correlation with traditional market benchmarks. Managers typically seek to exploit disparities in pricing relationships of like instruments and profit from mispricing.
- *Fixed Income Arbitrage.* These funds try to profit from price discrepancies between related interest rate securities.
- *Event Driven.* These managers seek to rely on anticipated occurrences such as mergers, bankruptcy, and so on. The profitability of these strategies generally relies on a timely conclusion of the expected event and the realization of expected returns.

    Each event within a portfolio tends to trade on the specifics of that deal and is generally not correlated with other events within a hedge fund's portfolio.

    Styles within this category include distressed securities, merger arbitrage, spin-offs, restructurings, and recapitalizations.
    - *Distressed Securities.* These types of funds invest in corporate bonds, loans, and other securities of companies that are highly leveraged, in financial difficulty, or appear likely to file for bankruptcy. The securities are purchased in anticipation of a recovery or the liquidation of assets. For example, let's say ABC Company files for bankruptcy. Because of this, its bonds trade at a substantial discount to its competitors. It is working on some of its problems and a hedge fund feels that it is positioned for recovery so it buys the bonds hoping for a rebound. The hedge fund faces two risks: ABC either doesn't recover and the bonds do nothing or drop in value, or ABC goes out of business and the bonds become worthless.
    - *Merger Arbitrage.* These types of funds attempt to capture the spread on announced mergers. For example, let's say ABC Company announces that it has reached an agreement to purchase XYZ Company for $50 per share, closing in six months. Before the announcement, XYZ was trading at $40 per share. Immediately after the announcement, shares of XYZ will go up, but not to the acquisition price of $50 per share due to the risk that the deal will not go through. Instead, XYZ might go up to $48.50 per share.

A merger arbitrage fund would buy XYZ for $48.50 per share and hold it until the merger is finalized for $50 per share. The main risk for this fund is if this deal falls through, XYZ would probably go back down to $40 per share or lower, creating large losses for the hedge fund.

- *Special Situations.* These types of funds invest in securities of companies involved in restructurings, spin-offs, liquidations, or privatizations. These investments are made in the anticipation of the expected event occurring and the possibility that the occurrence will increase the value of the hedge fund's investment.

- *Capital Structure Arbitrage.* These types of funds invest in multiple financial instruments of the same company that the manager feels have become mispriced in relation to each other. For example, if two sets of bonds from ABC Company have the same basic risks but one is priced higher than the other by an amount more than it should be, a fund might buy the lower-priced one and sell the higher-priced one short.

- *Long/Short.* Long/short strategies combine long positions in securities with short positions in other securities in order to reduce exposure to overall market movements. These strategies are predominantly used in stock markets and typically involve leverage. Long/short managers will seek to profit from successfully predicting one company's future value relative to another company's future value, or decline in future value. For example, a long/short manager might buy shares of Coke and sell short an equal amount of shares of Pepsi. They are not betting what direction the market will go—just that Coke will outperform Pepsi. Unlike market neutral funds, long/short funds do not usually have a neutral exposure to the market.

- *Equity Non-Hedge.* These funds are predominantly long only but have the ability to hedge if they want to.

- *Global Macro.* These strategies speculate on the direction of prices in stocks, bonds, currencies, and/or commodities. They are either driven by a mechanical system or are discretionary. The returns of these strategies tend to be quite volatile and are based on the manager's advantages in knowledge, research, the ability to find both temporary pricing anomalies, and market inefficiencies.

- *Private Real Estate.* Private real estate investments are nonpublic partnerships to participate in commercial real estate deals.
- *Managed Futures.* Chapter 14 is devoted to managed futures. In short, managed futures typically use a mechanical system to identify trends in financial and commodity futures contracts.

Evaluating Hedge Funds

Mutual funds are hard to evaluate, and hedge funds are even harder. Investors who decide that hedge funds are right for them must do their homework to make sure the fund they are looking at is appropriate. They need to do due diligence, look at the returns, look at the risks, and look at the diversification.

Due Diligence: Investors and advisors must ask three key questions when looking at a hedge fund investment:

1. What does the return stream look like? For example, how volatile is it from year to year? How has it done when the market has gone up, and how has it done when the market has gone down?
2. What risks are being taken to achieve these returns?
3. How does this investment help the investors' overall asset allocation?

Returns: Most hedge funds have a targeted return. It is essential for prospective investors to know what that is so they will have a better understanding of what they are investing in and have a way to determine if the fund is meeting expectations. Volatility is also key. Are the returns consistent and steady, or is holding the fund like riding a roller coaster? This can be determined by looking at month-to-month return data and the standard deviation.

Risks: It is essential for prospective investors to understand what risks the hedge fund is taking. Is it using leverage? If so, how much? They should also ask about the maximum drawdowns in the past to gauge what the worst-case scenario might be.

Diversification: Once investors understand the returns and the risks, the question becomes how does this investment help the current portfolio? It is important to know how the prospective fund is correlated to existing investments. Noncorrelated investments could help reduce the overall risk of the clients' portfolio.

Top-Performing Funds

Although it is essential that you use the four evaluation techniques listed above to assess hedge funds, you may also choose to use hedge funds that are known to produce superior results. For instance, below is a list of the top 10 performing hedge funds. This list, which originally included the top 50 performing funds, was based on the average annual return over the previous three years as of October 2007. They were ranked by *Barron's* Online in an October 2007 article entitled "Hedge Fund 50." According to the article, the top 10 at the time were as follows:

1. RAB Special Situations Fund (RAB Capital, London): 47.69%
2. The Children's Investment Fund (The Children's Investment Fund Management, London): 44.27%
3. Highland CDO Opportunity Fund (Highland Capital Management, Dallas): 43.98%
4. BTR Global Opportunity Fund, Class D (Salida Capital, Toronto): 43.42%
5. SR Phoenicia Fund (Sloane Robinson, London): 43.10%
6. Atticus European Fund (Atticus Management, New York): 40.76%
7. Gradient European Fund A (Gradient Capital Partners, London): 39.18%
8. Polar Capital Paragon Absolute Return Fund (Polar Capital Partners, London): 38.00%
9. Paulson Enhanced Partners Fund (Paulson & Co., New York): 37.97%
10. Firebird Global Fund (Firebird Management, New York): 37.18%

Because of the unavailability of reliable figures, the top 50 list excludes funds such as Renaissance Technologies' Renaissance Medallion Fund and ESL Investments' ESL Partners (each thought to have returned an average of over 35% in the previous three years) and funds by SAC Capital and Appaloosa Management, which might otherwise have made the list.

The list also excludes funds with a net asset value of less than $250 million. The returns are net of fees.

Highest-Earning Hedge Fund Managers

Investors may also look at hedge fund managers' earnings to ascertain the fund's success rate. Even though a hedge fund manager's earnings are not made public, there are several publications that estimate how much they make. Below are some of the highest-earning hedge fund managers:

Trader Monthly's list of top 10 earners among hedge fund managers in 2007:

1. John Paulson, Paulson & Co.: $3 billion+
2. Philip Falcone, Harbinger Capital Partners: $1.5 to $2 billion
3. Jim Simons, Renaissance Technologies: $1 billion
4. Steven A. Cohen, SAC Capital Advisors: $1 billion
5. Ken Griffin, Citadel Investment Group: $1 to $1.5 billion
6. Chris Hohn, The Children's Investment Fund: $800 to $900 million
7. Noam Gottesman, GLG Partners: $700 to $800 million
8. Alan Howard, Brevan Howard Asset Management: $700 to $800 million
9. Pierre Lagrange, GLG Partners: $700 to $800 million
10. Paul Tudor Jones, Tudor Investment Corp.: $600 to $700 million

Trader Monthly's top three in 2006:

1. John D. Arnold, Centaurus Energy: $1.5 to $2 billion
2. Jim Simons, Renaissance Technologies: $1.5 to $2 billion
3. Eddie Lampert, ESL Investments: $1 to $1.5 billion

Trader Monthly's top three in 2005:

1. T. Boone Pickens, BP Capital Management: $1.5 billion+
2. Steven A. Cohen, SAC Capital Advisers: $1 billion+
3. Jim Simons, Renaissance Technologies: $900 million to $1 billion

In comparison, *Institutional Investor*'s top three earners among hedge fund managers in 2007 were:

1. John Paulson, Paulson & Co.: $3.7 billion
2. George Soros, Soros Fund Management: $2.9 billion
3. Jim Simons, Renaissance Technologies: $2.8 billion

Institutional Investor's 2005 top earner was Jim Simons with $1.6 billion, and their 2004 top earner was Edward Lampert of ESL Investments, who earned $1.02 billion during the year.

As you can see, the reports indicate different winners. Therefore, it is important that investors do their due diligence in evaluating hedge funds as an investment vehicle.

How Do Investors Access Hedge Funds?

Hedge funds typically have minimum investments of $1 to $5 million. Many of the best managers will no longer take money from individual investors. Therefore, to achieve an appropriate level of diversification across strategies and managers, an investor should have at least $10 to $25 million to invest in hedge funds. Most investors do not have the financial resources to create a diversified hedge fund portfolio or the expertise to do the due diligence necessary on hedge funds. Because of this, we generally recommend that most investors consider hedge fund of funds or mutual funds that follow hedge fund type strategies.

Hedge Funds of Funds

Because of the difficulty in picking hedge fund managers and high minimum investments, many investors turn to a fund of funds approach. A hedge fund of funds has a manager who allocates money to other hedge funds. Typically, the manager will diversify fund investments over a number of different hedge fund styles and managers. This will tend to water down returns and add another layer of fees, but it also reduces the risk that any one manager will underperform and reduce overall volatility. Many funds of funds charge a 1% annual management fee and 10% of profits, so this makes an already expensive vehicle even more expensive. Just as with any money manager, there are good funds of funds managers and others not so good; the good ones are worth their fee and the not so good ones aren't. Some funds use a multistrategy approach whereas others might allocate money to managers in a single strategy such as long/short. Funds of funds typically have minimum investments in the $100,000 to $10 million range. The number of underlying managers a fund has can vary widely but generally will range from 20 to 100.

Advantages of a fund of funds include:

- *Access to Established Hedge Funds.* A fund of funds can sometimes gain access to hedge funds that either have high minimums or don't take money from individual investors.
- *Access to Up-and-Coming Managers.* Funds of funds might have knowledge of up-and-coming managers who could be tomorrow's stars.
- *Due Diligence.* Funds of funds are experts at choosing and monitoring hedge funds.
- *Risk Reduction.* By combining multiple funds over multiple strategies, investors can mitigate the risk of a hedge fund blowup.
- *Ease of Investment.* Investors can get access to a diversified portfolio of hedge funds at much lower minimums than if they tried to create a hedge fund portfolio on their own.

A fund of funds comes at a cost since it adds a second layer of fees to the underlying hedge fund. Some detractors would not use a fund of funds for this reason. However, I look at it as an investor is paying for the guidance and experience, access to talent, risk management, and daily fund management that a fund of funds offers. Another disadvantage is that funds of funds tend to be very fickle when it comes to the returns of their underlying hedge fund returns. If a good fund has a bad year, they will often pull all their money out. Because of this, some hedge funds no longer accept money from funds of funds.

Investors still need to do due diligence on a fund of funds to make sure the investment objective and experience of the management team are in line with what they are looking for.

The most common types of funds of funds are as follows:

- *Diversified.* These funds invest in a variety of strategies among multiple managers.

- *Conservative.* These funds invest in hedge funds that follow more conservative strategies such as market neutral, fixed income arbitrage, and convertible arbitrage.
- *Market Defensive.* These funds invest in hedge funds that are either uncorrelated to the market, like managed futures, or will profit in a market decline like short biased.
- *Strategic.* These funds try to generate superior returns by investing in opportunistic strategies like emerging markets, global macro, and so on.

Mutual Funds That Follow Hedge Fund Strategies

Due to the popularity of hedge funds and the high minimum investments, many mutual funds have come out through the years that employ hedge fund like strategies. These funds are available to nonaccredited investors and do not have performance-based fees. Investors who are not accredited but would benefit from alternative investments may want to consider these funds.

Hedge Funds vs. Mutual Funds

Because hedge funds operate as limited partnerships, they are largely unregulated and are free from many of the constraints of mutual funds with regard to diversification and the use of leverage. This can be a good or a bad thing. Hedge fund compensation is largely incentive based; again, this can be good or bad. Some other issues of hedge funds that we talked about previously include the illiquidity and tax issues. If you are not an accredited investor or qualified purchaser, then you have no choice but to use mutual funds if you want to follow some traditional hedge fund strategies.

Mutual funds must adhere to stricter rules than hedge funds regarding leverage, illiquid securities, derivatives, and short positions. Recent history shows that mutual funds that follow hedge fund strategies have been able to come close to matching hedge fund index returns, albeit with higher volatility. Table 9.3 compares mutual funds that follow hedge fund strategies with hedge funds.

Mutual funds also have four advantages to hedge funds:

1. You do not need to be an accredited or qualified investor.
2. Mutual funds are transparent and liquid.

Table 9.3   Comparative Performance of Mutual Funds and Hedge Fund Indexes 2001–2005

	Annualized Return	Standard Deviation	Maximum Drawdown
Mutual Funds			
Equity market neutral	5.1%	3.3%	−4.1%
Convertible arbitrage	5.4%	3.8%	−5.8%
Event-driven	4.9%	6.4%	−5.4%
Long/short equity	5.3%	11.9%	−22.2%
Average	5.2%	6.3%	−9.4%
Hedge Fund Index			
Equity market neutral	6.0%	1.7%	−1.5%
Convertible arbitrage	6.5%	3.1%	−5.4%
Event-driven	4.9%	2.7%	−2.3%
Long/short equity	5.9%	5.4%	−7.0%
Average	5.8%	3.2%	−4.0%
S&P 500	0.6%	14.9%	−38.9%
Lehman Aggregate Bond Index	5.9%	4.0%	−3.6%

3. Mutual funds can be held in brokerage accounts and are portable.
4. Tax reporting is much easier with mutual funds.

Moving On to Asset Classes

Now that we have covered the different types of investment vehicles you can use in your portfolio, in Part III we will talk about the asset classes you should have in your endowment type portfolio.

PART
III

ENDOWMENT ASSET CLASSES AND INVESTING STRATEGIES

There are a number of different asset classes and a number of ways to define each of them. For our purposes in this book, we will talk about five asset classes: absolute return, stocks, bonds, real assets (which includes managed futures), and private equity. For each asset class, I will describe its role in a portfolio and the range of how much an investor would want in it. It is also important to note that not every investment will comfortably fit into an asset class. For example, I like a mutual fund called the Permanent Portfolio. It has a fixed allocation to gold, silver, Swiss francs, bonds, growth stocks, real estate, and natural resources stocks. Therefore, it could fit anywhere in an allocation. I choose to put it in real assets since the bulk of the fund is invested in that asset class. When you use skill-based managers, it is likely that many of them will straddle different asset classes. The simplest solution is to use the appropriate asset class where the bulk of the investments are.

Chapters 10 through 15 in Part III begin with an explanation of the role that each specific asset class should have in your portfolio, how each should be expected to perform (remember, of course, that past performance doesn't predict future results), what you can expect from the asset class, what you can benchmark it against, and a range of how much of your portfolio should go into that asset class.

Chapters 16 and 17 in Part III covers some other endowment investing strategies: in-house and portable alpha.

CHAPTER

Absolute Return

Role in Portfolio:	Stability
Performance Expectation:	3% to 7% real return, should be able to generate stable returns over just about any market environment. Will significantly underperform the market during periods like 1995–1999 when stocks were going up like crazy.
Benchmarks:	Hedge Fund Research Performance Index, fund of funds index, LIBOR+, T-bills+, inflation+
Allocation:	0% to 40%

The objective of absolute return investments is to beat inflation with a low correlation to stocks and bonds. Absolute return strategies do this by eliminating beta as much as possible, by having little to no market exposure, and trying to generate performance entirely from alpha. Absolute return investments are the anchor of the portfolio. Specifically, absolute return seeks to outperform inflation by 3% to 7% and should particularly shine in flat or down stock markets. In strong up markets, like the period from 1995 to 1999, absolute return will generally underperform. My definition of absolute return investments encompasses the following:

- Market neutral hedge funds, fund of funds, or mutual funds
- Conservative hedge fund of funds
- Mutual funds that have a hedge fund of funds format
- Convertible arbitrage hedge funds or mutual funds

- Fixed income arbitrage hedge funds, fund of funds, or mutual funds
- Merger arbitrage hedge funds or mutual funds

The bulk of many endowment portfolios consists of absolute return types of investments. You cannot replicate the strategies of endowments like Harvard and Yale without including absolute return strategies in your portfolio.

Absolute Return Mutual Funds

More and more mutual funds are coming out that have an absolute return focus which is blurring the line between mutual funds and hedge funds. Some examples include:

- *Alpha and Beta Hedged Strategies*. These funds are the only ones of their kind. They invest in a portfolio of hedge funds just like a hedge fund of funds does. However, instead of investing directly into these hedge funds, they get the information on the fund's holdings and create a mirror portfolio that is held at a bank. The Beta Hedged Strategies takes more risk than the Alpha Hedged Strategies.
- *Absolute Strategies*. Absolute Strategies is similar to the Alpha and Beta Hedged Strategies in that it allocates money to outside managers. The difference is that the managers it uses are all regular money managers (not hedge fund managers) that follow strategies similar to hedge funds. This keeps expenses lower than the Alpha and Beta but somewhat limits the universe of money managers to choose from.
- *Permanent Portfolio*. The Permanent Portfolio could fit into any asset class. I prefer to include it under Absolute Return because it seeks to be an all weather fund and provide absolute returns. The fund has fixed percentages in the following assets:
  - 20% in gold bullion
  - 5% in silver
  - 10% in Swiss franc–denominated assets
  - 15% in U.S. and foreign real estate and natural resources stocks
  - 15% in aggressive growth stocks
  - 35% in U.S. T-bills, bonds, and other dollar-denominated assets

- *Arbitrage Fund and Merger Fund.* These funds are merger arbitrage funds. Merger arbitrage funds buy shares of companies that have announced mergers or takeovers, hoping to profit on the difference between the price after the announcement and the merger-takeover price. For example, ABC Company might announce that they are buying XYZ Company for $50 per share to close in three months (XYZ was at $40 before the takeover was announced). Immediately after the announcement, XYZ shares will go up, but not to $50 because the deal could fall through in the three months until the takeover date. XYZ might go up to $49, with the difference reflecting the risk of something going wrong. A merger arbitrage fund would buy XYZ at $49 and hold onto it for three months when they would sell their shares to ABC for $50.

These are just a few of the absolute return mutual funds out there. More and more continue to come out every day.

Objectives of Absolute Return Investments

Absolute return investments have the following objectives:

- *Increased Diversification.* In previous chapters we talked about how all sectors of the stock market have become well correlated to each other. Absolute return investments seek low to negative correlation with stocks and bonds, which can reduce the risk and increase the return of a portfolio.
- *Low Correlation to Traditional Assets.* Table 10.1 shows some absolute return categories like the HFRI Equity Market Neutral Indexes versus traditional assets like the S&P 500, the Russell 2000, and the Lehman Aggregate Bond Index. In each case, the correlation between this absolute return index and traditional indexes was very low.
- *Lower Portfolio Volatility.* Table 10.2 shows the returns and volatility (standard deviation) of the HFRI Equity Market Neutral Index versus the S&P 500 and the Lehman Aggregate Bond Index. The S&P 500 is almost 5 times more volatile than the Market Neutral Index. You may also notice that the S&P 500 had a higher return, which is to be expected. Absolute return investments are not a substitute for stocks. If you look at the

Table 10.1 Correlation of Market Neutral and Other Assets

Correlation Coefficient (Jan 1994–Jun 2007)	Goldman Sachs Commodity Index	HFRI Equity Hedge Index	HFRI Equity Market Neutral Index	HFRI Fixed Income (Total)	HFRI Sector: Real Estate Index	Lehman Aggregate Bond Index	Russell 2000 Index (DRI)	S&P 500 DRI
Goldman Sachs Commodity Index	1.000	0.212	0.133	0.142	−0.001	0.057	0.131	−0.004
HFRI Equity Hedge Index	0.212	1.000	0.367	0.569	0.384	−0.012	0.866	0.685
HFRI Equity Market Neutral Index	0.133	0.367	1.000	0.252	0.269	0.170	0.255	0.158
HFRI Fixed Income (Total)	0.142	0.569	0.252	1.000	0.416	0.118	0.524	0.390
HFRI Sector: Real Estate Index	−0.001	0.384	0.269	0.416	1.000	0.067	0.510	0.387
Lehman Aggregate Bond Index	0.057	−0.012	0.170	0.118	0.067	1.000	−0.073	0.029
Russell 2000 Index (DRI)	0.131	0.866	0.255	0.524	0.510	−0.073	1.000	0.717
S&P 500 DRI	−0.004	0.685	0.158	0.390	0.387	0.029	0.717	1.000

Source: PerTrac HFRI: Hedge Fund Research, Inc.

Table 10.2   Rate of Return and Risk for Market Neutral Funds

Risk Table Annualized (Jan 1994–Jun 2007)	Annualized ROR	Standard Deviation	Sharpe—5.00%	Sortino—5.00%
HFRI Equity Hedge Index	14.28%	8.58%	1.04	1.85
HFRI Equity Market Neutral Index	7.96%	2.96%	0.96	1.78
HFRI Fixed Income (Total)	8.19%	2.91%	1.05	1.55
HFRI Sector: Real Estate Index	9.87%	6.52%	0.73	1.13
Lehman Aggregate Bond Index	6.05%	3.78%	0.28	0.38
S&P 500 TR	10.72%	14.09%	0.45	0.55

Market Neutral Index versus the Lehman Index, it had a lower volatility than bonds and a higher return. This is why the large endowments use absolute return investments as a bond substitute. We will talk more about bonds in a later chapter.

- *Accessing the Best and Brightest Talent.* Absolute return investments don't have to be in hedge funds, but one of the advantages of using hedge funds is that the best and brightest money managers tend to be there. There are four main reasons why the top portfolio managers tend to prefer the hedge fund structure:
  1. Incentive compensation allows them to earn substantially more than mutual fund managers and ties their earnings more to performance. In Chapter 9 on hedge funds, you may have noticed a lot of managers earning more than $1 billion.
  2. Wider variety of investment options and strategies to pursue.
  3. Privacy of investment ideas versus mutual fund managers who need to publish their holdings.
  4. The ability to take larger positions and invest in illiquid investments.

Table 10.3   Return and Risk for Hedge Funds of Funds vs. S&P 500

1990–2005	Return	Standard Deviation (Risk)
S&P 500	10.55%	14.32%
Hedge funds of funds; HFRI Fund of Funds Index	9.89%	5.54%

Table 10.4   Hedge Funds of Funds Down Months vs. S&P 500 Down Months

Cumulative down months S&P 500	HFRI over same period
–91%	.02%
Cumulative down months for Lehman Bond Index	HFRI over same period
–35.2%	36.8%

Types of Absolute Return Investments

Absolute return investments can be hedge funds of funds, mutual funds that follow a hedge fund of funds format, true market neutral hedge funds, and certain arbitrage strategies.

Table 10.3 is a chart of the S&P 500 and hedge funds of funds as measured by the HFRI Fund of Funds Index from 1990 to 2005.

The funds of funds gave up a little bit of return, but had almost one-third of the risk of the S&P 500.

Table 10.4 is a chart of the funds of funds compared to the down months in the S&P 500 and bonds, as measured by the Lehman Bond Index. What this shows is that in the months when the S&P 500 has been down in total, funds of funds have been up slightly. During the down months for bonds, funds of funds were up significantly.

These characteristics are why college endowments use absolute return investments as bond substitutes. They have had historical returns much higher than bonds and risk much lower than stocks. They have also shown an ability to do well when stocks and bonds are down. Table 10.5 shows the risk return of some specific absolute return strategies: convertible arbitrage, equity market neutral, and merger arbitrage versus stocks and bonds.

Just like the hedge funds of funds, these strategies had bondlike risk, with higher (except for equity market neutral) returns than bonds.

Table 10.5   Risk/Return of Absolute Return Strategies vs. S&P 500 and Lehman Bond Index: January 1998–August 2006

	Convertible Arbitrage	Equity Market Neutral	Merger Arbitrage	S&P 500	Lehman Aggregate Bond
Annualized returns	6.6%	2.3%	6.8%	5.1%	5.8%
Standard deviation	4%	3.7%	3.8%	15.5%	3.6%
Maximum drawdown	−10%	−6%	−4.6%	−44.7%	−3.6%

Source: Bloomberg, Hedge Fund Research, Inc.

Mutual Funds That Have an Absolute Return Focus

Every month there are more and more mutual funds coming out that seek to provide investors with an absolute return type of investment strategy. So far, there are four ways that fund companies have structured these funds:

1. Funds that track a hedge fund index: Goldman Sachs Absolute Return Tracker Fund and Rydex Absolute Return Strategies are two funds in this category.
2. Funds that invest in other mutual funds that follow hedge fund type strategies: New Century Alternative Strategies falls into this category.
3. Funds that invest in other hedge funds through a mirror approach: Alpha Hedged Strategies and Beta Hedged Strategies are actual funds of hedge funds. They farm out money to actual hedge funds but instead of being managed directly by those funds, a mirror portfolio is created with the exact same investments for the fund.
4. Funds that invest with other money managers who follow hedge fund type strategies: Like Alpha and Beta Hedged Strategies, the Absolute Strategies funds also use outside managers. However, they use money managers who follow hedge fund-like strategies but which are not hedge funds.

Market Neutral Mutual Funds

Market neutral strategies seek to exploit inefficiencies in similar or related securities, often using arbitrage. For example, a portfolio might be 50% long stocks with attractive characteristics and 50% short stocks with unattractive characteristics. Other strategies might be to go long convertible bonds and short the underlying stock. Market neutral strategies aren't necessarily as risk free as the name might lead one to believe. Because *market neutral* is in the name doesn't mean that the strategy is really market neutral. When evaluating market neutral funds, you need to find out how neutral they actually are. Many of the mutual funds that claim to be market neutral really have a long bias. Also, market neutral strategies tend to be low return. To counter this, market neutral hedge funds use leverage whereas mutual funds do not. Because of the lack of leverage and perhaps because the best talent is at mutual fund companies, most market neutral mutual funds have not had the best performance records.

Market neutral funds usually seek a modest spread over and above a risk-free rate such as T-bills. Because of their structure they are designed to underperform in a bull market.

The Anchor of Your Portfolio

Absolute return investments make up the bulk of many endowment portfolios. It used to be difficult for individual investors to access them, but with the proliferation of absolute return mutual funds, they are available for investors of all sizes.

Whether you choose to access absolute return investments through hedge funds, funds of funds, or mutual funds, this will be the anchor of your portfolio.

11

Stocks

Role in Portfolio:	Returns
Performance Expectation:	Your stock investments should be beating the S&P 500 on a risk-adjusted basis. That doesn't necessarily mean beating the market; it means adding alpha. It means that if you are taking less risk than the market, then you might not have as high a return as the market but you should have a higher return than would be expected given the level of risk you are taking.
Benchmarks:	S&P 500, Dow Jones Industrial Average, MSCI EAFE, etc.
Allocation:	0% to 40%

The famed financier J. P. Morgan was once asked his opinion about what the stock market would do on a certain day. His answer was that it will fluctuate. That is the one thing we can be certain of in the stock market. Since 2000, investors have seen stocks have periods of high returns followed by periods of losses or low returns. Investors have also seen longer-term trends. From 1964 to 1981, the Dow Jones Industrial Average gained just $\frac{1}{10}$ of 1%. From 1982 to 2000 it gained over 1000%. Over time, markets will fluctuate; therefore it is beneficial for investors to have a flexible investment approach with the stock part of their portfolios.

During periods like 1982 to 2000, index funds were doing well; since they tracked the market a rising tide lifted all boats. During periods like 1964 to 1981, index funds performed poorly. In such times it is important to be able to identify the areas that might do well regardless of what the broader market is doing. Stocks should be the cornerstone of any portfolio; they will provide the growth over long periods of time that many of your other asset classes will not. However, as we have seen in the market during 2008, stocks are not always a safe place to put your money. Extreme care should be taken to identify the best money managers for the stock portion of your portfolio.

Your stock investments could include the following:

- Flexible money managers that primarily invest in stocks
- Long/short funds
- Long bias market neutral funds
- Global macro hedge funds
- Style box-based money managers who focus on stocks
- Index funds or ETFs

Endowments like Harvard and Yale use stocks as the growth part of their portfolio. Stocks usually come second to absolute return investments in many endowment portfolio allocations. Without stock market exposure in your portfolio, you will never be able to experience the types of growth that endowment portfolios do.

Investing Globally

In previous chapters, we talked about how the U.S. and international stock markets have become much more highly correlated. So does that mean that investors should shun international stocks? The answer is an emphatic no. It is important to remember from our discussion of correlation, that two highly correlated assets don't move the exact same amount at the same time. It means that there is a high degree of likelihood that the direction of returns is related, but not the magnitude. So, if U.S. stocks are up 10%, that doesn't necessarily mean international stocks will also be up 10%. It does mean that many of the factors that impact U.S. stocks also impact international stocks, which is why we need other assets in our portfolio to provide diversification from stocks. I would argue that not only should investors have international exposure but they should also have more international exposure than U.S. exposure.

There are many reasons why investors need to think globally: the weakening of the U.S. dollar, the ability to have higher returns in global markets, the fact that the United States is declining in its share of the global marketplace, and changes in emerging market economies. However, most investors have what I call home market myopia—just because they live somewhere, they think they need to have some or all of their money invested there. Let's say there was a developed country called Madeupia. Madeupia had a well-developed stock and bond market and a well-developed economy. However, Madeupia was in a deep recession that looked like it would continue for some time. On the other hand, there were many other countries in the world that were doing very well and had much better investment prospects. If I live in Madeupia, should I invest the bulk of my assets there and ignore the global opportunities around me? That would be crazy. I am often asked by journalists how much U.S. investors should have in overseas investments. I normally give a politically correct answer like 30% to 40%, but in actuality there is no reason that a U.S. investor should not have 100% of his or her investments overseas if the opportunities are better from a risk/return standpoint. An added benefit to using skill-based money managers is that they generally have flexibility to go anywhere in the world where they see opportunities.

Declining Dollar

Investors often overlook the impact of currency exchange rates on returns when investing overseas. This is not a concern when the dollar is strong, but over the past several years we have seen the dollar in a decline. If the dollar continues to decline, an international investment that has the same local currency return as a U.S. dollar investment will significantly outperform when exchange rates are taken into account.

In Table 11.1 we have a U.S. dollar investment and a euro investment that both return 10%. If the dollar subsequently declines versus the euro, the returns of the euro investment will be substantially higher once it is brought back into dollar returns. This shows how important exchange rates can be in investing in non-U.S. stocks.

Table 11.1   Impact of Exchange Rates

	U.S. Dollar	Exchange Rate	Euro
Initial investment	$100	$1 = 1 euro	100 euros
Local currency return	10%		10%
Value in local currency	$110		110 euros
Dollar equivalent value assuming dollar decline	$110	$1.25 = 1 euro	$137.50

Source: SEI.

Higher Potential Returns in Global Markets

Table 11.2 shows that despite increased correlations, there is a wide dispersion of returns among global markets from 2005 to 2007. It also shows that the U.S. market has been near the bottom in returns over those three years.

Table 11.2   Returns of Global Markets

Rank/ Year	2007	Return	2006	Return	2005	Return
1	Luxembourg	84.78	Luxembourg	157.80	Japan	25.69
2	Finland	50.09	Spain	49.43	Denmark	25.67
3	China	44.46	Portugal	48.97	Austria	25.52
4	Bermuda	44.36	Singapore	47.97	Norway	23.84
5	Hong Kong	40.89	Ireland	46.22	Netherlands	19.07
6	Germany	35.98	Norway	44.91	Australia	17.64
7	Greece	32.90	Sweden	44.85	Finland	17.47
8	Norway	30.81	Denmark	39.55	Switzerland	17.18
9	Australia	30.05	Austria	37.84	Greece	16.35
10	Singapore	28.21	Germany	36.96	Singapore	15.40
11	Denmark	25.86	Belgium	36.64	Luxembourg	10.74
12	Portugal	25.24	Greece	34.67	Germany	10.70
13	Spain	23.98	Italy	34.08	Sweden	10.59
14	Netherlands	19.92	France	33.32	France	10.24
15	France	12.27	Australia	32.50	Belgium	9.67
16	New Zealand	9.84	Finland	31.05	Hong Kong	8.59
17	United Kingdom	8.35	United Kingdom	30.58	United Kingdom	7.99
18	Italy	7.26	Hong Kong	30.20	**United States**	**4.91**
19	Switzerland	6.06	Switzerland	28.23	Spain	4.52
20	**United States**	**5.49**	New Zealand	17.40	New Zealand	3.48
21	Austria	2.65	**United States**	**15.79**	Italy	3.46
22	Sweden	1.33	Bermuda	10.35	Portugal	−0.51
23	Belgium	−2.72	Japan	6.41	Ireland	−2.69
24	Japan	−4.13				
25	Ireland	−18.50				

Source: SEI, FactSet.

When Wayne Gretzky, the hockey legend, was asked what made him so great he replied that he skated to where the puck was going to be, not where it was. The international markets are where the puck is going to be in the investing world. In 1970 the U.S. market made up 66% of the global marketplace. By 2036 it is projected to make up only 24%. (See Table 11.3.)

By 2050 China is expected to surpass us as the world's largest economy, as shown in Table 11.4.

Why BRIC (Brazil, Russia, India, and China)?

We are big believers that the best returns for the foreseeable future will come from the emerging markets, particularly the so-called BRIC countries: Brazil, Russia, India, and China. There are a number of reasons for this, including:

- Indian GDP is projected to be more than twice Japan by 2020. (Source: CLSA)
- Chinese GDP is projected to be more than twice U.S. by 2020. (Source: CLSA)
- These countries have higher GDP growth rates and corporate profit growth rates than the developed world.

Table 11.3   United States vs. the World

Date	United States	World
1970	66%	34%
2005	44%	56%
2036 (Projected)	24%	76%

Source: Merrill Lynch.

Table 11.4   Top World Economies

Five Top Economies 2004	Five Top Economies 2050 (Projected)
United States	China
Japan	United States
Germany	India
United Kingdom	Japan
China	Brazil

Source: Hamish Mcrae—The World in 2020.

- Political stability is increasing in these countries.
- Sophisticated capital markets are developing in these countries.
- The rise of the middle class in BRIC countries will spike demand for consumer goods and services.

The BRIC countries also have diverse sources of growth and returns: Brazil is strong in commodities; Russia is home to 20% of the world's oil reserves and 35% of its natural gas; India is strong in technology and outsourcing; and China is a strong manufacturing center.

The wealth transfer that we talked about at the beginning of the book is shifting wealth from our economy to emerging economies, specifically Brazil, Russia, India, and China. This wealth transfer is creating a middle class that is beginning to demand the same goods and services as the U.S. middle class. These economies are therefore shifting from primarily export driven (where they live and die with the economic situation of the countries they are exporting to) to imports and internal production for their own citizens.

This is creating and will continue to create huge opportunities in these markets. The path will not be straight up, and these markets will continue to be volatile. However, for the longer term your portfolio should include money managers who are invested in BRIC countries.

BRIC Countries and Infrastructure

Infrastructure is likely to be an area of excess returns going forward, especially in the BRIC countries. Infrastructure includes roads, bridges, railroads, public transit, airports, seaports, water and sewer systems, electrical power grids, and communications networks.

Due to the future growth in emerging markets and the need to repair and replace infrastructure in developed markets, the stock part of your portfolio may be a good place for money managers that focus on infrastructure stocks. In the United States, our infrastructure is growing older and older. According to the American Society of Civil Engineers, we would have to invest $1.6 trillion in our infrastructure to bring it into good repair. Electricity use in China, India, and Latin America is growing between 4% and 5% per year according to Booz Allen Hamilton. Infrastructure in those countries must be updated to keep pace with demand.

Cost estimates to upgrade global infrastructure vary between $32 and $41 trillion over the next 25 to 30 years (according to studies by Britain's Foresight Programme and Booz Allen Hamilton).

A larger, more urban population is to blame for the growing need to repair and develop infrastructure. According to the United Nations, by 2030 there will be 8.3 billion people on Earth, and 60% of them will be living in cities. This will put tremendous pressure on existing infrastructure.

China is undergoing the biggest infrastructure boom in history. Their current five-year plan, set to expire in 2010, calls for the following:

- $175 billion for railroads
- $200 billion for airports and subways
- $80 billion for highways

According to Merrill Lynch, they spend 36% of their GDP on infrastructure.

India's finance minister told legislators in 2007 that they need to spend 8% (up from 5%) of GDP on infrastructure in order to sustain its current economic growth rate.

According to Merrill Lynch, Russia is spending 16% of its GDP on infrastructure and Brazil is spending 9%.

There are a growing handful of money managers and mutual funds that specialize in investing in companies engaged in infrastructure development. Some examples of mutual funds include Kinetics Water Infrastructure and U.S. Global MegaTrends Fund. There are also a number of mutual funds that invest in India and China, or invest globally with a large allocation to India and China. Some examples are as follows:

- *Matthews China and Matthews India.* These funds invest exclusively in China and India, respectively.
- *Ivy Asset Strategy and BlackRock Global Allocation.* These funds allocate their assets globally based on where they see the best opportunities.

Long/Short Investments

In addition to global investments, your stock allocation is also where you should have long/short investments. Table 11.5 shows

Table 11.5 Risk/Return for Portfolio A and B for the Periods January 1990 and January 1998 to August 2006

	Portfolio A		Portfolio B	
Risk/Return Statistics	Since 1998	Since 1990	Since 1998	Since 1990
Annualized return	4.3%	9.2%	6.9%	11.7%
Standard deviation	17.4%	15.4%	13.6%	12.3%
Maximum drawdown	−47.6%	−47.6%	−32.7%	−32.7%
Months to recover	N/A	N/A	34	34

Source: Absolute Return Strategies: A Class of its Own, Geronimo Financial Asset Management, October 2006.

the advantage of adding long/short investments to an aggressive portfolio. Portfolio A is 100% invested in stocks as follows: 33% S&P 500, 33% Russell 1000 Growth, and 33% Russell 2000. Portfolio B has 23% in the S&P 500, 23% in the Russell 1000 Growth, 23% in the Russell 2000, and 30% in long/short investments represented by the HFR Equity Hedge Index.

Since 1990, Portfolio A would have returned 9.2% a year with a standard deviation of 15.4%. This portfolio would have suffered a 47.6% drawdown starting in 2001 from which it would not have recovered as of August 2006. Portfolio B with a 30% allocation to long/short would have returned 11.7% a year over the same period with a standard deviation of 12.3%. The worst drawdown would have been 32.7%, from which it would have recovered in 34 months. So, by adding long/short investments to this portfolio, we would have increased the return *and* lowered the risk.

Table 11.6 shows the benefits of adding Long/Short (HFRI Long/Short Index), Multi-Strategy (HFRI Multi-Strategy Index), and Market Neutral (HFRI Market Neutral Index) Investments to a balanced portfolio of 50% stocks and 50% bonds. From 1990 to August of 2006, the balanced portfolio (Portfolio A) would have returned 9.2% per year with a standard deviation of 7.5% and a maximum drawdown of 14.7% requiring 14 months to recover. By contrast, adding 30% of the skill-based managers (Portfolio B) would have produced annual returns of 10.1% per year, a standard

Table 11.6   Risk/Return for Portfolios A and B for the Periods January 1990 and January 1998 to August 2006

Risk/Return Statistics	Portfolio A		Portfolio A	
	Since 1998	Since 1990	Since 1998	Since 1990
Annualized return	6%	9.2%	6.8%	10.1%
Standard deviation	7.4%	7.5%	5%	5.3%
Maximum drawdown	−14.7%	−14.7%	−5.4%	−5.4%
Months to recover	14	14	3	3

Source: Absolute Return Strategies: A Class of its Own, Geronimo Financial Asset Management, October 2006.

deviation of 5.3%, and a maximum drawdown of 5.4%, from which it would have taken three months to recover.

Long/Short Mutual Funds

So many long/short mutual funds have been coming out that Morningstar now has an entire category for them. Be careful though, because sometimes funds get misplaced, like the Rydex Managed Futures fund, which Morningstar classifies as long/short but is really managed futures.

Some examples of funds are TFS Market Neutral, Diamond Hill Long/Short, and ICON Global Long/Short.

130/30 Funds

Over the past couple of years there has been an explosion of new 130/30 funds into the marketplace. These funds use 100% of their NAV to purchase stocks long; they then sell short up to 30% of their NAV and use the proceeds of the short sales to buy more stocks. The net result is that they are long approximately 130% of the portfolio and short 30%. So, for example, if the NAV of the XYZ 130/30 fund was $100, they would hold $130 worth of stocks and sell $30 worth of stocks short.

We believe that 130/30 funds will become more prevalent and popular. We also believe that it is a viable investment strategy.

However, just like any strategy there will be good managers and bad managers. Since these funds have not been around very long, it is difficult at this point to figure out which is which. Also, because selling stocks short takes a different skill set than buying them long, I would wait on these funds to see how they do on the short side.

Stocks Are the Growth Engine of Your Portfolio

Nothing else in your portfolio has the ability to provide as much growth as stocks. For most endowments, stocks are the first or second largest portfolio allocation and this should probably be the case for most investors. Your stock investments should include global skill-based managers and funds that are not constrained to be long only.

CHAPTER 12

Bonds

Role in Portfolio:	Stability
Performance Expectation:	This will probably be the lowest-performing part of your portfolio. Your allocation here should be higher during periods of decreasing interest rates and during periods where other investment strategies are going haywire. As of this writing in 2008, we have a much larger allocation to bonds than usual because of the dislocations in global markets.
Benchmarks:	Lehman Brothers Aggregate Index
Allocation:	0% to 40%

Most endowments like Harvard and Yale use bonds very sparingly because after inflation they do not offer very attractive returns. However, these endowments still do have a modest exposure to bonds, and individual investors should have at least that.

Your bond investments could consist of any of the following:

- Individual bonds
- Bond mutual funds
- Fixed-income hedge funds
- Bond ETFs

The Destructive Power of Inflation

One of the most interesting things in looking at the portfolios of large endowments is that their main goal is to reduce risk, yet they have very little invested in bonds. Typically, when individual investors look to reduce the risk of their portfolio, they increase their bond exposure, so why don't the endowments do the same? The endowments realize that after inflation they are not getting much in return from bonds. For individual investors, it's even worse because we have to deal with taxes and inflation.

At today's interest rates, bonds have the lowest expected return of any of the asset classes that endowments use. Table 12.1 shows Treasury bond yields as of July 22, 2008.

At the same time, the Consumer Price Index (CPI), which measures inflation, was up 5% from June 2007 to June 2008. That means that an investor in any Treasury bond or a five-year CD would be losing money in real terms by buying bonds. That doesn't even account for taxes.

This is why large endowments tend to have very low allocations to bonds. They know that after inflation they are virtually guaranteed to lose money.

How much of an impact can inflation have on your portfolio? Consider the following examples of the value of $100,000 over three 10-year periods as shown in Table 12.2: 1977–1986, 1987–1996, and 1997–2006. Table 12.2 shows the decline in the value of

Table 12.1   Treasury Bond Rates

Treasuries	Yield (%)
1-Month bill	1.353
3-Month bill	1.501
6-Month bill	1.924
2-Year note	2.683
5-Year note	3.435
10-Year note	4.089
30-Year bond	4.653
5-year CD, annual yield	4.12

Table 12.2   Buying Power of $100,000

Period	Buying Power of $100,000 at the End of the Period
1977–1986	$51,686
1987–1996	$69,398
1997–2006	$78,442

Source: SEI, Economy.com.

what $100,000 would buy during these periods using the Consumer Price Index (CPI) as our measure of inflation.

During all of these periods, the value of $100,000 declined significantly due to inflation. In fact, a dollar at the start of 1976 would have been worth 26 cents by the end of 2006.

You may have noticed that Table 12.2 doesn't assume that the investor earns anything on the $100,000; they just stick it under their mattress. In real life this is not what most investors do.

Many investors, especially after the technology bubble collapse of 2000, fled stocks as too risky for the safety of bonds and CDs. However, the large endowments would argue that bonds and CDs are actually the riskiest investments you can own, primarily due to inflation. Table 12.3 is a chart of the returns on CDs from 1983 to 2007 if taxes and inflation are factored in.

The other reason that endowments have low allocations to bonds is that it is very hard for bond managers to add alpha. Bill Gross from PIMCO is commonly thought of as one of the best, if not the best, bond managers in the business. His flagship bond mutual fund is the PIMCO Total Return. Over the past three years, the fund has only been able to generate an alpha of .43. Compared to his peers that's great, but because bonds yield so little and the market is so efficient, it is very difficult for the best of managers to outperform by much.

In a previous chapter, we talked about how endowments use absolute return investments as a bond substitute. Since most individuals don't have access to the caliber of absolute return managers that the endowments do, you will probably want some bonds in your portfolio to add stability. For that reason, we recommend higher allocations than the Yale endowment.

Bond Basics

Bonds are basically loans. When you buy a bond from the government or a corporation, you are lending them money for a certain term (the maturity date on the bond). In exchange for the loan, the bond promises to pay you a fixed amount of interest (unless it is a floating rate loan) and then give you back principal at maturity. Because the interest rate is fixed, the bond's price will fluctuate during its life with market interest rates. For example, let's say you buy a bond yielding 5% for $1,000. A year later, interest rates have

Table 12.3   Real Return of Six-Month CDs—After Taxes and Inflation for Investors in Maximum Federal Income Tax Bracket

Year	CD Rate (%)	Maximum Federal Tax Rate (%)	Inflation Rate (%)	Real Rate of CD Return (%)
1983	9.65	48.0	3.20	1.82
1984	11.17	50.0	4.30	1.28
1985	8.54	50.0	3.60	0.67
1986	6.70	50.0	1.90	1.45
1987	7.21	38.5	3.60	0.83
1988	8.18	28.0	4.10	1.79
1989	9.46	28.0	4.80	2.01
1990	8.49	28.0	5.40	0.71
1991	6.06	31.0	4.20	−0.02
1992	3.82	31.0	3.00	−0.36
1993	3.34	39.6	3.00	−0.98
1994	5.05	39.6	2.60	0.46
1995	6.16	39.6	2.80	0.92
1996	5.61	39.6	3.00	0.78
1997	5.87	39.6	2.30	1.25
1998	5.58	39.6	1.60	1.77
1999	5.59	39.6	2.20	1.18
2000	6.79	39.6	3.40	0.70
2001	3.69	39.1	2.80	−0.55
2002	1.81	39.1	1.60	−0.50
2003	1.23	35.0	2.30	−1.50
2004	1.75	35.0	2.70	−1.56
2005	3.79	35.0	3.40	−0.94
2006	5.33	35.0	3.20	0.26
2007	5.23	35.0	2.80	0.60

Source: Lipper Inc. Taxes are for the highest federal income tax rates in effect during the periods shown prior to the rate change in 2003. This information does not constitute tax advice. Inflation rate is based on the change in the Consumer Price Index (CPI) as determined by the U.S. Bureau of Labor Statistics. CD income is calculated using the six-month annualized average monthly CD rate reported by the Federal Reserve. Performance reflects reinvestment of income. For illustrative purposes only, not intended to predict or depict the performance of any investment. Past performance does not guarantee future results.

increased to 6% and you want to sell your bond. Nobody would buy your bond yielding 5% when they could buy similar bonds yielding 6%, so your bond would have to go down in price to entice a buyer. Because of this, bonds have an inverse relationship with interest rates—when interest rates rise, bond prices go down, and when interest rates fall, bond prices go up. Bond prices also have an inverse relationship with inflation—as inflation increases, bond prices go down, and yields go up to account for the fact that the interest the bond is paying isn't worth as much.

Bond Ratings

There are two major bond rating firms: Standard & Poors (S&P) and Moody's. These companies give bonds ratings which give investors an idea of the potential risk of default. The higher the rating, the lower the interest that the issuer has to pay. Individual investors need to balance between the safety of their bond and yield. A higher rating means you may sleep better, but you won't have as much return potential.

S&P Ratings.   Below are the investment grades given by S&P.

Investment Grade

- **AAA:** The best-quality borrowers, reliable and stable (many of them governments)
- **AA:** Quality borrowers, a bit higher risk than AAA
- **A:** Economic situation can affect finance
- **BBB:** Medium class borrowers, which are satisfactory at the moment

Noninvestment Grade (Also Known as Junk Bonds)

- **BB:** More prone to changes in the economy
- **B:** Financial situation varies noticeably
- **CCC:** Currently vulnerable and dependent on favorable economic conditions to meet its commitments
- **CC:** Highly vulnerable, very speculative bonds
- **C:** Highly vulnerable, perhaps in bankruptcy or in arrears but still continuing to pay out on obligations
- **CI:** Past due on interest
- **R:** Under regulatory supervision due to its financial situation
- **SD:** Has selectively defaulted on some obligations
- **D:** Has defaulted on obligations and S&P believes that it will generally default on most or all obligations
- **NR:** Not rated

Moody's Ratings.   Below are the investment grades given by Moody's.

Investment Grade

- **Aaa:** Obligations rated Aaa are judged to be of the highest quality, with minimal credit risk.
- **Aa1, Aa2, Aa3:** Obligations rated Aa are judged to be of high quality and are subject to very low credit risk.
- **A1, A2, A3:** Obligations rated A are considered to be upper medium-grade and are subject to low credit risk.
- **Baa1, Baa2, Baa3:** Obligations rated Baa are subject to moderate credit risk. They are considered to be medium-grade and as such may possess certain speculative characteristics.

Speculative Grade (Also Known as High Yield or Junk Bonds)

- **Ba1, Ba2, Ba3:** Obligations rated Ba are judged to have speculative elements and are subject to substantial credit risk.
- **B1, B2, B3:** Obligations rated B are considered speculative and are subject to high credit risk.
- **Caa1, Caa2, Caa3:** Obligations rated Caa are judged to be of poor standing and are subject to very high credit risk.
- **Ca:** Obligations rated Ca are highly speculative and are likely in, or very near, default, with some prospect of recovery of principal and interest.
- **C:** Obligations rated C are the lowest rated class of bonds and are typically in default, with little prospect for recovery of principal or interest.

Special

- **WR:** Withdrawn Rating
- **NR:** Not Rated
- **P:** Provisional

Bond Maturities

Generally, a bond that matures in one to three years is referred to as a short-term bond. Medium- or intermediate-term bonds are generally those that mature in 4 to 10 years, and long-term bonds are those with maturities greater than 10 years. The longer the term the more the price of a bond will fluctuate due to changes in interest rates.

Table 12.4   Size of the World's Bond Markets as of 9/30/07

Market	(%)
United States	38
Europe	37
Asia	17
Latin America	4
Canada	2
Australia	2

Source: BIS, December 2007.

Think Globally

When we talked about stocks, we talked about the importance of not having home market myopia. The same applies with bonds. More than half of the bonds in the world are outside of the United States. Whereas domestic bonds have two sources of return—income and capital gains—global bonds (that don't hedge currency risks) have a third potential source of return in the form of currency exposure (of course, this could also produce losses if the dollar is appreciating). Table 12.4 shows the largest bond markets.

Table 12.5 shows the best-performing bond markets from 2002 to 2007. It shows that since 2002 North America has been either at the bottom or second to last in performance each year. Whereas past performance is no guarantee of the future, I think this makes a great case for adding global bonds to a portfolio.

Types of Bond Funds and Managers

There are many different types of bond mutual funds and money managers, including:

- *Hard Currency.* One of the best uses for your bond market allocation is to get nondollar exposure. Many funds that invest in global bonds hedge their currency risk so the only appreciation or depreciation you receive is from interest and capital gains. Funds that don't hedge can also have gains and losses as the currencies that the bonds are denominated in move versus the dollar. Some of these funds take it a step further and make their investment decisions based on how much

Table 12.5　Global Bond Market Performance 2002–2007

2002	2003	2004	2005	2006	2007
Eastern Europe, 27.15%	Western Europe, 23.09%	Eastern Europe, 21.89%	Latin America/ Caribbean, 5.3%	Eastern Europe, 12.44%	Eastern Europe, 15.48%
Western Europe, 27.07%	Africa/ Middle East, 14.5%	Western Europe, 15.1%	North America, 2.33%	Western Europe, 11.49%	Western Europe, 11.78%
Africa/ Middle East, 19.71%	Latin America/ Caribbean, 13.52%	Africa/ Middle East, 9.91%	Africa/ Middle East, 1.54%	Latin America/ Caribbean, 7.44%	Asia, 9.43%
Latin America/ Caribbean, 15.15%	Eastern Europe, 11.67%	Latin America/ Caribbean, 9.71%	Eastern Europe, 1.49%	Africa/ Middle East, 6.12%	Africa/ Middle East, 8.88%
Asia, 14.17%	Asia, 10.26%	Asia, 6.05%	Western Europe, 7.95%	North America, 4.53%	North America, 7.79%
North America, 10.28%	North America, 4.91%	North America, 4.94%	Asia, 11.87%	Asia, 17%	Latin America/ Caribbean, 7.52%

Source: Zephyr StyleADVISOR.

of a certain currency they want exposure to. They then usually invest in money market accounts and short-term bonds denominated in these currencies. These funds can be a great tool to get nondollar exposure into a portfolio. An example of a fund that specializes in this area is the Merk Hard Currency Fund. This fund invests primarily in short-term government debt of countries that have sound fiscal and monetary policy, and it does not hedge its currency risk. Most foreign bond funds hedge their currency risk so that their returns come entirely from the bonds they are buying and not from movements in the dollar. The Merk fund tries to profit from a falling dollar and picks its investments based on which currencies the money manager feels will outperform the U.S. dollar.

- *Emerging Market Bonds.* Emerging markets are comprised of nations that are considered to be developing. This generally includes Africa, Eastern Europe, Latin America, Russia, the Middle East, and Asia, excluding Japan. Emerging market bonds are bonds issued by emerging market governments and companies. They tend to offer attractive yields compared to developed country bonds. Bonds issued in local currencies can also benefit from appreciation of the local currency versus the dollar.

- *Treasury Inflation Protected Securities.* TIPS were introduced by the federal government in 1997 and are designed to help investors protect their portfolios from rising inflation. Like traditional Treasury bonds, they pay a fixed rate of interest, but their principal, to which the interest rate is applied, is linked to the current rate of inflation. Also, like traditional Treasury bonds, TIPS are backed by the full faith and credit of the U.S. government.

- *Floating Rate.* Floating rate money managers invest in floating rate loans issued by banks. When banks make loans to corporations, the interest rate usually fluctuates with LIBOR. When interest rates go up, the loan rate goes up, and when interest rates go down, the loan rate goes down. This gives these types of bonds protection from rising rates: As other bonds are losing their value, floating rate bonds should hold up. The risk with floating rate bonds is that they are usually made to below-investment-grade companies. This is mitigated by the fact that the loans are backed by specific collateral at the company.

- *High-Yield (Junk) Bonds.* High-yield bonds are issued by companies below investment grade. Because of this they have a risk of default and often will trade more like stocks than bonds. High-yield bonds have a higher yield than risk-free government bonds to account for the risk of default.

- *Government Bonds.* These are bonds issued by the U.S. government and are therefore free from default risk. They still have interest rate risk, especially if they are longer-term bonds. Interest from government bonds is free from state and local income taxes.

- *Agency Bonds.* These are bonds issued by Fannie Mae and Freddie Mac. They have been in the news recently because these two agencies have been having financial difficulties.

These bonds are issued to finance the mortgage activity of these two agencies. They have the implied backing of the government, so they are still rated AAA, but because they are not actually government bonds, they provide a slightly higher yield.

- *Mortgage-Backed Bonds.* These are bonds backed by home mortgages. Many money managers in this area have been hurt by the subprime meltdown as they reached for yield into the subprime market and got burned.

- *Collateralized Mortgage Obligations.* CMOs are the most complex type of bonds. They are pools of home mortgages that are split up into tranches. As people refinance or prepay their mortgages, each tranche gets paid off. The tranches are set up to provide different risk-reward profiles for investors with differing goals. The early tranches are the safest, while the later tranches can be so risky that they are often referred to as toxic waste. Because this area is so complex, most investors should not be buying CMOs directly.

- *Corporate Investment Grade.* These are bonds issued by investment grade companies. They still have default risk but not the same risk as high-yield bonds.

- *Municipal Bonds.* These are bonds issued by states and municipalities. They are free from federal and state taxation if you buy bonds issued by your state. Municipal bonds are particularly appropriate if you are in a high tax bracket. The way to compare municipal bonds with taxable bonds is to figure out the taxable equivalent yield. This is computed by taking the yield on the municipal bond and dividing it by 1−your tax rate. So, for example, if a municipal bond is yielding 4% and your tax rate is 30%, then the taxable equivalent yield is 5.71% (4% ÷ 1 − 30%). You would then use the 5.71% to compare the municipal bond to other taxable bonds.

- *Total Return Bond Managers.* Total return bond managers allocate among all the different types of bonds depending on which sectors they think will perform the best.

- *Laddered Bond Portfolios.* Instead of using a bond money manager, you could also decide to create your own laddered bond portfolio. A bond ladder is constructed by buying bonds with different maturities, for example you might have a one-year bond, a two-year bond, a three-year bond, and so on. That way, you always have something coming due, so if interest rates are increasing you can reinvest that money at the higher rate. You also always have some longer-term bonds that will benefit if interest rates go down (bond prices move inversely with interest rates).

Keep in mind that it can be expensive to buy individual bonds, especially in small amounts. Brokerage firms do not charge a commission on bonds; they earn a spread, which is not disclosed. For example, let's say you call up your broker to buy XYZ Company bonds; he will then call the trading desk to find out how much they are trading for. The trader may be willing to buy the bonds for 104 and sell them for 105; this is the trader's profit on the trade. The broker can then mark the bond up, within reason, so that once they get to you they are now 106. You have paid a 2-point markup, but it is never disclosed to you on the confirmation.

Endowments Don't Like Bonds but You Should Still Have Some

Bonds are not very popular with many large endowments, especially Harvard and Yale. However, they can provide stability to a portfolio and should not be completely ignored by investors.

13

Real Assets and Commodities

Role in Portfolio:	Inflation hedge, return
Performance Expectation:	This will be the most volatile part of your portfolio, but it is also the part that will be uncorrelated with the rest.
Benchmarks:	Dow Jones AIG, Goldman Sachs GSCI, NAREIT
Allocation:	0% to 25%

Rising inflation, stock market declines, and the surge in commodity prices have increased investors' attention to real assets. (For the purposes of this chapter real assets and commodities will mean basically the same thing. The only difference is that real assets encompass real estate, which is not a commodity.) There were 150 institutional investors polled in an article in *Pensions & Investments* in January 7, 2008. Half of them said that they expected to place more than 10% of their portfolios into real assets over the next three years. This is up from only 15% of respondents in the same poll taken in 2005.

Commodity prices have skyrocketed over the past few years and many prognosticators, myself included, expect them to continue to rise. Demand for oil and other commodities has increased from the rapid development in China, India, and other emerging market countries. As a strong middle class continues to develop in these countries, we expect demand for commodities to increase. Agricultural commodities have also been increasing as we look for sources of alternative energy from renewable resources such as corn.

Stocks and bonds are financial assets; commodities and real estate are real assets. Real assets help protect a portfolio from inflation since the value of these assets should increase as inflation increases. The CPI is the most common measure of inflation. As of this writing, inflation is around 5%, which is near a three-year high. Inflation peaked in April 1980 at 14%. Inflation impacts the value of bonds and their fixed interest payments because the payments stay the same but their real value declines by 5% (the current inflation rate) per year. Inflation can also negatively impact stocks if it happens during an environment where the economy is slow, such as we are dealing with today. Higher oil and commodity prices are hurting a number of companies in a variety of industries. For this reason, ownership of real assets can provide a hedge because the value of the assets should increase with inflation and can mute the impact of falling stock and bond prices.

Real assets can include the following:

- Stocks of companies engaged in energy production, industrial products, forest products, base metals, precious metals, and agriculture
- Managed futures—see Chapter 14
- Real Estate Investment Trusts—public and private
- Physical commodities
- Structured notes that track commodity prices
- ETFs and ETNs that track physical commodities or commodity indexes
- Commodity mutual funds
- Commodity stock mutual funds
- Alternative energy
- Managed futures mutual funds
- Real asset hedge funds or funds of funds
- Private real estate

Real Assets

Endowments like Harvard and Yale have large exposures to real assets because they have the ability to hedge against rising inflation and provide attractive returns.

Benefits of real assets/commodities:

- *Ownership of Real Assets/Commodities.* Unlike companies whose stock prices are driven by future earnings potential, most natural resources companies own real assets today that have value. Also, unlike technologies and products that can become obsolete, natural resources such as oil in the ground, trees in the forest, and gold in a mine all have value, both today and in the future.
- *Benefit from the Developing World.* As the world's developing economies like China and India continue to expand, their demand for natural resources also expands. Since there is a finite supply and no limit to demand, this can lead to an increase in prices of these resources.
- *Inflation Hedge.* This global growth has also created inflation as the prices of natural resources rise. By owning these assets and the stocks of companies involved in developing these assets, an investor can protect his or her portfolio from inflation.

Main real asset risks:

- *Volatility.* Real assets, commodities in particular, tend to be more volatile than financial assets.
- *Regulatory, geopolitical risk, and economic risk.* Commodities are susceptible to a number of external risk factors including weather, politics, trade policy, and interest rates.

Hot Commodities

Over the past three-, five-, and ten-year periods, commodities have outperformed the market. Table 13.1 is a chart of the three-, five-, and ten-year returns of two of the most prominent commodity

Table 13.1 Returns of DJ-AIG and GSCI vs. S&P 500 as of 4/30/08

Returns	3-Year	5-year	10-year
DJ-AIG	15.71%	16.67%	10.92%
GSCI	14.80%	19.34%	12.53%
S&P 500	8.23%	10.62%	3.89%

Source: Dow Jones, Standard & Poor's.

indexes: the Dow Jones AIG (DJ-AIG) and the Goldman Sachs Commodity Index (GSCI). Over all of those time periods they have handily outperformed the S&P 500.

The outperformance comes with a price. Table 13.2 shows the standard deviation of those same indexes versus the S&P 500. The commodity indexes have been much more volatile than the stock market.

The next obvious question is whether adding an asset this volatile into a portfolio makes any sense. Just like everything else we have been talking about, it all depends on how highly correlated it is to what you already have.

Table 13.3 is a correlation matrix between the DJ-AIG, GSCI, and the S&P 500. The two commodity indexes are highly correlated

Table 13.2   Standard Deviation of DJ-AIG and GSCI vs. S&P 500 as of 4/30/08

	3-Year	5-year	10-year
DJ-AIG	15.28%	14.41%	15.11%
GSCI	21.42%	20.77%	22.25%
S&P 500	8.91%	8.74%	14.75%

Source: Dow Jones, Standard & Poor's.

Table 13.3   Correlation of Commodities vs. S&P 500

	1	2	3
1. Dow Jones AIG Commodity Index	1	.83	.09
2. Goldman Sachs Commodity Index	.83	1	−.03
3. S&P 500	.09	−.03	1

Table 13.4   70/30 Portfolio

Fund	Percentage
Vanguard 500 Index	36%
Vanguard Int Bond Index	30%
Vanguard Total Intl Index	20%
Vanguard Mid-Cap Index	7%
Vanguard Small-Cap Index	7%

at .83 but neither are correlated with the S&P 500. The GSCI actually has a slight negative correlation with the stock market.

From our discussions in this book about correlation, adding commodities to a portfolio should be beneficial. Table 13.4 is a basic portfolio of index funds with 70% in stocks and 30% in bonds.

Table 13.5 shows the statistics for the portfolio.

Table 13.6 adds a fund that seeks to match the return of the DJ-AIG, changing our new portfolio.

Table 13.7 shows the statistics for this portfolio.

Once again, lack of correlation did the trick. Not only did adding the commodity fund increase performance but it also lowered the risk of the portfolio.

Investable Commodities

Below are some commodities that can be invested in through mutual funds, futures contracts, or ETFs and ETNs:

- Oil
- Natural gas
- Copper
- Gold
- Silver
- Corn
- Cotton
- Soybeans
- Wheat
- Cattle
- Coal

Table 13.5   Return and Risk for 70/30 Portfolio

Period	3-year	5-year
Average annual return	9.68%	11.82%
Standard deviation	6.38%	6.75%
Sharpe ratio	.82	1.23
Alpha	2.45	2.97

Source: Compiled by Matthew Tuttle using information from Vanguard as of 4/30/08.

Table 13.6   Adding Commodities

Fund	Percentage
Vanguard 500 Index	32%
Vanguard Int Bond Index	30%
Vanguard Total Intl Index	16%
Vanguard Mid-Cap Index	6%
Vanguard Small-Cap Index	6%
PIMCO Commodity Real Return	10%

Table 13.7   Returns and Risk with Commodities

Period	3-year	5-year
Average annual return	10.15%	12.24%
Standard deviation	5.75%	6.35%
Sharpe ratio	.98	1.36
Alpha	3.41	4.12

Source: Compiled by Matthew Tuttle using data from Vanguard and PIMCO as of 4/30/08.

How to Invest in Commodities

Commodities can be accessed through managed futures (see Chapter 14), commodity ETFs, commodity index mutual funds, and commodity stock mutual funds.

Commodity ETFs and mutual funds track commodity indexes. The mutual funds either track the Dow Jones-AIG Index or the GSCI Commodity Index. Table 13.8 shows the weightings on the Dow Jones-AIG Index, and Table 13.9 shows the weightings of the GSCI.

The two main mutual funds that invest in these indexes are the PIMCO Commodity Real Return, which invests in the Dow Jones-AIG, and the Oppenheimer Commodity Strategy Total Return, which invests in the GSCI. The main difference in the indexes is that the GSCI has 77% in energy while the Dow Jones-AIG has approximately 35% in energy.

Most commodity ETFs invest in next-generation commodity indexes created by investment banks that insist they are better than the traditional Dow Jones-AIG and GSCI. Some of the most popular ETFs and ETNs include the Rogers Intl Commodity Index Total

Table 13.8   Dow Jones-AIG Index Weightings

Name	Exchange	Weight
Aluminum	London Metal Exchange (LME)	7.12
Soybean oil	Chicago Board of Trade (CBOT)	2.87
Corn	Chicago Board of Trade (CBOT)	6.16
Coffee	Coffee, Sugar, Cocoa Exchange (CSCE)	2.59
Crude oil	New York Mercantile Exchange (NYMEX)	14.94
Cotton	New York Cotton Exchange (NYCE)	2.00
Gold	Commodity Exchange Inc. (New York) (COMEX)	6.47
Copper	Commodity Exchange Inc. (New York) (COMEX)	6.84
Heating oil	New York Mercantile Exchange (NYMEX)	4.58
Live cattle	Chicago Mercantile Exchange (CME)	4.45
Lean hogs	Chicago Mercantile Exchange (CME)	3.02
Natural gas	New York Mercantile Exchange (NYMEX)	15.37
Nickel	London Metal Exchange (LME)	1.85
RBOB	New York Mercantile Exchange (NYMEX)	4.35
Soybean	Chicago Board of Trade (CBOT)	7.04
Sugar	Coffee, Sugar, Cocoa Exchange (CSCE)	2.38
Silver	Commodity Exchange Inc. (New York) (COMEX)	2.54
Wheat	Chicago Board of Trade (CBOT)	3.36
Zinc	London Metal Exchange (LME)	2.06

Source: DJ Indexes.com as of May 30, 2008.

Return (RJI) and the Rogers Intl Commodity Index Agriculture Total Return (RJA).

Commodity Stock Mutual Funds

Commodity stock mutual funds invest in companies that are involved in commodities. Like gold stocks, these stocks generally move in the same direction as commodities prices but they can diverge. Some of the more popular funds in this area are Van Eck Global Hard Asset and Ivy Global Natural Resources. DWS has a hybrid fund (the DWS Commodity Securities Fund), which puts half of its assets into commodity stocks and half of its assets into the GSCI Commodity Index.

Real Estate

Real estate investments in portfolios usually include investments in office, retail, residential, and industrial properties, typically made through real estate investment trusts (REITs). These investments

Table 13.9 GSCI Weightings: S&P GSCI Components and Dollar Weights (%) (July 25, 2008)

Energy	77.01	Industrial Metals	6.26	Precious Metals	1.93	Agriculture	11.57	Livestock	3.23
Crude oil	40.64	Aluminum	2.29	Silver	0.23	Wheat	3.18	Live Cattle	1.89
Brent crude oil	15.00	Copper	2.76	Gold	1.70	Red Wheat	0.75	Feeder Cattle	0.34
RBOB gas	4.46	Lead	0.32			Corn	3.22	Lean Hogs	1.00
Heating oil	5.46	Nickel	0.49			Soybeans	2.07		
Gas oil	5.58	Zinc	0.40			Cotton	0.74		
Natural gas	5.86					Sugar	0.89		
						Coffee	0.50		
						Cocoa	0.22		

Source: Goldman Sachs.

Gold: The Safe Haven

For lack of a better place to put it, we place gold in the energy and natural resources sector. It deserves its own section because it doesn't fit neatly into any other section. Even though it is a natural resource, it is also much more: Gold is also a currency. Unlike the dollar and the euro, gold exists in a relatively fixed supply and it cannot be inflated or deflated by government policy. Because of this, it is a true store of wealth and tends to rise in value when investors are worried about the value of currencies.

Gold investments can be made through gold ETFs and gold stock mutual funds.

- *Gold ETFs.* Gold ETFs move in tandem with the price of gold; they give a pure play on the gold price. The most popular gold ETF is the SPDR Gold Shares (GLD), which is backed by actual gold bullion.
- *Gold Stock Mutual Funds.* Gold stock mutual funds are not the pure play on gold that the ETFs are. These funds buy stock of companies involved in the gold business. Normally, shares of these companies will move in tandem with gold prices, but that isn't always the case.

It is important to keep in mind that if you are using skill-based mutual funds, they may have exposure to gold as well.

can be in either public or private vehicles. Public real estate investments are usually accessed through REITs, either in mutual funds that buy REITs or individual REITs that are traded like stocks.

The Real Estate Investment Trust Act of 1960 created REITs. The act allowed investors to pool money into a REIT which would be managed by a professional firm that would acquire and manage properties.

Advantages and Risks of REITs

REITs have a number of advantages:

1. REITs provide a high current income since they pay out almost all of their earnings as dividends. (See Table 13.10.)

Table 13.10   U.S. REITs Offer Attractive Dividend Yields—Current Yields as of 3/31/08

Equity REITs	4.9%
10-Year T-bill	3.5%
Utilities	3.3%
S&P 500	2.3%
3-Month T-bill	1.4%

Source: Cohen & Steers.

Table 13.11   U.S. REITs Have Provided Solid Returns—10-Year Total Return ended 3/31/08

Equity REITs	10.7%
Global bonds	7.1%
Non-U.S. equity	6.6%
U.S. bonds	6.0%
S&P 500	3.5%

Source: Cohen & Steers.

Table 13.12   U.S. REITs Have a Low Correlation with Other Asset Classes—10-Year Correlations ended 3/31/08

Equity REITs	1
S&P 500	.33
Non-U.S. equity	.29
Global bonds	.08
U.S. bonds	.03

Source: Cohen & Steers.

2. Historically, REITs have provided competitive total returns versus the broader stock market. (See Table 13.11.)
3. REITs have a low correlation with stock and bond markets. (See Table 13.12.)

REITs also carry risk. The main risks of investing in REITs include these three risks:

1. The oversupply of REITs due to new construction which could hurt prices.

2. A decline in economic activity could cause a decline in REIT prices.

3. A reduction in capital and liquidity could cause a decline in REIT prices.

Going Global with REITs

Just like all your other investments, you need to think globally when investing in REITs. Some reasons to invest in global REITs include these three:

1. *Participation in the Growth of REITs Globally.* Many countries have created REIT-like structures expanding the investment environment for REITs.

According to Cohen & Steers, in 1994 only five countries had REIT legislation; now there are 21. Also according to Cohen & Steers, only 8.4% of the world's $17.2 trillion of total real estate has been securitized in REIT structures. As these structures continue to emerge and evolve worldwide, it is likely that many private owners will utilize them to bring much more investable real estate to the market.

2. *Participation in the Growth of Global Economies.* As economies grow, especially in the emerging markets, demand is stimulated for real estate. Investing in REITs provides investors with a direct way to play in that growth.

As more and more countries go global, they provide less and less exposure to their local markets. Local real estate investments might be the best pure play on local economic growth. Table 13.13 is a chart of the local exposure of multinational stocks versus real estate securities for four countries.

3. *More Diversification.* Global REITs provide an extra layer of diversification to U.S. stocks and bonds.

Private Real Estate versus Public REITs

Private real estate is a form of private equity and is accessed through limited partnerships that are available only to accredited investors or qualified purchasers.

Table 13.13   Local Exposure of Multinational Stocks vs. Real Estate Securities

Country	Largest Company	Local Index Weight	Percent of 2006 Revenue from Home Country	Largest Real Estate Company	Percent of 2006 Revenue from Home Country
United Kingdom	BP	7%	21%	Land Securities Group	100%
Switzerland	Novartis	16%	37%	PSP Swiss Properties AG	100%
Hong Kong	HSBC	20%	13%	Sun Hung Kai Properties	99%
Australia	BHP Billiton	12%	13%	Westfield Group	44%

Source: Cohen & Steers.

Private and public REITs are very different types of investments. Private REITs have a number of differences from public REITS:

1. Private REITs have a fixed share price versus public REITs whose share price fluctuates based on the market. This can be good and bad. A private REIT won't go down when public REITs are going down, but it also won't appreciate when public REITs are appreciating.
2. Private REITs are usually taken public or liquidated after a period of time.
3. Private REITs usually pay a higher dividend than public REITs.
4. Private REITs typically have high upfront fees, ranging from 5% to 16%.
5. Private REITs are sold through offerings and are then closed to new investors.
6. Redemption of private REIT shares could be difficult, if not impossible.

Protecting from Inflation

Real assets are the part of your portfolio that protects from inflation and is not correlated with stocks and bonds. As such, endowment type portfolios use real assets to protect from the ravages of inflation and individual investors should as well. In the next chapter, I will discuss a component of real assets: managed futures.

14

Managed Futures

Role in Portfolio:	Inflation hedge, return
Performance Expectation:	Managed futures are a component of real assets. Whereas real assets need commodity or real estate prices to go up, managed futures just need a trend, either up or down. Managed futures will most likely have a negative correlation with everything else in your portfolio. This also might be a risky area, prone to large drawdowns.
Benchmarks:	Barclay's CTA Index
Allocation:	0% to 15%

Managed futures are a component of real assets. Individual investors don't usually have access to some of the sophisticated real asset strategies that endowments use. Therefore, they can often get caught on the wrong side when the prices of real assets like oil are declining. Unlike the types of investments that I described in the previous chapter, managed futures have the flexibility to go long and short commodity and financial futures. This can provide investors with protection from price declines and allow them to profit regardless of market direction. This can provide investors with very attractive returns, protection from inflation, and an asset that has negative correlation with everything else in your portfolio.

How Futures Work

Just as the name implies, managed futures are a managed portfolio of futures. Futures contracts are agreements between buyers and sellers to establish a price today for items to be delivered at some point in the future. In this way, farmers can sell wheat at a fixed price months before they harvest it, portfolio managers can hedge a portfolio of stocks by selling S&P 500 futures short, and so on. Futures allow people to manage the risk of prices going up or down in the future. They do this by offering the following three features:

1. *Forward Pricing.* Unless goods are sold and consumed immediately, there is a risk of a price change. Futures markets provide a means to determine prices months or years in advance. For example, Table 14.1 shows the contracts that are being traded for gold as of this writing.
2. *Liquidity.* Since futures contracts are so widely traded, most have a tremendous amount of liquidity, allowing prices to be determined efficiently and trades to be executed easily.
3. *Storability.* A trader can sell a contract obligating him to deliver a certain amount of a commodity without having to actually own that commodity. Any time before the last day of trading for the contract month, he can buy a futures contract for the same commodity and cancel out his position. Most futures contracts are settled this way without someone actually delivering or taking delivery of a commodity.

There are futures contracts on agricultural commodities like corn, cotton, and soybeans; there are futures contracts on cattle and pork bellies; there are futures contracts on gold and other metals; and there are financial futures that are based on stock indexes, bonds, and currencies. According to BarclayHedge Ltd., as of the end of 2007, there was more than $205 billion invested in managed futures. Table 14.2 shows some of the markets that managed futures funds trades.

Table 14.1   Gold Prices

Expiration	Last Price ($ per oz)
June 2008	907.2
July 2008	911.5
August 2008	912.3
October 2008	917.7
December 2008	921.0
February 2009	930.9

Prices as of 5/27/08, 11:10 AM EST.

Table 14.2   Markets Traded by Managed Futures

Stock Indexes:	S&P 500, Dow, NASDAQ, Dax, Cac 40, Hang Seng, FTSE, Australian Spi, Nikkei, Euro Stoxx50, Russell 2000, Etc.
Currencies:	U.S. dollar, euro, British pound, Swiss franc, Japanese yen, Mexican peso, Australian dollar, Canadian dollar, Turkish lira, New Zealand dollar, etc.
Bonds:	U.S. Treasury bonds, gilts, U.S. 10-year T-note, Japanese bond, Australian bond, etc.
Interest Rates:	Euribor, Eurodollar, LIBOR, Euroyen, Euro Bobl, Euro Swiss, etc.
Grains:	Corn, Soybeans, Soybean Oil, Soybean Meal, Wheat, etc.
Energy:	Crude Oil, Heating Oil, Natural Gas, Gas Oil, Brent Crude, etc.
Metals:	Gold, Copper, Silver, Copper, Platinum, Zinc, Nickel, etc.
Agricultural:	Coffee, Cotton, Sugar, Cocoa, Orange Juice, etc.
Livestock:	Live Cattle, Pork Bellies, Lean Hogs

They Don't Have to Be Risky

Generally, when people think about futures, they assume that they are high risk. This is because the margin requirement on futures is only a small amount compared to the total value of the contract. Margin for futures is not the same as margin for stocks. It is basically a good faith deposit that gains and losses are subtracted from daily. If your loss is large and your margin goes below a specified amount, then you will be required to put up more money—this is a margin call. This is why futures are one investment that you can lose much more than you put in.

For example, the margin requirement on the gold futures contract on the Chicago Board of Trade is $4,555/contract. The gold contract is for 100 ounces of gold, at today's price of $906/oz, which means that the contract controls $90,600 worth of gold. That is a lot of leverage which can maximize gains but it can also maximize losses. Today gold is up $6.60/oz, which means that if I held one futures contract, I would have a profit of $660 for the day. Based on my initial deposit of $4,555 I would be up 14.4% in just one day! While that sounds like a great return, it can work the other way as well. The maintenance margin on gold is $3,300/contract. Let's say gold ended the day down $20/oz. If that happened I would have a loss of $2,000 ($20 × 100 oz). That would be subtracted from my margin account leaving it at $2,555, below the maintenance margin of $3,300. I would now be required to put up more money to get back up to $3,300; if I didn't have it, then my contract would be liquidated. As an even more drastic example, let's say that over a period of time gold went down $200/oz. In this case, not only would my initial margin be wiped out but I would also have to come up with another $15,455, which might wipe me out as well. Because of the high amount of leverage and the possibility of losing more than you deposit, it is very hard for individuals to make money in the futures market, and it can be a very risky proposition.

Managed futures, however, are different. These are pools managed by one or more commodity trading advisors (CTAs) who generally use much less leverage than they are allowed to, trade a large and diversified basket of futures, and use stops to manage risk.

CTAs are required to register with the U.S. government's Commodity Futures Trading Commission (CFTC) before they can offer themselves to the public as money managers. CTAs are also required to provide disclosure documents and certain books and records which are reviewed by the National Futures Association (NFA), a self-regulatory watchdog organization.

Managed Futures

There are a number of ways to set up managed futures accounts and a number of different trading strategies that managed futures funds might employ.

Types of Accounts. Managed futures funds can either be managed as a commodity pool or an individual account at a futures brokerage firm. In a commodity pool, investor funds are commingled not unlike a mutual fund. Typically, minimum investments for commodity pools will be lower than individual accounts. In an individual account, the client sets up an account at a futures brokerage and authorizes the CTA to place trades on his or her behalf and deduct fees.

Trading Strategies. The trading strategies of CTAs will either be discretionary, mechanical, or a combination of both. Discretionary traders rely on their analyses of different markets to make buy-and-sell decisions. Mechanical traders create complex computer systems that generate buy-and-sell signals automatically. These traders rarely override the computer. Some traders might use a mix of both. They may use a computer to generate signals but then use their own judgment about whether to act on the signals.

Mechanical Systems. Most mechanical systems are based on some sort of trend following. Trend following is a type of technical analysis. Trend followers develop complicated computer systems that analyze current price action to determine if the price of a futures contract will go up or down. The system generates signals to either buy the futures contract, sell the contract closing out a buy, sell it short, or buy it back to cover a short position. Trend followers realize that approximately 60% of the time they will be wrong, so they seek to cut their losses short and ride their winners.

Trend following doesn't get a lot of press because trend followers try to fly under the radar screen as much as possible. They realize that the more people who trade similar systems, the harder it will be for them to make money as more people are entering the same trades at the same time.

Trend Following versus Fundamental Analysis

Fundamental investors often have little regard for trend following and technical analysis. They believe that if they spend hours researching a commodity or any other investment, they may be able to find hidden gems that others miss. Trend followers believe that the market will tell you where it wants to go. They also understand that they don't need to be right most of the time to still make large amounts of money. If they can control their risk and just catch a few major trends each year, then they can do very, very well. Fundamental analysis may do well in finding securities that are undervalued or should increase in price but it could take a while—and a lot of pain—for others to realize this as well.

History of Trend Following

Trend following became popular in the mid-1980s when two successful trend following traders, Richard Dennis and Bill Eckhardt, made a bet. If you have ever watched or heard of the movie *Trading*

Places, this was very similar. In *Trading Places* two brothers who ran a commodities firm bet that they could turn a successful commodities trader into a criminal and turn a criminal into a successful commodities trader. Dennis and Eckhardt didn't go quite that far, but they had the same idea. Dennis believed that top traders could be taught, while Eckhardt thought it was a skill you were born with. To test it out, they placed a classified ad looking for traders who they would train in their system for two weeks and then let them trade the company's money for a share of the profits. These traders became known as the Turtles. Some of these traders washed out, but the experiment was still a great success as many of the traders put up impressive numbers—some even had years when their returns were well over 100%. The Turtles used a fairly basic system: When the prices of the markets they traded broke out of a price range (highest or lowest price of the past 20 days), then they would buy if the price broke out to the upside, or sell if the price broke out to the downside. They also had sophisticated risk management techniques as far as how large their positions were and when they would sell. Positions' size was based on the volatility of the futures contract: More volatile futures were smaller positions than less volatile positions. Stops (orders to close out a position) were also based on volatility. To take advantage of winning trades, they would add to positions if they moved in the direction of the trend.

The Turtles didn't look at any of the fundamental factors regarding these markets. They didn't care about supply and demand or what they thought a market was going to do; the system generated signals and they traded them. Those that washed out of the program tended to be the ones who overrode the signals or didn't take as large a position as they should have. When the program was disbanded in the late 1980s, many of the Turtles went out on their own and formed CTA firms. The Turtles also inspired second and third generations of trend traders.

The Turtles' strategy was high risk/high return. In order to make managed futures palatable to investors, very few CTAs trade with the same level of risk that the Turtles did. The Turtle system is also now very widely known in the industry and doesn't work nearly as well as it did when it was kept secret. Most, if not all, former Turtles now trade different systems that they have developed throughout the years.

Countertrend Systems

Some managed futures funds include countertrend strategies. A successful trend following system will typically only be right 40% of the time. In those 40% of trades where they are correct, they hope to get a few large trends that will make up the bulk of their performance. However, being wrong most of the time can create a lot of volatility. Countertrend systems can reduce that volatility. Countertrend systems seek to profit from mean reversion—the tendency for assets that get out of line to revert to where they used to be. For example, let's say we did an analysis that showed that most of the time gold and silver move together. We then come across a period where gold is going up and silver is going down. A countertrend system might either sell gold short, assuming it will go back down to keep pace with silver again, or buy silver, assuming it will go back up to keep pace with gold (or both). Countertrend systems tend to be right a higher percentage of the time than trend following systems; however, the profits also tend to be lower.

Benefits of Managed Futures

One of the main benefits of managed futures is that they have a historically low or no correlation to stocks and bonds. Table 14.3 shows the correlation between the S&P Diversified Trend Index (S&P DTI) and stocks (S&P 500) and bonds (Lehman Aggregate Bond Index). The S&P DTI is an index of 50% financial futures and 50% commodity futures that goes long or short based on price momentum.

Historically managed futures have had a negative correlation to stocks and a very low correlation with bonds. Therefore, adding managed futures into a portfolio can add significant diversification benefits. Table 14.4 shows the returns and risk of managed futures versus stocks and bonds.

Table 14.3   Managed Futures vs. Stocks and Bonds as of January 1985–December 2007

	S&P 500 Index	Lehman Aggregate Bond Index
Correlation to S&P DTI	−.075	.035

Source: Bloomberg & FactSet. Correlations are subject to change.

Table 14.4   Annualized Returns of Managed Futures, Stocks, and Bonds, as of 12/31/07

Annualized Returns as of 12/31/07	S&P DTI	S&P 500 Index	Lehman Aggregate Bond Index
1-Year	10.66%	5.49%	6.97%
3-Year	7.96%	8.62%	4.56%
5-Year	8.43%	12.83%	4.42%
10-Year	8.77%	5.91%	5.97%
Jan 1985–Dec 2007	11.5%	12.83%	8.55%
Standard deviation Jan 1985–Dec 2007	5.95	14.69	4.29
Standard deviation 3-yr	5.76	7.83	2.78
Standard deviation 5-yr	6.8	9.07	3.64
Sharpe ratio Jan 1985–Dec 2007	1.43	0.67	1.29

Source: Bloomberg & FactSet.

Table 14.5   Best and Worst Months in the S&P 500 1985–2007

5 Worst Months			5 Best Months		
Date	S&P 500	S&P DTI	Date	S&P 500	S&P DTI
Oct 97	−21.54%	−2.08%	Jan 87	13.47%	1.32%
Aug 98	−14.46%	2.80%	Dec 91	11.44%	3.06%
Sep 02	−10.87%	−1.56%	Mar 00	9.78%	−1.01%
Feb 01	−9.12%	1.57%	May 90	9.75%	−.83%
Aug 90	−9.04%	5.23%	Jul 89	9.03%	−.20%

Source: Bloomberg & FactSet.

As Table 14.5 shows, during the worst months for the stock market, managed futures held up well. During the best months for the stock market, managed futures didn't do as well.

On the flip side, as Table 14.6 shows, when managed futures had bad months, the market had some pretty good months. When managed futures had its best months, we saw some fairly bad months for stocks.

As Tables 14.5 and 14.6 show, managed futures have generated attractive returns versus the S&P 500 and don't move in the same direction at the same time.

Table 14.6   Best and Worst Months in the S&P DTI 1985-2007

	5 Worst Months			5 Best Months	
Date	S&P DTI	S&P 500	Date	S&P DTI	S&P 500
Mar 85	−4.72%	0.07%	Sep 90	8.04%	−4.87%
Apr 05	−3.26%	−1.90%	Sep 04	5.63%	1.08%
Jul 91	−2.41%	4.66%	Aug 90	5.23%	−9.04%
Dec 02	−2.38%	−5.87%	Mar 89	5.02%	2.33%
Oct 99	−2.36%	6.33%	Dec 87	4.26%	7.61%

Source: Bloomberg & FactSet.

Table 14.7   Effects of Adding Managed Futures 1980-2007

	S&P 500 Portfolio	Managed Futures Portfolio	Portfolio Return	Standard Deviation (Risk)
S&P 500 only	100%	0%	13.0%	14.7
90/10	90%	10%	13.2%	12.6
80/20	80%	20%	13.4%	11.3
70/30	70%	30%	13.7%	10.7
Managed futures only	0%	100%	15.0%	16.7

Source: CISDM CTA Equal Weighted, S&P 500 Index.

Adding managed futures to a portfolio of stocks can also increase returns *and* lower risk. For instance, Table 14.7 shows the impact of adding managed futures (represented by the CISDM Index) to a stock portfolio. The CISDM index is an index of CTAs. Adding just 10% can increase the return and lower risk.

Investing in Managed Futures

Managed futures can play a very important role in portfolios and can be accessed by individuals in many different ways: through mutual funds, managed futures funds, managed futures funds of funds, and individual accounts managed by CTAs.

   Mutual Funds. As of this writing there are only two man-
      aged futures mutual funds that I am aware of: the Rydex
      Managed Futures Fund and the Direxion Commodity

Trends Strategy. The Rydex fund seeks to mimic the performance of the S&P DTI. According to the Rydex Funds Quarterly Fact Sheet on the fund, as of 3/31/08 the average annual return of the A Shares at NAV since inception (3/2/07) has been 12.04% versus 16.09% for the S&P DTI. While the performance has still been impressive, it has lagged its benchmark. The Direxion fund only has exposure to commodity futures while the Rydex fund has exposure to commodity and financial futures.

Managed Futures Funds. Managed futures funds are another way to access managed futures. Like hedge funds, these are private investments and usually charge incentive fees and a percent of assets managed. Minimum investments on some of these funds can be as small as $5,000. Because most managed futures funds use trend following systems, they tend to be very highly correlated to each other. However, there are differences. Some funds take more risk than others. Some funds use only trend following while others use counter-trend systems as well.

Managed Futures Funds Can't Advertise, Either

You may be wondering why you haven't heard of managed futures before. The main reason is that managed futures funds have to follow the same rules hedge funds do about advertising. You may remember a few years ago when a company called Superfund started running strange ads. The president of the company came on and told you he had a product but because of regulations, he couldn't tell you anything about it. For most people, the curiosity was so great they had to go to the Superfund web site where they found out it was a managed futures fund.

As an investor you need to look at the returns and the month-to-month volatility to see what you can tolerate. Managed futures are also unlike other investments in that periods of underperformance don't necessarily mean anything is wrong with the manager. There are periods when the markets just don't trend. A CTA could have the best trend following system ever, but if the markets aren't trending, the system won't make money. Historically, we have seen nontrending periods followed by trending periods, so the key to managed futures investing is to pick a fund with drawdowns that you can tolerate and hold through the drawdown in the expectation that when the markets turn around the fund will as well.

TWM Global Diversified Fund

I am such a big believer in managed futures that we manage an internal managed futures fund called the TWM Global Diversified Fund. We combine a number of mechanical systems to decide what to buy and sell on a given day. Our system designer is the quintessential computer geek. It is always amazing to see how he can take sophisticated financial concepts and turn them into computer code. The core of our fund is a sophisticated trend following system. Surrounding the trend following system are several countertrend systems to limit volatility and enable us to hopefully make money in years when markets are not trending.

Managed futures should be an integral part of your real assets investments since they have the ability to go long and short, whereas typical real asset investments are long only.

The Future Is Now

Managed futures can add a number of benefits to your portfolio: the ability to profit regardless of market direction, noncorrelation with stocks and bonds, and potentially very attractive returns, just to name a few. Next, we move on to private equity.

15

Private Equity

Role in Portfolio:	Return
Performance Expectation:	Because of the illiquidity premium, private equity should provide returns that are 2% to 4% higher than the S&P 500.
Benchmarks:	S&P 500
Allocation:	0% to 15%

Private equity is the one asset class in this book that some readers will not be able to access. You need to be an accredited investor and minimum investments can be high. Even though there is an ETF that invests in the stocks of publicly traded private equity firms, it is not the same as investing in private equity itself. As of this writing, there is no mutual fund or other investment vehicle that can replicate an investment in private equity. Even though it can certainly enhance a portfolio, private equity is not vital to achieving the investment results you are looking for. It is important to talk about, however, because many endowments like Harvard's and Yale's are able to get substantial returns from their private equity portfolios. If you can get access to good private equity managers, then it definitely should be a part of your portfolio.

What Is Private Equity?

Private equity is equity investments in companies that are not publicly traded on any stock market. Private equity can refer to a number of different types of private investments, but it is usually comprised of buyouts, venture capital, and special situations. Private equity seeks to do the following:

- Invest in nonpublic, less efficient markets
- Uncover target companys' operational and pricing inefficiencies
- Improve target companys' medium- and long-term performance
- Align manager-owner interests
- Execute an exit strategy (initial public offering, recapitalization, sale, etc.)
- Provide attractive returns with low correlation to other assets and historical outperformance of public markets

Private equity encompasses three main strategies: leveraged buyouts, venture capital, and special situations.

You've Probably Heard about Private Equity Before

If private equity doesn't seem familiar to you, then think harder. If you watched the movie *Pretty Woman*, Richard Gere's character was in private equity. *Barbarians at the Gate* is the story of how two private equity firms, KKR and Forstmann Little, battled it out for RJ Reynolds.

Leveraged Buyouts

Leveraged buyouts (LBOs) occur when a private equity fund borrows money (usually using the earnings and/or assets of the target company as collateral) to take a public company private. The goal of the fund is to unlock value through operational changes, selling off divisions, and so on, and then bring the company public again at a higher price. The usual steps a private equity company takes in a buyout are shown in Table 15.1.

LBO companies are usually more mature and generate operating cash flows.

Venture Capital

Venture capital funds provide early stage financing for new businesses in return for large ownership stakes. Venture funds work on the law of large numbers. Since they are working with newer

Table 15.1 Leveraged Buyout Steps

Source	Enhance Value	Exit
Identify target company	Create a management incentive structure to align manager's interest with owner's	Identify possible buyers
Conduct due diligence	Focus on long-term returns	Execute exit strategy: IPO Recapitalization Sale to strategic or financial buyer
Explore ways to add value	Add new managerial talent	
Structure financing of buyout	Improve operations, governance, capital structure, and strategic positioning	
Purchase at an attractive price		

companies, it is likely that most will not meet expectations, but the ones that do can reap significant gains. Venture funds seek to sell their stake in the future for more than they paid. Venture capital is usually broken up into stages. Early stage venture capital is given to start-up companies whereas late stage venture capital is given to more mature companies that don't yet have the cash flow to fund future growth. The earlier the stage, the more risk and return potential the investment has.

Special Situations

Special situations encompass a number of different investment strategies that don't exactly fit into buyouts or venture capital. An example of a special situation could be investing in the securities of distressed companies expecting a turnaround.

Private Equity Exit Strategies

Private equity firms seek to monetize their investments through one of the following three methods:

1. *Initial Public Offering.* Shares of a company taken private or a company that was provided venture capital are sold to the public allowing the private equity firm to cash out.

2. *Merger or Acquisition.* Shares of a company taken private or given venture capital are merged with or acquired by another company allowing the private equity firm to cash out.
3. *Recapitalizations.* Money is distributed to shareholders or new debt is issued to cash out a private equity firm.

Why Private Equity?

The two main reasons why private equity makes sense in a portfolio is the opportunity for higher returns and a low correlation to other assets. Markets always reward investors for taking risks. Since private equity funds lock up money for long periods of time, investors usually get an illiquidity premium. According to Venture Economics, private equity has outperformed the stock markets by 4.31% per year. Table 15.2 shows the returns of private equity versus stocks.

Private equity has also historically had a low correlation to public markets as shown in Table 15.3.

Private Equity Investment Considerations

Private equity has a number of issues that investors need to be aware of.

Table 15.2 Venture Capital and Buyout Funds Have Outperformed the Public Markets—Growth of $100 from December 1985 to December 2004

S&P 500	$517
NASDAQ	$614
Buyouts	$932
Venture capital	$2,002

Source: Cambridge Associates.

Table 15.3 Correlation Matrix

	Buyouts	Venture Capital	S&P 500	NASDAQ
Buyouts	1	0.64	0.66	0.47
Venture capital		1	0.35	0.54
S&P 500			1	0.57
NASDAQ				1

- *J-Curve.* Investors who commit money to a private equity fund will most likely have to wait a number of years for the portfolio companies to all be resold so they can be paid back. During the early years of the investment, the portfolio companies are usually carried at cost so investors will not see paper gains. Also during the early years, fees are taken out and unprofitable investments are unwound. This creates a phenomenon known as the *J-curve,* where private equity funds generally have negative returns for the first few years. This can sometimes be mitigated by buying secondary private equity funds that have been around for a number of years and are out of the J-curve, but these are often hard to find.
- *Diversification by Vintage Year.* The ultimate return of a buyout fund has a lot to do with the nature of the debt markets from the beginning of the fund to the end of its investment period and the IPO market when it is trying to bring companies public. Because of this, it is very important to diversify private equity funds by vintage years and have funds that start in a number of different years. This can often be difficult for the individual investor but may be easier with a private equity fund of funds.
- *Capital Calls.* When investors buy a stock or mutual fund, they decide how much they want to invest and they usually invest the full amount. Private equity is different. Investors commit to invest a specific maximum amount of money, but it is not needed by the fund until they find investments they want to make. Because of this, private equity funds will make capital calls from time to time up to the investors' maximum commitments.
- *Manager Dispersion.* The dispersion in the performance of the top private equity fund managers and the bottom fund managers is extremely large. According to Cambridge Associates, the top private equity managers earn 10% more per year than the median private equity managers. Also, the top managers tend to stay at the top. According to McKinsey & Company, if a private equity fund manager is in the top 50%, they have a 73% chance that their next fund will also be in the top 50%. If a manager is in the bottom 50%, they only have a 28% chance that their next fund will be in the top 50%. The best deals tend to gravitate toward the best fund managers and

the top tend to stay on top. Because of this, picking the best fund managers is extremely important. Unfortunately, the best of the best usually have high minimums or don't want your money at all.

Other Investment Considerations

Other considerations when investing in private equity include:

1. *High Investment Minimums.* Most private equity funds have minimum investments of $1 million or more that can be drawn down by the manager at his or her discretion over a number of years.
2. *Limited Liquidity.* Investments in a private equity fund can be locked up for years before you start seeing returns. While it may be possible to sell interests in private equity funds, there is no organized secondary market. Unlike a hedge fund where you can ask for your money back at specified times, you have no such ability with a private equity fund.
3. *Unfunded Commitments.* Commitments to a private equity fund are drawn down over time as new investments are found. If the fund manager can't find enough opportunities, it may not use as much money as you had initially hoped to allocate to the fund. For example, if you want to commit $1 million to a private equity fund, it is possible that a manager might only use $500,000 of it, leaving you with half of the allocation you had initially planned for.
4. *Investment Risks.* LBOs are generally highly leveraged, heightening the chance that the company taken private will not be able to meet its debt obligations and could file for bankruptcy. Venture capital investments are even more risky as the firms that receive venture capital are unproven.

Investing in Private Equity

An investor in a private equity fund becomes a limited partner in that fund. As a result the investor will only benefit from private equity investments made by the firm in the fund itself, not in any other funds it may offer.

For most investors, we believe the best way to access private equity is through a fund of private equity funds instead of going directly to individual funds. This way, an investor can usually access managers who might otherwise be unavailable, can more easily diversify across vintage years, and have an expert picking the underlying managers. There are also fund of funds available for low minimum investments for qualified investors (who have net worth of $1.5 million or more) or qualified purchasers (who have investment assets of $5 million or more).

Largest Private Equity Firms

According to a 2008 ranking by Private Equity International, the 10 largest private equity firms in the world are as follows:

1. The Carlyle Group
2. Goldman Sachs Principal Investment Area
3. TPG
4. Kohlberg Kravis Roberts
5. CVC Capital Partners
6. Apollo Management
7. Bain Capital
8. Permira
9. Apax Partners
10. The Blackstone Group

The Allure of Private Equity

Many endowments are able to earn substantial returns from their private equity portfolios. If you can access private equity, it should be a part of your portfolio because over time, good managers have been able to deliver returns that are better than those you could have gotten in the public equity markets.

16

Managing Some of Your Money In-House

Harvard's endowment and some others operate what is called a *hybrid model*. Some of the money is invested with outside managers, and some is invested internally. Individual investors can mimic this as well, assuming you are comfortable managing some of your money yourself or using the strategy of an advisor. For the purposes of this chapter, when I talk about managing money "in-house" I mean any strategy that you follow that does not involve investing in an actively managed mutual fund, separately managed account, hedge fund, hedge fund of funds, and so on. These could be strategies that you do on your own or you could use an advisor. These internal investments can be in stocks, bonds, futures, ETFs, and so on. Whatever you decide to use, you or your advisor should have a well-thought-out methodology that has a low correlation with the money managers you have chosen.

ETF Strategies and Advantages

Because of their variety and ease of use, I think ETFs make sense for investors who want to manage some of their portfolio internally. I believe that for most people it is easier to pick the direction of certain markets than it is to pick the direction of certain stocks. ETFs also make it easy to use leverage, to go short, to invest in commodities, and to invest in currencies. The ability to access these markets and strategies makes it relatively simple to create an internal

Table 16.1   Leveraged ETFs—Closing Price Information as of 6/27/08 Ultra MarketCap

Fund	Ticker (View Chart)	NAV	NAV Change	Market Price	Market Price Change	Benchmark Index
Ultra QQQ	QLD	$74.69	$0.03	$75.07	$0.21	NASDAQ-100 Index
Ultra Dow30	DDM	$60.65	−$1.15	$60.95	−$1.13	Dow Jones Industrial Average
Ultra S&P500	SSO	$61.32	−$0.45	$61.11	−$0.57	S&P 500 Index
Ultra MidCap400	MVV	$70.11	−$0.57	$69.80	−$0.79	S&P MidCap 400 Index
Ultra SmallCap600	SAA	$50.33	−$0.51	$50.29	−$0.57	S&P SmallCap 600 Index
Ultra Russell 2000	UWM	$48.38	−$0.05	$48.42	$0.11	Russell 2000 Index

Source: ProFunds web site.

Table 16.2   Leveraged ETFs—Closing Price Information as of 6/27/08 Ultra Style

Fund	Ticker (View Chart)	NAV	NAV Change	Market Price	Market Price Change	Benchmark Index
Ultra Russell1000 Value	UVG	$41.72	−$0.44	$41.85	−$0.39	Russell 1000 Value Index
Ultra Russell1000 Growth	UKF	$57.06	−$0.28	$57.06	−$0.46	Russell 1000 Growth Index
Ultra Russell MidCap Value	UVU	$43.13	−$0.37	$43.35	−$0.35	Russell Mid-Cap Value Index
Ultra Russell MidCap Growth	UKW	$56.24	−$0.16	$56.09	−$0.35	Russell Mid-Cap Growth Index
Ultra Russell2000 Value	UVT	$37.49	−$0.41	$37.59	−$0.39	Russell 2000 Value Index
Ultra Russell2000 Growth	UKK	$52.02	$0.42	$52.00	$0.28	Russell 2000 Growth Index

Source: ProFunds web site.

Table 16.3   Leveraged ETFs—Closing Price Information as of 6/27/08 Ultra Sector

Fund	Ticker (View Chart)	NAV	NAV Change	Market Price	Market Price Change	Benchmark Index
Ultra Basic Materials	UYM	$100.74	$1.97	$100.80	$2.03	Dow Jones U.S. Basic Materials Index
Ultra Consumer Goods	UGE	$54.23	−$1.66	$54.51	−$1.84	Dow Jones U.S. Consumer Goods Index
Ultra Consumer Services	UCC	$40.16	−$0.39	$40.25	−$0.35	Dow Jones U.S. Consumer Services Index
Ultra Financials	UYG	$20.82	−$0.52	$20.85	−$0.51	Dow Jones U.S. Financials Index
Ultra Health Care	RXL	$51.75	$0.51	$52.20	$0.80	Dow Jones U.S. Health Care Index
Ultra Industrials	UXI	$57.83	−$0.29	$57.94	−$0.44	Dow Jones U.S. Industrials Index
Ultra Oil & Gas	DIG	$116.86	$1.90	$117.30	$2.06	Dow Jones U.S. Oil & Gas Index
Ultra Real Estate	URE	$27.98	−$0.52	$27.92	−$0.54	Dow Jones U.S. Real Estate Index
Ultra Semiconductors	USD	$48.95	−$0.55	$48.93	−$0.68	Dow Jones U.S. Semiconductors Index
Ultra Technology	ROM	$59.12	−$0.57	$59.13	−$0.64	Dow Jones U.S. Technology Index
Ultra Telecommunications	LTL	$68.62	−$1.02	$68.74	−$2.19	Dow Jones U.S. Select Telecommunications Index
Ultra Utilities	UPW	$73.68	−$1.09	$73.55	−$1.43	Dow Jones U.S. Utilities Index

Source: ProFunds web site.

portfolio that is not correlated to your other investments. In addition to our internal managed futures fund, my company also runs an internal ETF strategy.

In this chapter I will discuss using ETFs to manage some of your money yourself, either through overlay strategies or as a more complete investment strategy.

Leverage

There are many ETFs that offer twice the exposure of a certain market. This can be good and bad as leverage magnifies gains and losses. ProShares and Rydex are two of the leaders in leveraged ETFs; some examples from ProFunds are included in Tables 16.1 to 16.3. As the tables show, there are a number of different types of

Table 16.4 Inverse ETFs—Closing Price Information as of 6/27/08 Short MarketCap

Fund	Ticker (View Chart)	NAV	NAV Change	Market Price	Market Price Change	Benchmark Index
Short QQQ	PSQ	$58.43	−$0.01	$58.45	$0.10	NASDAQ-100® Index
Short Dow30	DOG	$68.14	$0.63	$68.04	$0.66	Dow Jones Industrial Average
Short S&P500	SH	$68.58	$0.25	$68.54	$0.20	S&P 500 Index
Short MidCap400	MYY	$61.12	$0.25	$61.10	$0.10	S&P MidCap 400 Index
Short SmallCap600	SBB	$74.39	$0.37	$74.18	$0.29	S&P SmallCap 600 Index
Short Russell2000	RWM	$77.08	$0.04	$77.16	$0.18	Russell 2000 Index
UltraShort QQQ	QID	$44.14	−$0.01	$44.00	$0.10	NASDAQ100 Index
UltraShort Dow30	DXD	$64.72	$1.18	$64.39	$1.11	Dow Jones Industrial Average
UltraShort S&P500	SDS	$67.13	$0.49	$67.07	$0.57	S&P 500 Index
UltraShort MidCap400	MZZ	$55.71	$0.45	$55.93	$0.63	S&P MidCap 400 Index
UltraShort SmallCap600	SDD	$74.97	$0.75	$74.89	$0.88	S&P SmallCap 600 Index
UltraShort Russell2000	TWM	$77.04	$0.07	$76.86	−$0.39	Russell 2000 Index

leveraged ETFs so whatever type of bet (long or short) you want to make, chances are there is an ETF for it.

As evidenced by looking at Tables 16.1 to 16.3, if I am very, very positive on utility stocks I could buy the Ultra Utilities ETF and have double the exposure to utilities. This would give me twice the exposure of just buying a regular nonleveraged ETF. This would also give me twice the downside if I am wrong, so I need to be careful.

The Ability to Go Short

There are also a number of inverse ETFs; these provide the opposite of the return of an index. Some of these are also leveraged. Some examples from ProShares are included in Tables 16.4 to 16.8.

Table 16.5 Inverse ETFs—Closing Price Information as of 6/27/08 Short Style

Fund	Ticker (View Chart)	NAV	NAV Change	Market Price	Market Price Change	Benchmark Index
UltraShort Russell1000 Value	SJF	$97.97	$1.00	$97.48	$0.63	Russell 1000 Value Index
UltraShort Russell1000 Growth	SFK	$72.32	$0.35	$72.31	$0.58	Russell 1000 Growth Index
UltraShort Russell MidCap Value	SJL	$93.20	$0.79	$93.34	$1.10	Russell Mid-Cap Value Index
UltraShort Russell MidCap Growth	SDK	$69.73	$0.20	$69.55	$0.36	Russell Mid-Cap Growth Index
UltraShort Russell2000 Value	SJH	$98.50	$1.08	$98.27	$0.86	Russell 2000 Value Index
UltraShort Russell2000 Growth	SKK	$73.12	−$0.61	$73.10	−$0.90	Russell 2000 Growth Index

These allow investors a much easier way than short selling stocks to express negative views on different asset classes. They also allow investors to tweak the risk exposure of their portfolios. For example, if you were scared that the market was going to go down but didn't want to take money away from your stock managers, you could put some of your money into inverse ETFs on the stock market that would profit in a market decline.

If I am negative on a sector, inverse ETFs make it much easier to monetize my view. Before inverse ETFs I would have either had to sell stocks short, which is not always easy and can't be done in an IRA; bought put options, which has a cost; or sold ETFs short, which also is not easy.

Using ETFs to Create Opportunistic and Hedging Overlays

Large endowments often use overlay strategies in their portfolio. They may use these strategies to reduce risk and take advantage of opportunity. The endowments will generally use futures or options contracts that would be too complicated for many individual investors. That's where ETFs can help individuals pursue some of the strategies of endowments.

Table 16.6   Inverse ETFs—Closing Price Information as of 6/27/08 Short Sector

Fund	Ticker (View Chart)	NAV	NAV Change	Market Price	Market Price Change	Benchmark Index
Short Financials	SEF	$77.17	$0.93	$77.15	$1.65	Dow Jones U.S. Financials Index
Short Oil & Gas	DDG	$69.52	−$0.57	$69.14	−$0.77	Dow Jones U.S. Oil & Gas Index
UltraShort Basic Materials	SMN	$28.82	−$0.58	$29.00	−$0.29	Dow Jones U.S. Basic Materials Index
UltraShort Consumer Goods	SZK	$82.39	$2.38	$82.31	$2.39	Dow Jones U.S. Consumer Goods Index
UltraShort Consumer Services	SCC	$100.46	$0.95	$100.34	$0.88	Dow Jones U.S. Consumer Services Index
UltraShort Financials	SKF	$150.87	$3.59	$150.76	$3.78	Dow Jones U.S. Financials Index
UltraShort Health Care	RXD	$85.88	−$0.86	$85.59	−$0.31	Dow Jones U.S. Health Care Index
UltraShort Industrials	SIJ	$67.83	$0.34	$67.90	$0.61	Dow Jones U.S. Industrials Index
UltraShort Oil & Gas	DUG	$27.66	−$0.45	$27.50	−$0.53	Dow Jones U.S. Oil & Gas Index
UltraShort Real Estate	SRS	$104.83	$1.84	$104.15	$1.42	Dow Jones U.S. Real Estate Index
UltraShort Semiconductors	SSG	$65.66	$0.72	$65.55	$0.71	Dow Jones U.S. Semiconductors Index
UltraShort Technology	REW	$63.53	$0.59	$63.30	$0.51	Dow Jones U.S. Technology Index
UltraShort Telecommunications	TLL	$67.46	$0.97	$67.61	$1.81	Dow Jones U.S. Select Telecommunications Index
UltraShort Utilities	SDP	$53.68	$0.77	$53.61	$0.88	Dow Jones U.S. Utilities Index

ETFs allow you to create an opportunistic part of your portfolio where you can move quickly. For example, when you saw financial stocks plummet during the summer of 2007 you could have used an ETF to sell them short. You could have used an ETF to go long oil and commodities, long gold, or short the dollar.

Portfolio Hedging Using ETFs

You can also use ETFs to control the beta of your portfolio. You may want to hedge the risk of your portfolio during periods of instability

**Table 16.7   Inverse ETFs—Closing Price Information as of 6/27/08
Short International**

Fund	Ticker (View Chart)	NAV	NAV Change	Market Price	Market Price Change	Benchmark Index
Short MSCI EAFE	EFZ	$81.11	−$0.18	$81.04	−$0.21	MSCI EAFE Index
Short MSCI Emerging Markets	EUM	$76.70	−$0.58	$76.55	−$0.55	MSCI Emerging Markets Index
UltraShort MSCI EAFE	EFU	$90.25	−$0.42	$90.06	−$0.44	MSCI EAFE Index
UltraShort MSCI Emerging Markets	EEV	$76.82	−$1.17	$76.53	−$1.07	MSCI Emerging Markets Index
UltraShort MSCI Japan	EWV	$79.48	−$1.30	$79.54	−$1.36	MSCI Japan Index
UltraShort FTSE/ Xinhua China 25	FXP	$86.58	−$0.65	$86.40	−$0.55	FTSE/Xinhua China 25 Index

**Table 16.8   Inverse ETFs—Closing Price Information as of 6/27/08
Short Fixed-Income**

Fund	Ticker (View Chart)	NAV	NAV Change	Market Price	Market Price Change	Benchmark Index
UltraShort Lehman 7- to 10-Year Treasury	PST	$70.76	−$0.37	$70.55	−$0.84	Lehman Brothers 7- to 10-Year U.S. Treasury Index
UltraShort Lehman 20+- Year Treasury	TBT	$68.94	−$1.28	$68.75	−$1.79	Lehman Brothers 20+-Year U.S. Treasury Index

Source: ProFunds web site.

or because of a change in your goals and objectives, but it may not make sense for you to sell your existing investments or reallocate. In this situation you can use an inverse ETF to reduce the overall beta (movement with the market) of your portfolio. Here's an example. If we construct a simple portfolio of 34% in the Fidelity ContraFund, 33% in the Fidelity Magellan Fund, and 33% in the Fidelity Small Cap Growth Fund, the portfolio has a beta of 1.17. This means that our portfolio should move 17% more than the market on the upside and the downside. If I want to reduce that beta, either temporarily or permanently, I could use an inverse ETF. If I change my portfolio and put 25% in the ProFunds Ultra Short S&P 500 (2 times the inverse return of the S&P 500) and keep 25% each in my other funds, the beta declines to .57. I can increase or decrease the percent in the ETF to change my beta to fit in with what I am trying to accomplish.

Other ETF Strategies: The Trend Is Your Friend

Some endowments use ETFs and index mutual funds to track market trends. Currently, oil and commodity prices are going up, financial stocks and the dollar are going down. If you thought this was likely to continue, you could buy long ETFs on oil and other commodities and buy short ETFs on financial stocks and the dollar. Just like our managed futures portfolio, we use trend following when we create ETF portfolios. We believe that the market will tell you where it wants to go. I may have my opinions (and I do), but the market doesn't ask me what I think; it will go where it is trying to go. Trend following doesn't try to outguess the markets, it tries to look at the prices and determine which way they will go. When you are right, trend following seeks to maximize your returns while protecting your gains. When you are wrong, trend following seeks to get you out with the least possible loss.

Our systems are very complex. The market declines of 2000–2002 and 2007–2008 proved that investors need a new way of thinking about their portfolios. Yet investors are still doing the same things that caused, and continue to cause, large losses. We know that market experts can't predict where markets are going to go, but we listen to them and act on their recommendations. We know that most money managers don't beat their index benchmark, but we also know that indexing doesn't protect us in a market decline. Gurus who can predict what stocks to buy get famous, until they crash and burn and are replaced by the next gurus.

The market decline that started in 2007 and the bankruptcies that followed were a true game changer in the investment industry. Buying and holding solid stocks used to be a valid investment strategy. However, at one point in time Fannie Mae, Freddie Mac, Lehman Brothers, and Bear Stearns were considered solid stocks. The indexing approach used to resonate with many fee-conscious investors. However, with the recent declines, we are getting perilously close to the first negative 10-year period in the market since the Depression.

What is the right answer? Although we can't predict where the markets are going to go, they do give us clues to where they want to go. We can't see these clues with the naked eye because our emotions and our need to be able to predict where things are going betray us. We may see oil prices going up, but we discount it because we fear that prices have already gone up too far too fast, and we are convinced that the supply-demand equation favors lower prices. We also might see the stock market show signs of recovery after a large decline; however, we don't act on the signals because we fear a new decline and the talking heads in the media are still negative. Our emotions and our beliefs that we, or someone else, know what is going to happen cause us to ignore what the markets are telling us.

At TWM we do things differently. Most people love to try to figure out whether the markets are going up or down. It is human nature to want to know this. Instead, we think in terms of statistics and probability. We use sophisticated computer systems that have been developed over many years, back tested, and proved by some of the smartest minds in the industry. These systems allow us to see what the markets are telling us, free of emotion and the noise of what the so-called experts are saying. We believe that creativity and judgment are best used designing and testing systems rather than in the emotionally charged environment of actual trading. When our systems tell us one thing while our emotions and our judgments are telling us something else, we are humble enough and confident enough in our technology that we listen to the system. When we are wrong, we don't double down or say things like "If we liked it at $50, then we'll love it at $40." Instead, we cut our losses and move on. Losses are our biggest enemy; we can't always avoid them, but we can minimize them. When we are right we don't have a predefined price target; we let the markets tell us when it is time to get out. Most investors buy more of their losers and cut their profits short. We cut our losses short and let our profits run. That way, we only need a few profitable trades each year to do well for our clients. We don't benchmark ourselves against a market index. To us, that is just a license for mediocrity. It would allow us to say things like "The market was down 20% and we were only down 18%, so we were successful." Our benchmark is zero; we don't want to lose any money. We won't beat it every

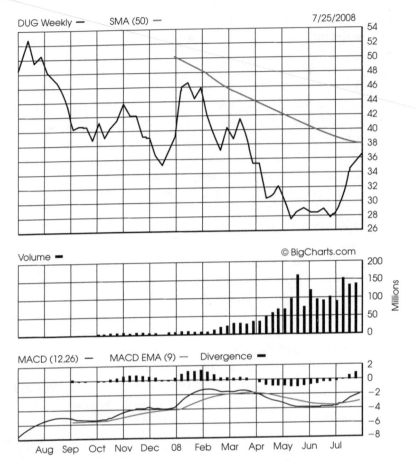

Figure 16.1   DUG Chart

month, quarter, or year but our overriding goal and passion are to protect our clients' assets and generate attractive returns.

Individual investors cannot duplicate our systems, but they can still utilize some of the same thinking. Individual investors can start with the charts of different ETFs to determine the overall trend.

Figure 16.1 shows a weekly chart for the ProShares Ultra Short Oil & Gas ETF (DUG), which seeks to provide double the inverse the return of an index of stocks in the oil and gas industry. Since oil and gas have been rising, this ETF has been going down. However, recently it broke out of its downtrend. Our system uses a number of proprietary indicators to try to determine whether this is a real breakout to the upside or whether the downside will continue, but individuals don't have to get that sophisticated. Personally, I believe that oil and gas will continue to go up long term, but I do not let my feelings affect what the chart and the numbers are telling me if it is something different.

Once we have determined that a position is worth taking, we use the volatility of the ETF to determine our position size, where we place stops, when we will buy more shares, and when we will start to scale out of a position.

Relative Value Trades

Another type of trade that endowments may do with ETFs is relative value trades. Let's say you aren't sure if markets will go up, but you think China will outperform the United States. You could buy an inverse S&P 500 ETF and an equal amount of a China ETF. That way you are effectively market neutral and will make money if China outperforms the United States, even if both go down. Of course if you are wrong and the S&P 500 goes up and China goes down, then you will take a beating.

Laddered Bond Portfolios

Because it is so hard for bond managers to add alpha, any endowments do bond management in-house, typically through a laddered bond portfolio. In a laddered bond portfolio, bonds are bought across the maturity spectrum. For example, you might own a one-year bond, a two-year bond, a three-year bond, a four-year bond, a five-year bond, and so on. That way, you always have something coming due that can be reinvested at higher rates if interest rates are going up. You also always have something long term that will benefit if interest rates are going down.

If you choose to manage some of your money in-house, make sure you have a well-thought-out strategy that preferably is not well correlated with your core investment approach.

Managing Some Money Yourself

Your overall skill and confidence with investing will determine how much, if any, money you should manage yourself versus farming it out to external money managers. If you do decide to manage some yourself, there are a number of strategies that you can use.

CHAPTER

17

Portable Alpha

Endowments and other institutional investors are always a few years ahead of individual investors. It took a number of years for individual investors to embrace traditional asset allocation. Then, after the market crash of 2000–2002, smart institutions realized there had to be a better way. Even though individuals are still invested in traditional asset-allocated portfolios, the institutions are creating portfolios that separate alpha from beta.

As I am sure you remember from earlier in this book, beta is the performance you get from just being in the market and alpha is out-performance. Beta is easy and cheap to get since you can just buy and index funds. Alpha is harder to find; you need to find money managers that consistently outperform the market or their benchmark. The traditional approach was to come up with an asset allocation and hire style-pure money managers. These money managers would generate beta just by being invested in the market. The hope is that they can make bets around their benchmarks, underweighting some sectors and overweighting others, so they can generate some alpha as well. In the traditional approach, alpha and beta are tied together.

So, for example, say you had an endowment that had come up with their asset allocation and hired XYZ Large Cap Growth money manager to manage their large-cap growth allocation. XYZ is a style box-based money manager. Let's assume XYZ Large Cap Growth's benchmark is the S&P 500 index. The endowment would expect XYZ to invest pretty close to the index weights and own many of the stocks in the index. Because of that, a lot, or most, of their performance would come from beta, just holding many of the allocations and stocks in the index. The endowment would also expect XYZ to slightly overweight or underweight stocks or sectors to try to outperform the index and generate some alpha. However, XYZ can't overweight or underweight too much because they would risk making a bad bet, underperforming the index, and getting fired. So it is very difficult for XYZ to generate alpha.

There are a number of reasons why traditional (style box-based) money managers have trouble outperforming their benchmark:

1. They must have minimum allocations to certain sectors to stay in line with their index even if they don't like the sector.
2. They cannot exceed certain percentages in any one security or sector. This makes it difficult to monetize positive viewpoints on securities and/or sectors.
3. They have minimal or no ability to sell securities or sectors short.
4. They are required to deliver performance within a certain minimum tracking error (deviation from the index).
5. There are limitations on the types of securities in which they can invest.

Also under the traditional approach, the endowment might have come across ABC Money Management. ABC doesn't have a benchmark; they are skill based; they invest in whatever they want, wherever they want, to try to generate alpha. Since ABC doesn't fit nicely into any style box, the endowment cannot use them even if their performance is great. They need to hope that XYZ and their other style box-based money managers can figure out some way to generate alpha—a very tall order.

Twenty years ago some smart institutions started to realize that there might be a better way. If they could separate alpha from beta, they could design more efficient portfolios and increase returns. At that point in history, a monkey throwing darts at a board could have earned 20%/year in the market, so the idea never really gained traction. Now that we are in a period of mediocre returns, more and more endowments and other institutional investors are converting to a portable alpha approach.

Portable alpha sounds complicated, but it's really not. The key is to separate money manager skill from market risk and return. As you remember from earlier in the book, beta is easy to find; you can invest in an index fund or an index ETF and you will get market returns. Alpha is not as easy to find, but it does exist if you look hard enough. There are many money managers who have consistently generated alpha over the years. In the portable alpha approach, instead of having money managers who generate beta and hopefully some alpha, the alpha and beta are split off into separate allocations. In the above example, if the endowment went to a portable alpha approach, they would fire XYZ and replace them with a passive exposure to the S&P 500 (this would usually be through futures, swaps, or other derivatives). Using products such as futures, which only require a small margin to control large market exposure, frees up cash that can be invested elsewhere to generate alpha. They would also fire their other style box-based managers and replace them with passive exposure to whatever index they wanted to replicate returns for: MCSI EAFE, Lehman Aggregate, and so on. This would become their beta portfolio. They would then hire ABC and other skill-based money managers with their free cash, who would then hopefully generate alpha. This would be their alpha portfolio. They would then combine their beta and alpha portfolios to create one big efficient portfolio. So instead of the old approach of trying to get alpha and beta from the same place, they split them into different portfolios and combined them. The alpha they are creating gets ported to their beta portfolio—hence the term *portable alpha.*

Leverage

Many investors look at the word *leverage* and ultimately think of high risk. Leverage doesn't have to be risky; it depends on how you use it. Homeowners use leverage to buy their homes, car buyers use leverage to buy cars, and so on. Using leverage wisely can enhance your portfolio; using it unwisely to make large speculative bets can wipe you out.

A Step-by-Step Process

Individuals can do pretty much the same thing. Let's say your benchmark is the S&P 500; you want to beat the index and you are willing to take some risk that your returns will not be quite in line with the index. Basically, there are two steps that demonstrate how portable alpha works.

Step 1: Replicate the Returns of Your Index

With some part of your portfolio, you need to replicate the returns of the S&P 500. Endowments do it by using futures contracts or swaps that allow them to put a little money down and get the returns of the index. As an individual investor, this usually isn't that easy for you. A better way would be to use a leveraged index fund. There are many S&P 500 index funds that give you 1.5, 2, or 2.5 times the daily return of the S&P 500 index.

Leveraged Index Funds

Leveraged index funds seek to provide 1.5, 2, or 2.5 times an underlying index. They do this by investing in futures and/or swap contracts on the underlying index. There are funds available now on a number of different stock indexes. Leveraged funds are not perfect; they attempt to magnify the daily return of the index so the yearly returns can be different than one might expect. The leveraged funds also have an interest cost to the leverage and an expense ratio that will cause returns to deviate somewhat from the underlying index. The returns of leveraged index funds will vary based on whether the market is increasing steadily, declining steadily, or is flat and volatile. This difference is because leveraged index funds change their market exposure with gains and losses. When a fund has gains, the assets go up, increasing index exposure. When the fund goes down, the assets go down, decreasing index exposure. To accurately create a portable alpha strategy using leveraged index funds, you must continually monitor the fund and buy and sell as necessary to keep your exposure in line with how you want it. Direxion Funds is one company that has a tool on its web site to help investors keep their fund at the level necessary to keep index exposure steady. The tool can be found at www.direxionfunds.com.

The Impact of Changing Market Exposure on Leveraged Index Funds.   Leveraged index funds seek to provide a multiple of the daily return of the underlying index. Because of this, when the market is up they are increasing market exposure and when the market is down they are decreasing exposure. This is caused by the structure of the funds. A leveraged fund's exposure is a product of its magnification level and its assets. Gains in the index increase the assets of the fund which causes an increase in exposure to the index. Conversely, a decline in the index reduces exposure to the index. In essence, leveraged index funds react to gains by becoming more aggressive and respond to losses by becoming more conservative. The examples in Tables 17.1 to 17.3 show how a fund that seeks to deliver 2 times the daily return of an index would react under different scenarios:

In Table 17.1, the fund's assets rise as the market rises. This causes market exposure to rise as well, which amplifies gains beyond what an investor would expect.

In this example, the fund returned 54.76% when we would have expected it to earn only 50%.

In Table 17.2, the fund's assets fall as the market falls, causing market exposure to fall as well, which protects the fund so it doesn't lose as much as an investor would expect.

Table 17.1 Market Rising

Index Value	Index Daily Return	Index Total Return	Index Total Return × 2	Actual Fund Daily Return	Actual Fund Total Return
100					
105	5.00%	5.00%	10.00%	10.00%	10.00%
110	4.76%	10.00%	20.00%	9.52%	20.48%
115	4.55%	15.00%	30.00%	9.09%	31.43%
120	4.35%	20.00%	40.00%	8.70%	42.86%
125	4.17%	25.00%	50.00%	8.33%	54.76%

Source: Direxion Funds.

Table 17.2 Market Declining

Index Value	Index Daily Return	Index Total Return	Index Total Return × 2	Actual Fund Daily Return	Actual Fund Total Return
100					
95	−5.00%	−5.00%	−10.00%	−10.00%	−10.00%
90	−5.26%	−10.00%	−20.00%	−10.53%	−19.47%
85	−5.56%	−15.00%	−30.00%	−11.11%	−28.42%
80	−5.88%	−20.00%	−40.00%	−11.76%	−36.84%
75	−6.25%	−25.00%	−50.00%	−12.50%	−44.74%

Source: Direxion Funds.

Table 17.3   Market Flat and Volatile

Index Value	Index Daily Return	Index Total Return	Index Total Return × 2	Actual Fund Daily Return	Actual Fund Total Return
100					
95	−5.00%	−5.00%	−10.00%	−10.00%	−10.00%
100	5.26%	0.00%	0.00%	10.53%	−0.53%
105	5.00%	5.00%	−10.00%	10.00%	9.42%
100	−4.76%	0.00%	0.00%	−9.52%	−1.00%
95	−5.00%	−5.00%	−10.00%	−10.00%	−10.90%
100	5.26%	0.00%	0.00%	10.53%	−1.52%

Source: Direxion Funds.

In this example the fund returned −44.74% when we would have expected it to lose 50%.

In a volatile market, gains can lead to increased exposure just before a loss, whereas losses can lead to decreased exposure just before a gain. (See Table 17.3.) In this example the fund returned −1.52% when we would have expected it to be flat.

So suppose you have a $1 million portfolio and use a fund that gives you 2 times the return of the index. Investing half of your portfolio, $500,000, into the fund has the same result as investing your entire portfolio into a nonleveraged index fund, but now you have an extra $500,000 to invest elsewhere. You could also choose a 2.5× fund, which would only require putting in $400,000 to get the same impact of having the entire portfolio in an index fund. Or, if you were more risk averse, you could use a 1.5× leveraged fund and put $666,666 into it. Direxion, Rydex, and ProFunds are the current leaders in providing leveraged index funds. Their web sites are as follows:

- http://direxionfunds.com/index.html
- http://profunds.com/
- http://proshares.com
- http://www.rydexfunds.com/index.shtml

Step 2: Pick Your Alpha Manager(s)

In Step 2, we identify a portfolio of money managers or different strategies that consistently generate alpha and are not that well correlated with the S&P 500 (have as little beta risk as possible).

Table 17.4   Portable Alpha Results

March 1997– June 2008	$1 Million in S&P 500	Portable Alpha Strategy: $500K in 2× S&P 500 & $500K in Hedge Fund of Funds
Annualized return	6.1%	11%*

*Return does not take into account fees charged by index funds and any potential market underperformance.

These are going to be your skill-based money managers. Earlier in the book I talked about a hedge fund of funds that has averaged 9.8% a year since March 1997. We could take $500,000 and invest it in the fund. Please note that I am not necessarily recommending a portfolio of half in a leveraged index fund and the other half in a hedge fund of funds. I am just trying to give you a simple example. Table 17.4 shows the results.

The portable alpha strategy almost doubles your return. Now keep in mind that it could have gone the other way if the fund of funds had lost money. Also, the higher the alpha allocation the more chance you have that your performance will be much different than your underlying index. The endowments call this *tracking error*. This can be good or bad, depending on how well your alpha investments do.

At first, this might seem to be some really advanced financial theory, but it really isn't. You use portable alpha in your daily life. Let's say you have $500,000 in cash, and you want to buy a house for $500,000. You have two choices. You can put all of your money down or you can put $100,000 down and take the other $400,000 and invest it. If you pay cash for the house and its value goes up, you do well, and if its value goes down you do poorly. If you only put $100,000 down, you still experience the appreciation and depreciation of your property, but you also have the extra $400,000 to invest. If you invest it wisely, your total return will be better than it would be if you had put all of your money in the house (assuming of course that the returns on your $400,000 beat the mortgage interest rate). I didn't include this in the example because a leveraged ETF or mutual fund has costs but not the same as a mortgage.

There are two key concepts to portable alpha. The first is that borrowing (through leveraged index funds) can increase return (also potentially increasing risk). Second, diversification has the ability to increase returns and potentially reduce risk. Portable alpha uses borrowing to improve a portfolio on two fronts: diversification (a portable alpha portfolio will be much more diversified than a traditional portfolio) and alpha generation.

Alpha-Generating Vehicles

Successful investment vehicles for a portable alpha strategy should have the following three characteristics:

1. Consistently outperform their benchmark
2. Low volatility
3. Low correlation to the markets (your sources of beta)

In short, you are looking for smart money managers who consistently outperform their benchmark but invest in such a way that they have little or no correlation with your sources of beta.

Portable Alpha

Some examples of alpha and beta sources are below. Portfolios can easily be customized based on how much risk you want to take versus how much you want to beat your benchmark by.

Beta Sources

- S&P 500
- Dow Jones Industrial Average
- Mid-cap stocks
- Small-cap stocks
- International stocks
- Emerging market stocks
- Fixed income

Alpha Sources

- Hedge fund of funds
- Market neutral
- Arbitrage fund
- Short-term bonds
- Skill-based money managers

Portable Alpha Mutual Funds

There are a few mutual funds that have adopted portable alpha approaches, including:

- *PIMCO StockPlus.* PIMCO funds have been pioneers in bringing the portable alpha concept to mutual funds. Their StockPlus funds use some of their cash to buy futures on the S&P 500 to replicate the index, and the remainder is invested in an actively managed bond portfolio.
- *RiverSource Absolute Return Currency & Income.* This fund seeks to return 3% more than cash. It invests in a portfolio of short-term bonds and then invests some money into a dollar neutral currency strategy. The bonds seek to replicate the return of cash and the currency investments are designed to deliver the extra 3%.
- *DWS Short Duration Plus Fund.* This fund is a normal short-term bond fund that takes a small percentage of assets and invests them in an alpha overlay that can include currency investments, global bond investments, and so on.

Portable Alpha Details

Because of the use of leverage in portable alpha, investors need to proceed cautiously and carefully monitor the risk of their portfolios. Investors in a portable alpha strategy run the risk that in any given year their alpha-generating vehicle(s) will not outperform the cost of leverage (internal fund expenses).

There are a lot of permutations to this. Since we can now find leveraged mutual funds on many indexes—bonds, small-cap stocks, emerging market stocks, mid-cap stocks, international stocks, and so on—you can design your beta allocation however you want—50% stocks/50% bonds, combine international stocks, emerging market stocks, and the S&P 500, and so on. You can also decide how much risk you want to take that your portfolio will not move in line with the index. If you are willing to take a lot of risk, you can use 2.5× leveraged funds and make your beta allocations 40% and your alpha 60%. If you don't want to take much risk, you can use 1.5× leveraged funds and make your beta allocation 66% and your alpha allocation 34%. You could also put a big chunk of your portfolio in cash or short-term bonds to water it down even more. The possibilities with portable alpha are almost endless.

The endowment types of portfolios we have been talking about until now are absolute return portfolios designed to beat inflation. Their performance shouldn't be too correlated with the market, because you will be very well diversified and have a lot of money managers that generate alpha but not a lot of beta. If you design these portfolios properly, they will lag in a large up market but should provide protection in a down market. Long term, this is great, but you have to live with the fact that during periods like 1995–1999 your friends will be bragging about their returns and you will have nothing to say. The flip side is that during periods like 2000–2002 when your friends are losing tons of money, you will get the last laugh. Portable alpha is designed to try to outperform an index or an allocation like 50% stocks/50% bonds, or the S&P 500. So it all depends on what you want your portfolio to do. If you are one of those people who would be very angry if the market was up 30% and you were only up 20% but you could also handle the market being down 20% and your portfolio being down 18%, then portable alpha could be for you. If you want to try for absolute returns, then ignore portable alpha.

Portable alpha can also be used at an asset class level. Some asset classes like large-cap U.S. stocks and government bonds are very hard to generate alpha in. Large stocks are fairly efficient since there is not much that an analyst can learn about a large company that everyone else doesn't already know. Government bonds are pretty plain vanilla investments so it is hard for the best of investors to generate much excess return. Let's say an endowment has $1 million allocated to large-cap U.S. stocks and wants to add some alpha. The endowment would use a futures contract on the S&P 500 which would give them the same $1 million exposure as they had before but with less than $1 million down. (This is because futures contracts only need a margin deposit that is a small percent of the amount of assets the contract controls.) The endowment will then take the extra money and invest it in one or more alpha-generating investments. Again, as an individual investor you probably don't want to be playing in the futures market. You can use a leveraged fund or ETF to replicate the asset class and then invest the rest of the money into alpha-generating investments.

Endowments use the same basic concept when they want to add alpha without interrupting their current allocation. For example, let's say you have 50% in large-cap stocks and 50% in bonds and don't want to change your allocation. Just as in the previous example, you could use a 2.5× index fund to reduce your cash exposure to large-cap stocks to 20% of your portfolio (50% divided by 2.5) and then reallocate the 30% into alpha-producing investments.

Future of Money Management

Many endowments and other institutional investors believe that portable alpha is the future of money management. They foresee a time when money management firms will either structure beta or be providers of alpha. All of the current style boxes and style box-based managers would morph into beta providers or alpha providers. I could definitely see this happening. It will take a while to catch on with individual investors, but once it does there is no real reason to go back to the traditional way of thinking.

PART IV

DESIGNING YOUR PORTFOLIO

Now that you have learned about the mistakes most investors make, how to diversify a portfolio, the benefits of using skill-based managers, and all of the asset classes endowments use, you can start applying these concepts to your personal situation. In Chapter 18, we will talk about how to use your risk tolerance to determine your portfolio allocation, and I will show you a few sample allocations. In Chapter 19, we will talk about how to choose money managers. In Chapter 20, we will talk about how you must design your portfolio around your goals and how to decide if you need help. Finally, in Chapter 21, we will talk about how to develop your own Investment Policy Statement, which will guide your investment decisions going forward.

CHAPTER 18

Suggested Allocations

Now that you have an understanding of diversification, skill-based money managers, the importance of avoiding large losses, all the different investment vehicles you can use, and the different asset classes that should be in your endowment portfolio, it is now time to decide on your asset allocation. In this chapter we will go over the steps you need to take to determine your asset allocation.

Step 1: Determine Your Risk Tolerance

How you allocate your assets will be the most important determinant of your investment success. Your asset allocation is guided by your goals and your tolerance for risk. One way to determine your risk tolerance is to answer a questionnaire. The following simple risk tolerance questionnaire can help you get a handle on how much risk you are willing to take in your investment portfolio.

Risk Tolerance Questionnaire from SEI Investments

Instructions: For each question, circle the number after the answer that is most appropriate. If you are doing this exercise with your partner, then both of you should circle an answer and either average your scores or come up with different portfolios for each of you.

1. When you think of the word *risk* in a financial context, which of the following words comes to mind first?	Score 1	Score 2
A. Thrill	5	5
B. Uncertainty	3	3

C. Opportunity	3	3
D. Danger	1	1

2. What is your greatest concern?

A. Underperforming the market	5	5
B. Not growing my assets significantly over time: I am willing to assume higher risk for higher return potential.	5	5
C. Losing more than a certain amount within a time frame	3	3
D. Losing money in a market downturn along the way	3	3
E. Not having certainty around achieving my wealth goal in the remaining time	1	1

3. If the market falls by 25 percent in a year, and you lose 20 percent, how do you feel?

A. Optimistic, because I beat the market by thinking long term	5	5
B. Uneasy with loss but I would stick it out	3	3
C. Unhappy with the loss to the point where I will sell	1	1

4. What describes you best?

A. I am long-term focused.	5	5
B. I am focused on preserving current wealth and have little tolerance for losses.	3	3
C. I want to plan long term but have a hard time shrugging off moderate to severe losses.	3	3
D. I am most concerned about targeting a final value of my assets: I don't mind if this approach sacrifices return potential.	1	1

5. If I look at my quarterly statement and there is a moderate loss, my primary reaction is:

A. How did my portfolio compare with the market benchmark or other relative measures of success?	5	5
B. I lost money and am unhappy but am willing to stick it through until a recovery.	3	3
C. I don't care about short-term losses as long as I reach a specific sum of money at a specific point of time in the future.	1	1

Overall Risk Score(s)

Average Risk Score (if scoring with partner)

Risk-Tolerance Scoring Guide

After adding your scores from the questionnaire, you have a total risk-tolerance score. This score will provide some guidance in choosing the appropriate investment strategies for each of your goals. Please keep in mind that a risk tolerance questionnaire is just a tool and has its limitations. If I asked you in 1999 about your risk tolerance and then asked you again at the end of 2002, chances are I would have gotten two very different answers. Always use your own judgment or seek the help of a financial planning professional.

Score

5–11	Risk Tolerance Low: Choose defensive or conservative/low-risk strategies
12–17	Moderate: Choose moderate-/medium-risk strategies
18–25	High: Choose aggressive/high-risk strategies

The Limitations of Risk-Tolerance Questionnaires

Risk-tolerance questionnaires are far from perfect. First of all, the market environment you are in when you answer the questions can have a huge impact. Second, usually one spouse is the family CFO and handles the finances. This spouse could influence the nonfinancial spouse to answer similarly even if he/she had a different view. Third, it is very hard for people to visualize how they would feel if their portfolio declined unless it actually does. In theory, you may think you will be fine if your portfolio drops by 20%, but in reality when you are looking at your statement and you see the actual losses it may still cause you to panic.

Step 2: Allocate Your Assets

We try to avoid losses as much as possible by using benchmarks and expected downside capture. This enables us to effectively allocate our assets. For example, an endowment type of portfolio would be benchmarked against inflation plus some spread. A moderate portfolio should have maximum downside capture of 50% versus the S&P 500; that means if the S&P is down 20%, worst case is you should be down 10%. Please keep in mind that worst case is just that— worst case. If you have a moderate portfolio, your target downside capture should really be around 25%, with the expectation that there will be times when it is better or worse.

Table 18.1 shows some suggested asset allocations based on our capital market views as of July 2008.

Table 18.1 Suggested Asset Allocations

	Defensive	Conservative	Moderate	Aggressive
Absolute return	20%	20%	38%	30%
Stocks	5%	12%	35%	48%
Bonds	72%	60%	14%	9%
Real assets	0%	5%	10%	10%
Cash	3%	3%	3%	3%

Of course, these allocations are only suggested. You need to consider your own circumstances and comfort level in determining your own allocation. Remember, your asset allocation decision will probably have the most impact on your performance. When coming up with your asset allocation, the absolute return, bonds, and cash will be your most stable investments. Your stock and real asset investments will be the riskiest.

You need to look at each asset class and formulate an idea of future returns. While past performance doesn't indicate future results, you can still use it to get a feel for where you think future returns are going to be. Don't get caught up in the trap of believing that just because something is going up it will continue to go up, and just because something is going down it will continue to go down. You can also cheat a bit if you want by looking at Yale's endowment online at http://www.yale.edu/investments/. Yale forecasts return expectations for the asset classes it uses. If you use their forecasts, then I would bump them down a bit since you don't have access to the same caliber of money managers that they do. Table 18.2 shows our long-term (10 to 20 years) return estimates as of July 2008 for various asset classes. Notice that for most asset classes, we are forecasting that projected returns will be lower than historical returns.

As Yale talks about in the report, asset allocation is part art and part science. You don't need fancy software to come up with a robust asset allocation; sometimes good judgment and common sense is the better way to go. Come up with your own forecasts and use them to develop a diversified asset allocation.

Step 3: Monitor Asset Allocation—It Is Not Static

Once you have figured out your asset allocation, you need to monitor it and make changes as necessary. Remember that your brain will try to get you to allocate more money to the asset class that is

Table 18.2 Long-Term Return Estimates for Asset Classes

Asset Class Group	Projected Return	Expense Adj.	Stan. Dev.	Tax-Free	Taxable	Stan. Dev.	Tax-Free	Taxable
Cash	Cash Equivalent	5.71%	0.00%	3.01%	3.85%	3.60%	0.80%	2.30%
Bond	Short-Term Bonds	7.51%	0.00%	4.34%	6.58%	5.70%	2.00%	2.60%
Bond	Short-Term Municipals	6.58%	0.00%	3.72%	6.58%	2.60%	1.50%	2.60%
Bond	Intermediate-Term Bonds	8.21%	0.00%	5.59%	N/A	5.90%	7.00%	N/A
Bond	Intermediate-Term Munis	6.76%	0.00%	9.62%	6.76%	5.85%	7.00%	3.80%
Bond	Long-Term Bonds	9.12%	0.00%	10.81%	N/A	5.90%	10.53%	N/A
Bond	High-Yield Bond	9.37%	0.00%	7.95%	N/A	7.40%	9.20%	N/A
Stock	Large-Cap Value Stocks	12.09%	0.00%	13.21%	N/A	8.10%	16.00%	N/A
Stock	Large-Cap Growth Stocks	11.51%	0.00%	16.65%	N/A	8.80%	19.50%	N/A
Stock	Small-Cap Stocks	16.71%	0.00%	19.80%	N/A	9.90%	22.20%	N/A
Stock	Small-Cap Value	16.42%	0.00%	17.71%	N/A	8.60%	19.30%	N/A
Stock	Small-Cap Growth	12.08%	0.00%	22.48%	N/A	11.10%	25.90%	N/A
Stock	International Developed Stocks	12.49%	0.00%	20.33%	N/A	8.90%	20.10%	N/A
Stock	International Emerging Stocks	12.31%	0.00%	27.97%	N/A	9.80%	27.50%	N/A
Stock	REIT	13.22%	0.00%	17.32%	N/A	8.40%	15.50%	N/A
Bond	Emerging Market Debt	9.77%	0.00%	11.50%	N/A	7.50%	20.50%	N/A
Absolute return	Absolute Return	12.57%	0.00%	9.00%	N/A	9.00%	9.00%	N/A
Stock	Tax-Managed Large Cap	12.57%	0.00%	17.50%	N/A	8.20%	17.50%	N/A
Stock	Tax-Managed Small Cap	16.71%	0.00%	22.20%	N/A	9.90%	22.20%	N/A
Absolute return	Real Asset	9.56%	0.00%	21.54%	N/A	9.00%	15.00%	N/A
Absolute return	Private Equity	12.57%	0.00%	29.00%	N/A	14.00%	29.00%	N/A
Stock	Opportunistic Equity	12.57%	0.00%	20.00%	N/A	9.00%	15.00%	N/A
Bond	Enhanced Fixed Income	8.55%	0.00%	10.00%	N/A	6.90%	10.00%	N/A

Source: Tuttle Wealth Management, LLC.

performing well and less to the one that isn't. You need to fight that impulse. Changes should be made when things have changed fundamentally in the markets. For example, the subprime crisis of 2007 fundamentally changed the markets. Going into 2008 we shifted to a much higher bond portion than normal because we believed stocks would be hurt by economic weakness, but we also believed that absolute return investments might not fare well, either. While absolute return investments are designed to deliver absolute return, they won't always be up to the task. In markets where there are severe dislocations and where assets that usually are not correlated become correlated, absolute return strategies can be hurt. Keep an eye on what's going on and how your portfolio is reacting to it. You don't want to change your asset allocation willy-nilly, but you do want to take a good solid look at it at least every quarter.

You can also use an opportunistic overlay like we do. A part of your portfolio can be managed to take advantage of short- and intermediate-term opportunities, while the bulk of your portfolio is invested for the long term.

Step 4: Rebalance Your Asset Classes

I am not a huge fan of the inflexible rebalancing that most investors do. For each asset class, you should have your target asset allocation and tolerance ranges. So, for example, you might decide to have a target allocation of 35% in stocks with a range of 30% to 40%. If your stock portfolio is going up, you wouldn't rebalance until it got to 40% of your overall portfolio. All rebalancing should also be done in conjunction with a review of your asset allocation.

Half the Battle

Deciding how your assets are going to be allocated is the most important step, but it is only half the battle. It provides a framework for the next chapter, which will discuss how to choose money managers to manage your asset allocation.

CHAPTER 19

Choosing and Managing Money Managers

The final implementation step in creating your endowment portfolio is picking the actual money managers to manage its different parts. Again, this is a very complex process and not for the faint of heart. Picking money managers and monitoring them takes work. If you are not willing to do that, then please get the help of a professional. We have visits from at least two money managers every week. We talk to many more over the phone, and I can't tell you how many e-mails I get from money managers we work with or are considering using.

For the remainder of this discussion, when I use the term *money manager,* I am referring to mutual funds, separately managed accounts, ETFs, hedge funds, funds of funds, and private equity. I will not discuss individual stocks or bonds here. They can be perfectly valid for your portfolio but require much more time and expertise to choose and monitor.

Looking at Qualitative Criteria

This chapter will explain the process we use to evaluate and choose money managers. If you are doing this on your own you are probably better off using just mutual funds and/or ETFs. You will need access to some sort of financial database such as Morningstar. A less-sophisticated approach might be to select one or two fund companies with a broad lineup of funds that you can research in depth.

Here are the steps you should follow:

- *Criteria.* The first thing we must do is define what type of manager we are looking for: stock, bond, real asset, and so on. In the previous chapter, you went through your risk tolerance and have decided on what asset classes you should have and what percent should be in each. Now you are ready to pick the money managers.
- *Philosophy.* We look for specialist money managers who have a clearly defined investment philosophy and style (not fixed to a style box but a style that they could explain), that has been consistently applied over many years. You will come across many funds that have not been around for many years. For those, you need to do a little extra homework on the manager to get a feel for what they were doing before the new fund was launched.
- *Discipline.* We then note how the firms put the philosophy into action and make sure there is some sort of discipline regarding decisions (similar to how we recommend individuals have a specific investment methodology).
- *Consistency.* We compare the managers' performance against the relevant benchmarks to determine whether their performance is consistent with their investment process and what we would expect.
- *Talent.* When you hire money managers, you would prefer that they are talented and good at what they do. We look for firms that are well managed and able to attract and retain the best investment talent. All things being equal, we prefer a team approach to managing money rather than relying on one star manager.
- *Money Managers Who Put Their Money Where Their Mouth Is.* We believe that you should invest with money managers who put their money in their own funds. It always amazes me how a fund can say how great it is, but the money manager won't put any of his or her own money in it. If I was managing a mutual fund and I had confidence in my investment skill, why wouldn't I put my own money in my fund?

  If you remember back to the mutual fund scandals of the past few years, they were by and large committed by people who didn't have their own money in their funds. If you had a substantial amount of money in your fund, would you commit a crime to the detriment of shareholders? Probably not. The last reason why I think this is important is that if portfolio managers have a lot of money in their own fund, they will care even more than I do if it is down.

- *Good at Managing Money, Bad at Marketing.* We look for companies who are good at managing money but who don't put a lot of time or money in marketing themselves. There is only so much money a mutual fund can handle. Even the best mutual fund manager can have too much money to invest. Mutual funds that have large positions in stocks can also have a hard time buying and selling without moving the market against them. For these reasons, we prefer smaller funds that few people have heard of. Once the public hears about a good fund, they pour money into it, which can hurt the fund's performance.

  Along those same lines, we prefer companies where the owners are the money managers. Their main goals tend to be performance, which is yours also. Large public money management firms have a conflict. The shareholders want to see earnings, which mean fees from assets. These firms tend to focus much more on gathering assets than on managing money. That is not to say that large money management firms don't have good managers and funds, but all things being equal, I would probably choose a smaller, less marketing-focused company over a larger asset gatherer.

- *Fit.* We might find a great manager, but she may be very similar to an existing manager we already use. We would rather find managers whose performance is not in line with other managers we are using. This is called *correlation*; we are looking for managers who have a low correlation with each other.

The Numbers

When choosing managers, you also need to look at the numbers.

- *Correlation.* You want money managers that aren't that correlated with the overall market or the other money managers in your portfolio. You don't need fancy software to figure out correlation. Just put the return numbers down next to the returns of the market and other managers you are using, and you will be able to get a pretty solid idea.

- *Modern Portfolio Statistics.* You want to look at the beta (looking for a low beta), alpha (looking for a high alpha), standard deviation (looking for a low standard deviation), and the Sharpe ratio (looking for a high Sharpe ratio). For mutual funds you can get these from Morningstar. Any hedge fund or fund of funds can also supply these numbers. Remember, you need to compare apples to apples; you can't compare these numbers for a bond fund and a stock fund.
- *Maximum Drawdown.* This is especially important for managed futures and hedge funds. It gives you an idea historically of the worst loss the manager has sustained. If it is beyond your comfort zone, then don't invest. I am not aware of a resource that gives you this information for mutual funds, but I wish one existed.

Look Beyond the Performance Numbers

It is not enough to know what the performance numbers of a money manager are, you also need to know how they got that performance. As of 6/3/08 the three-year average annual return of the Caldwell & Orkin Market Opportunity fund was 11.30% a year. That beat the S&P 500 by 4.50% a year. That looks like a great return, but we need to examine those numbers more thoroughly. Table 19.1 shows the performance history of the fund from January 1, 2000, to May 31, 2008.

Even though the three-year average annual return is great, it was all caused by 2007 when the fund was up 33.1%. Every other year has been mediocre, to say the least. A review of their web site

Table 19.1   Caldwell & Orkin Market Opportunity Performance

Performance History 05-31-08	2001	2002	2003	2004	2005	2006	2007	05/2008
Total return %	−3.8	2.9	−6.6	−1.0	−0.1	7.4	33.1	−4.9
±Index	8.1	25.0	−35.3	−11.9	−5.0	−8.4	27.6	−1.1
± Category	−9.2	0.9	−15.0	−6.1	−4.9	0.2	28.7	−4.2
% Rank in category	92	52	94	100	78	38	1	86

Source: Caldwell & Orkin.

Table 19.2   Hussman Strategic Growth Performance

	2001	2002	2003
Total return %	14.7	14.0	21.1

Source: Hussman Funds.

shows that a lot of that year's performance was from being short the right companies at the right time. I have nothing against this fund, but the track record makes it hard to believe that they can repeat what they did in 2007.

Hussman Strategic Growth is another example. Table 19.2 shows the fund's performance from 2001–2003.

As you can see, the results are very impressive. However, if we now look at the performance from 2001 to May 31, 2008, in Table 19.3, it doesn't look quite as good.

Table 19.3   Hussman Strategic Growth Performance—Extended

Performance History 05-31-08	2001	2002	2003	2004	2005	2006	2007	05/2008
Total return %	14.7	14.0	21.1	5.2	5.7	3.5	4.2	0.3
± Index	26.6	36.1	−7.6	−5.7	0.8	−12.3	−1.3	4.1
± Category	9.3	12.0	12.6	0.1	0.9	−3.7	−0.3	1.0
% Rank in category	8	20	23	32	38	84	50	31

Source: Hussman Funds.

Markets are constantly changing. Strategies that worked in one market environment don't necessarily work in a different environment. Again, I have nothing against this fund, but purely looking at the numbers might lead me to believe that the strategy does not work very well in this type of environment.

Most people just look at performance, but to design a robust portfolio you must go beyond that. Performance is important, but it is equally, if not more, important to know how the money manager achieved that performance. Was it generated from a well-timed bet on a certain sector or was it generated by the consistent application of a well-thought-out investment philosophy? Let's say I am looking at two funds to decide which one I would rather invest in: Caldwell & Orkin Market Opportunity and BlackRock Global Allocation A. (Please note that BlackRock Global has a front-end load, which I

Table 19.4   BlackRock Global Allocation A vs. Caldwell & Orkin Market Opportunity

Fund	3-Year Average Annual Return
BlackRock Global Allocation A	13.03%
Caldwell & Orkin	12.48%

Table 19.5   BlackRock Global Allocation A

Performance History 05-31-08	2001	2002	2003	2004	2005	2006	2007	05/2008
Total return %	1.9	−8.0	36.0	14.3	10.3	15.9	16.7	1.5
±- Index	4.4	−0.9	8.8	1.1	3.1	4.0	8.7	1.5
± Category	5.1	−5.8	10.7	−1.0	3.8	−0.7	5.3	2.6
% Rank in category	31	70	10	61	12	53	14	15

Source: BlackRock Funds.

Table 19.6   Caldwell & Orkin Market Opportunity

Performance History 05-31-08	2001	2002	2003	2004	2005	2006	2007	05/2008
Total return %	−3.8	2.9	−6.6	−1.0	−0.1	7.4	33.1	−4.9
± Index	8.1	25.0	−35.3	−11.9	−5.0	−8.4	27.6	−1.1
± Category	−9.2	0.9	−15.0	−6.1	−4.9	0.2	28.7	−4.2
% Rank in category	92	52	94	100	78	38	1	86

Source: Caldwell & Orkin.

am ignoring for this analysis.) The three-year average annual return for each is shown in Table 19.4.

The performance is nearly identical, but we need to look beyond average annual returns. First, let's look at the year-by-year numbers in Tables 19.5 and 19.6.

BlackRock has had fairly consistent performance year in and year out, while Caldwell & Orkin had the one great year that drove up its three-year number.

That analysis is helpful, but we are still not done. We also need to look at the risk-adjusted numbers: standard deviation, Sharpe ratio, and alpha. Table 19.7 shows the numbers for each.

In the case of these two funds, alpha is not much help as Morningstar calculates it against two different indexes. However, it

Table 19.7 BlackRock Global Allocation vs. Caldwell & Orkin Market Opportunity

Fund	Standard Deviation	Sharpe Ratio	Alpha
BlackRock Global	5.74	1.74	5.68*
Caldwell & Orkin	8.14	0.84	7.40**

* Alpha calculated on Dow Jones Moderate Portfolio Index.

** Alpha calculated on S&P 500.

isn't really that necessary since standard deviation and Sharpe ratio tell the story. BlackRock has generated slightly higher returns and has taken much less risk to do it. In this comparison, the BlackRock fund wins just based on the numbers.

You are still not done, however, as you now want to go beyond the numbers and read the prospectus, annual and semiannual reports, and talk to the fund company to get a comfort level with the fund's philosophy and how it fits into your portfolio. Many fund companies will have well-educated people who can tell you about the fund, its managers, and its objectives. Unfortunately, many others will not.

As a financial advisor, I have an advantage as most fund companies have wholesalers who are responsible for getting the word out about their funds. They tend to be very knowledgeable not only about their funds but also about their competitors, and can be a great source of knowledge.

Time to Monitor

As mentioned in Chapter 18, once you have diversified and chosen your investments, you must monitor them constantly to make sure they are performing as you would expect. There are a number of events that could cause you to consider replacing money managers.

- *Change in Organization.* When you invest your money with money managers, you need to keep up with them and what they are doing. A good hedge fund of funds will know their managers so well that they know what they eat for breakfast. You don't have to hire a private investigator (however, if you are talking about millions of dollars you might want to), but you do have to keep track of what is going on. Read the reports that they send and look for warning signs. Some signs might be a portfolio manager leaving, research staff leaving, and so on.

- *Poor Performance.* Keep in mind that you are expecting each manager to generate performance relative to something. An absolute return manager will not keep track with the S&P 500 during a large up year, and you wouldn't expect him to. However, if the market is down 10% and your absolute return manager is down 12%, then something might be wrong. You should have expectations for each manager on how they should perform based on their style and mandate. If they don't perform as expected, you need to do some research to figure out why. If you don't like the answer, then consider moving on.

- *Fast Growth.* Fast growth is good for money managers' fees, but may not be good for investors. An index fund based on a large and diverse index like the S&P 500 can grow to just about any size, but a mutual fund that buys very small stocks cannot. Keep an eye on money growth and performance. Also keep an eye on whether growth in assets results in a change in investment objective.

- *Better Managers.* You should always be on the lookout for better money managers than what you currently have. We always have a backup group of money managers that didn't make the first cut, but that we track for the future. Often this is because they haven't been around long enough or they invest in a style that we don't think we need right now, but might need in the future.

- *Red Ferrari Syndrome.* This is something that mostly applies to hedge fund managers. When hedge fund managers start out, they are usually hungry to be successful and work 80 hours a week to try to uncover the best investments and have great performance. Once they become successful, they sometimes have the tendency to go out and buy fancy cars, fancy houses, and spend more time going to the right parties with the right people than managing money. Hedge funds require a higher degree of scrutiny than do mutual funds. You probably don't need to watch over the personal life of your mutual fund manager, but your hedge fund manager is a different story. If the performance isn't what it used to be, if the attention to detail isn't what it used to be, or if you keep seeing your hedge fund manager in the society pages instead of the business pages, then he or she could have Red Ferrari Syndrome.

- *Calling in Rich.* This is another issue related to hedge fund managers, and it is somewhat related to Red Ferrari Syndrome. Since most hedge fund managers have most of their money in their own funds, their investment style might change as they get richer. For example, when managers are just starting out, they may take high risks to achieve high returns. As their funds and their net worths grow, they may decide that they no longer need to grow their money and they become more interested in preserving it. This may make a fund manager who has historically taken large risks and delivered large returns much more conservative in his investment style. While this might be great for him, it may not be what investors are looking for. Keep an eye on communications from the fund and see if things change as the fund gets larger and the manager gets richer.

How Much to Allocate to Each Manager

Once you have chosen your money managers, you have to figure out what percent of your portfolio you will allocate to each one. We typically will not allocate more than 5% to any one money manager unless they are a bond fund, which will be less volatile; a fund of funds which gives us access to many money managers; or tracking an index where we don't have to worry about manager skills. There are cases where we find exceptional managers and will go over 5%, but rarely 10%. Let's say you decide to have 20% in stocks and have found four money managers who are uncorrelated to each other and everything else looks good. I would not be averse to giving 5% to each one. You can get more complex and use volatility to decide how much to allocate to each one or sometimes a simple approach works just as well. You want to make sure that the performance, or lack thereof, of any one manager cannot have a huge effect on your portfolio. Even the best money managers have off months, quarters, and years.

You Are Almost Ready to Go

You have now determined your asset allocation and your money managers, but you're not done yet. The next step is to put it all together and integrate your portfolio into your personal situation. Chapters 20 and 21 will focus on this.

20

Putting It All Together

Endowments invest their money for a reason. They need to be able to generate enough money for their university to meet its spending objectives and they need their assets to last indefinitely. What is your reason for investing? This chapter will focus on determining how you are investing your money in an endowment type portfolio.

Changing Your Views about Investing

In this book we talked a lot about investor mistakes and a need for new thinking. Nowhere is this better illustrated than the technology bubble of the late 1990s and the subsequent collapse. Endowments invest their money based on their goals of generating respectable real returns so that they can spend according to policy. Individual investors typically invest to beat the market with no real thought to what they are really trying to accomplish. During the bull market of the 1980s and 1990s, it was easy to overlook this flaw, as everyone was making truckloads of money. When you are earning 20% per year, then you are probably achieving your goals by default. The decline of 2000–2002 and the subsequent market uncertainty highlighted this issue and started an entirely new field of study called behavioral finance. With the understanding that individual investors didn't behave rationally, behavioral finance practitioners sought to understand how they actually did behave. This study is summarized in the following table.

Table 20.1   Traditional View vs. Individual Investor View

	Traditional View of Market Risks and Goals	Individual Investor's Actual View of Risks and Goals
Objective	• Seek performance in line with the markets	• Achieve goal • Protect against loss • Generate income • Growth
Risk measure	• Standard deviation • Risk relative to benchmark	• Risk of loss • Risk of not meeting goal
Return measure	• Annualized return • Cumulative return	• Reaching target goal value • Absolute return • Stable return stream • Stable cash flow
Reference point	• Return relative to benchmark	• High watermark • Goal attainment

In the next few sections we will discuss each of these issues.

Objective

The traditional view of investing was to always beat or match some benchmark. This was played out in the whole argument over whether it was better to buy index funds and match the return of the market, or to buy actively managed funds to try to beat the market. Beating or matching the market, however, is irrelevant (and perhaps dangerous) if you don't achieve your goals. Assume that you are 55 and your goal is to retire at 65, and you want me to design a plan to get you there. Now it's 10 years later, and I have some good news and some bad news. The good news is that over the 10 years, the market averaged 6% per year and your portfolio averaged 7% per year. We beat the market. The bad news is that you still have to work another 10 years until you can retire. Are you happy? You beat the market, but you are nowhere near reaching your goal.

Another objective that individual investors have is to protect against loss no matter what the market does. Assume you walked into my office in 2000 with $1 million to invest. I come back to you at the end of 2002, again with some good news and some bad news. Your portfolio is now worth $700,000; we lost $300,000, but we beat the market over that period. Are you happy? I doubt it.

If you are retired, you might also want to generate income to maintain your lifestyle. You need a certain amount coming in every month, regardless of what the market does.

Risk Measure

The traditional view of investing measures risk by either standard deviation or risk relative to a benchmark like the S&P 500.
Unfortunately, most individual investors do not know what standard
deviation means. (I do define it in the Appendix, which is at the very
end of the book.) Let's say you are a client of mine, and again I have
some good news and bad news. The bad news is that your portfolio
lost $100,000 this month. The good news is that the overall standard
deviation of the portfolio is only 4 while the standard deviation of
the S&P 500 was 10. Are you happy with that? Again, I doubt it.

When individual investors think about risk, they think about the
risk of losing money or the risk of not achieving their goal. Nobody
has ever asked me what the standard deviation of their investment
portfolio was.

Return Measure

The traditional view looks at return as annualized or cumulative
return. When individual investors look at those numbers, they
only tell part of the story. Individual investors also need to look at
their progress toward their goals, whether they lost any money, and
whether they had a stable return stream and/or a stable cash flow.

I believe that this decade will be the decade of absolute return.
Investors won't care as much about trying to match or beat the
market. They will be more concerned with beating zero, or beating what they could earn on a short-term CD. I have talked a lot
about this throughout the book. Finally the mutual fund industry
is starting to develop more and more products that focus on absolute return. That is what our firm is concerned with. We don't care
about beating the market; we just don't want to lose money.

How the market does is irrelevant (or should be) to the individual. Progress should be measured by how close you are to achieving
your goal. Think about it. If your goal is to generate $50,000 per
year (indexed for inflation) for the rest of your life, does it really
matter what your investments are doing in the market if you are
able to achieve your goal?

Reference Point

The traditional view uses return versus a benchmark as the reference
point. Individual investors look at goal attainment. Individual investors

also look at the high watermark of their portfolio. For example, let's say you came to me with $1 million in 1995. By the end of 1999, let's assume your portfolio had grown to $2 million. Are you happy with that? Who wouldn't be happy about doubling their money? Now let's say that at the end of 2002 your portfolio had declined to $1.5 million. How do you look at that? Do you look at the fact that you started with $1 million and gained $500,000 over seven years or do you look at the fact that you had $2 million and you lost $500,000? Most individual investors look at this as a loss of $500,000. They use the high watermark, in this case $2 million, as their reference point for gains and losses.

Goals-Based Investing

Understanding that individual investors don't behave rationally means that we can do one of two things: We can try to educate individuals to behave rationally (like how my wife tries to educate me to put the toilet seat down, take out the garbage, and mow the lawn), or we could design portfolios for the way investors actually behave. Since I believe in taking the path of least resistance, I believe in designing portfolios for the way you actually think. Goals-based investing, which was developed by SEI Investments, does that.

Goals-based investing rests upon two key tenets:

1. You have unique goals and objectives.
2. Each goal requires a unique portfolio.

The traditional way to manage money involves figuring out a client's risk tolerance and his or her needed or expected portfolio return, and then creating a diversified portfolio. Although this approach is valid, it has a number of limitations.

1. It assumes that you have one risk input, meaning you either prefer low, medium, or high risk. How individuals think about risk, however, tends to depend on their goal. For example, the risk you would be willing to take if your goal was to generate income to fund your lifestyle would probably be drastically different from the risk you were willing to take if you were saving up to buy a boat.
2. Traditional theory assumes that all goals have the same priority and time frame. This is not true. Some goals are more

important than others and can have vastly different time horizons. Because goals have different time frames and priorities, different portfolios for each goal may be warranted.

Constructing Goal-Based Portfolios

Constructing a goal-based portfolio is a four-step process.

Step 1: Define and Categorize Your Goals

Your endowment portfolio goals generally fall into one of four categories: want-to-now, want-to-later, have-to-now, and have-to-later. Want-to-now goals are things that you would like to have now. Want-to-later goals are goals that you would like to have later. Have-to-now goals are goals that you must have now. Have-to-later goals are goals that you must have later. The have-to goals obviously take precedence over the want-to goals. Table 20.1 shows the different types of goals investors have.

Goals-based investing would have a different portfolio for each of these types of goals. For example, if your have-to-now goal is to fund your current lifestyle, the objectives for this portfolio may be to protect against market declines and allow you to maintain your spending level. On the other hand, a want-to-later goal might be to save enough money to buy a boat. The objectives for this portfolio may be to aggressively grow assets for the long term.

Step 2: Allocate Your Resources

Once your goals have been identified, you must figure out how much resources you have to allocate to each goal. This is also where prioritization comes into play; it is possible that you will not have enough resources to fund all of your goals. Figure 20.1 shows the difference between the traditional approach versus a goals-based approach.

Table 20.2   Types of Goals

Want-to-Now Goals	Want-to-Later Goals	Have-to-Now Goals	Have-to-Later Goals
Short time horizon	Long time horizon	Short time horizon	Long time horizon
Low-priority	Low-priority	High-priority	High-priority

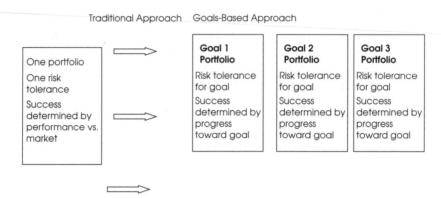

Figure 20.1   Traditional Approach vs. Goals-Based Approach

The traditional approach has one portfolio and one risk tolerance, and success is determined by performance versus the market. This one portfolio is expected to meet the needs of each goal. The goals-based approach has one portfolio for each goal, one risk tolerance for each goal, and success is determined by progress toward the goals. (See Table 20.3.) For example, if you have two goals—one to retire comfortably and the other to buy a boat—it is likely that you would invest money differently for each. Also, the success or failure of your strategy is not whether you beat the market, it is whether you achieve each of your goals.

The goals-based approach increases the likelihood of achieving your goals and manages the limitations of traditional investment theory, since there is no longer one risk input.

Endowments have it easy. They have only one goal—to generate high enough real returns to spend according to plan. Individuals can have many different goals.

Table 20.3   Different Goals Have Different Strategies

Goal	Portfolio Objective	Strategy
Maintain current lifestyle	Competitive return/control risk of loss	Stability focused
Future retirement	Competitive returns while protecting portfolio value at retirement date	Time focused
Leave pool of money to children—Legacy	Competitive returns while controlling risk vs. the market	Market focused
Discretionary money	Aggressive returns	Growth focused

Step 3: Determine Your Risks and Challenges

Table 20.4 lists some of the goals you might have and what risks and challenges you may face in trying to achieve those goals.

Spend some time to think about what your goals are and categorize them by want-to-now, want-to-later, have-to-now, and have-to-later. Then write down all the challenges and risks you can think of for each goal.

Be sure that your goals align with your risk tolerance, or else you will need to make some changes to one of them or to each. For example, let's say I have $100,000 and I want to retire in 10 years and be able to generate $25,000 per year from my portfolio. Let's also assume that I am very conservative. Something has to give as a very conservative portfolio has no real chance of achieving my goals. I either need to change my goals, be willing to accept more risk, or both.

Now that you have your goals, you will use them to create your Investment Policy Statement, which we will talk about in the next chapter.

Table 20.4   Goal Examples

Life Goals	Real Risks and Challenges
Current lifestyle	Have I saved enough? Do I have enough for my current lifestyle? Will unexpected expenses derail my other goals?
Charitable contributions	What if I don't have enough to contribute?
Vacation home	What if I don't have enough money to buy a vacation home? What if I don't grow my money aggressively enough?
Retire at 65	Can I afford to take on new hobbies or travel as much as I would like to? Will my spouse want to retire before me or after me? What if I can't work until 65? What if the cost of my lifestyle increases?

Step 4: Track Your Progress

When you are focused on your goals, tracking your performance is a little different. Again, while it is nice to beat the market, it isn't that relevant to your goals. If your goal is to generate $50,000 per year in income and to grow your portfolio to keep pace with inflation,

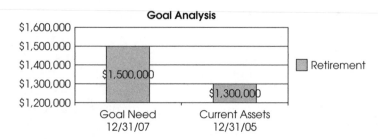

Figure 20.2   Goal Analysis

how did you do or how are you doing relative to your goal? You can use many free Internet programs to figure out how much money you need to reach your goals. You can then benchmark where you are versus where you need to be.

Figure 20.2 is an example of a simple tracking method you can employ. You can create this tracking method in an Excel spreadsheet.

Do You Need Help?

Now that you have the components for designing your investment plan, the next question is should you hire someone to help you or should you do it yourself?

In his landmark book, *Values-Based Financial Planning*, Bill Bachrach identified three different types of investors: do-it-your-selfers, collaborators, and delegators.

Do-it-yourselfers are people who make all of their decisions by themselves. They typically work with discount brokers and enjoy studying the markets and financial products and strategies. To be an effective do-it-yourselfer, you need to be as knowledgeable and competent as a professional, which means that someone else would reasonably hire you to manage their finances. Let's say I walked into your office one day, and I told you that I had no clients and had never really managed money before other than my own. I go on to tell you that I watch CNBC from time to time and read *Money* maga-zine, so I think I have a pretty firm grasp on financial matters. Even if I make a mistake, I am sure that I will learn from it and not make it again. Would you hire me? Probably not. If you explained your personal finance qualifications, would anyone hire you? If not, why should you hire yourself?

Another thing you might want to think about is this. Suppose you are very knowledgeable about investments. You do your homework on a particular mutual fund. You know the manager's track record, the standard deviation compared to like funds, the expense ratio compared to like funds, the alpha, the style, and the Sharpe ratio. Let's assume all of this work takes you three hours, and the fund has a 10% return. Now let's assume another investor works with a competent financial professional who does the work for him, and he also gets a 10% return. Instead of spending three hours on research, he went out to play golf or played with his children or grandchildren. Which investor had the better return: the investor who earned 10% or the investor who earned 10% and lost three hours of time?

That being said, if you enjoy doing the work and are good at what you do, then being a do-it-yourselfer might be for you.

Collaborators are people who make lots of their own decisions but look to a professional for help in certain areas. They might research their own investments and then call their stockbroker to just run it by them. A collaborator is usually either someone who wants to be a do-it-yourselfer but isn't confident enough yet or someone who wants to be a delegator but hasn't found anyone he or she trusts to delegate to. A collaborator is usually better off working with a financial products salesperson or finding a financial planner to delegate to.

A *delegator* is someone who would rather spend time not worrying about money. Delegators need to work with an investment advisor and/or financial planner to whom they can comfortably delegate all their financial affairs. A delegator realizes that there are more important things in life than money, such as financial health, mental health, relational health, spiritual health, and physical health. Of all these areas, financial health is the only one a person can delegate. (While life would be great if someone else could do your workout for you, I guarantee that this won't work.) Delegators delegate their financial health so that they can focus on those other areas.

A delegator realizes that there are only 168 hours per week and that the quality of life is directly related to how those 168 hours are spent. You could spend them watching CNBC, reading the *Wall Street Journal* and *Money* magazine, and watching over every aspect of your finances, or you could spend them playing golf, spending time with your family, and traveling. A delegator realizes that financial planning is not about how the hot fund of the month is performing, it's about quality of life.

For every activity in our life, we can do one of four things: delegate it, drop it, do it, or delay it—the four Ds. Our ability to delegate will directly affect what we can get done during the day and, ultimately, the quality of our lives.

Delegate It

So many people seem to have a problem with delegation. Either we are control freaks and are afraid to delegate something to somebody else, or we are worried that we cannot afford to delegate work to somebody else. I recently hired a new operations manager for my company and delegated to him all of the administrative tasks that I didn't enjoy doing and that I didn't need to do. Another advisor I talked to thought I was crazy to hire someone to do what I could do myself. He has always done everything himself, yet he is constantly struggling to stay in business while my practice is thriving. In the short-term, profitability was down, but in the long run it increased because I was able to concentrate more on the important things that only I can do.

Drop It

I once heard a story from a successful financial advisor at a large brokerage firm. All of the other advisors in his firm had in-boxes on the corner of their desks to receive the reams of reports and memos that were dropped off during the day. Instead of having an in-box, this advisor put a large recycle box at the corner of his desk. Whenever anyone would drop something on his desk, he would immediately sweep it into the box unread. That might sound crazy, but this advisor was one of the most successful in his office. While others spent time poring over documents that weren't important, he spent his time building his business.

How much of what takes up your time on a day-to-day basis could you just drop? How much time would that free up for what is more important?

Do It

In a perfect world, you would only do those tasks you enjoy doing and those tasks that only you can do, everything else would be delegated or dropped. Imagine the quality of your life if the only things

Table 20.5   How Do You Spend a Week?

Task	Is it delegable? (Y/N)	Are you the only one who can do it? (Y/N)	Do you enjoy doing it? (Y/N)	Can it be dropped? (Y/N)

in your to-do box were the tasks that you enjoyed doing or that only you could do.

How do you structure your life this way? Use the worksheet in Table 20.5, take an ordinary week, and note every activity you do. Next to the activity, indicate whether it is delegable, indicate if it is something that only you can do, then indicate whether it is something you enjoy, and finally indicate whether it is something that can be dropped.

Once you have your list, sort out those things that can be dropped and drop them. Sort out those things that do not require your attention and can be delegated, and find someone to delegate them to. You will be left with a list of worthwhile things.

Different Types of Advisors

To make things even more complicated, there are a number of different types of advisors and a number of different ways advisors get compensated. Methods of compensating advisors generally fall into one of four categories: fee-only, fee-based, commission, and hourly.

Fee-Only. Fee-only advisors are solely compensated by fees, either charged as a percentage of assets they manage, a retainer, and/or a financial planning fee. Fee-only advisors do not sell products and will either use no commission insurance products or refer insurance needs to a commission-based insurance advisor. A fee-only advisor could be a good choice for a financial delegator.

Fee-Based. Fee-based advisors will usually be compensated by a mix of fees and commissions. For example, a fee-based advisor may charge a fee to manage assets but might earn commissions on insurance products. A fee-based advisor could be a good choice for a financial delegator.

Commission. Commission-based advisors generally earn commissions on investment and/or insurance products. A commission-based advisor could be a good choice for a do-it-yourselfer or collaborator.

Hourly. Hourly advisors usually give advice on an as-needed basis; they sell no insurance or investment products and don't manage any assets. They charge based on an hourly rate. An hourly advisor could be a good choice for a do-it-yourselfer or a collaborator.

Advisors also work in different locations as brokerage firm advisors, insurance company advisors, and independent advisors.

Brokerage Firm Advisors. Advisors in brokerage firms could either be fee-only, fee-based, or commission-based. How they get compensated is ultimately their choice. When dealing with a brokerage firm, you are usually dealing with a company with a household name, which may give you a comfort level. Brokerage firms tend to have proprietary products and incentives to sell them. They also tend not to have that much sophistication with insurance products.

Insurance Company Advisors. Insurance company advisors could either be fee-based or commission-based. It is unlikely that they will be fee only. When dealing with an insurance company, you are also usually dealing with a household name. Insurance companies also have proprietary products and quotas to sell them. They tend to not be as sophisticated on the investment side.

Independent Advisors. Independent advisors can either be fee-only, fee-based, commission-based, or hourly. When dealing with independent advisors, they are usually not household names. But they have no proprietary products to sell, and therefore there will be fewer conflicts of interest.

My Firm

I spent a few years in a large brokerage firm and a few years working for large insurance companies. I did not like the focus on proprietary products and sales quotas. I felt that it was difficult to put client needs ahead of the needs of the firm. Because of this, I made the decision to become independent. I had a choice of either joining an independent broker and still being able to earn commissions on investments or becoming a registered investment advisor (RIA) and giving up my ability to earn commissions on investments. I decided on the RIA route and have never looked back. I do maintain my insurance license and ability to earn commissions on insurance because I believe that if I refer insurance needs to a commission-based advisor who only gets compensated if insurance is sold, there will still be a conflict of interest. Since I am doing the work anyway, then I might as well earn the commission. This makes me fee-based. My practice focuses on the recurring revenue that comes from our fees so that insurance commissions are not a major focus.

Designations

There are hundreds of designations that advisors can have. Some of them have rigorous requirements, whereas others can be obtained in a couple of hours. This is an area where many regulators are cracking down, so don't judge an advisor solely based on designations.

In my practice I made the decision to become a certified financial planner (CFP) practitioner. While I don't believe that this makes me smarter than anyone else, I do believe that there should be one respected designation for the financial planning field like the CPA is for accountants. I believe that the CFP designation will ultimately be that.

Advisor Criteria

Here are some things you should look for when searching for an advisor. You should look for someone who:

- Has been providing advisory services for compensation for at least five years
- Has a clean regulatory record
- Has worked often with people similar to you
- Routinely provides recommendations in the same areas that are of concern to you
- Takes the time to learn of your needs before offering recommendations to you

- Considers the tax implications of their strategies before recommending them to you
- Will review your status in all major areas of personal finance, including investments, insurance, taxes, real estate and mortgages, college and retirement issues, employer-provided benefit plans, and estate planning, and offer you recommendations as warranted.

Your First Meeting with an Advisor

There are many magazine articles, web sites, and books that will give you lists of questions to ask prospective advisors. In their view, your first meeting with an advisor should be all about your asking them questions. I disagree. I believe that your first meeting with an advisor should be all about his or her asking you questions. Let's say you wanted to know if I was a good golfer or not. What would be the best way to find out? Would you rather ask me, or would you rather watch me play golf? If you just ask me about my golf game, I could tell you about my great handicap, all the courses I have played, and how great I am; you might even believe me. If you watch me play golf, however, it won't take you very long to find out that I have no idea what I am doing. The same holds true for a financial advisor. You can ask an advisor all the questions you want, but the only way to truly know if he is competent is to watch him work, and the only way to watch him work is to see how he handles a first meeting with a prospective client.

Often, when I tell people this, the response is that they just don't know enough about the industry to know if someone is good at what he or she does. I don't believe that's the case. You may not understand the industry, but after meeting with someone for an hour or so you should have a pretty good feeling about whether you feel she is competent or not. For example, one day a few years ago my son, who was two at the time, was having problems with eczema on his legs. We brought him to the medical practice we always go to, and a doctor we had never worked with came into the room. Instantly it was clear that he was the oldest doctor in the practice, so my first thought was that maybe he was the founder and the most experienced partner. Then my son got a little cranky. Now I know nothing about medicine, but I figure pediatricians are used to dealing with cranky kids. This guy started getting cranky himself, like this was the first time he ever saw a cranky child. Now I also have to figure that eczema is a pretty common childhood ailment and that any pediatrician should be able to prescribe something right on the spot, but this doctor had to go out and get a desk reference guide and look up the treatment for eczema. Again, I don't know anything about medicine, but common sense would dictate that there should be a cream that can cure or help it. I later found out that there is a cream to treat eczema, but this doctor prescribed an oral steroid and a second drug to counteract the side effects of the steroid. He also told me that the medicine tasted so bad that I would have to force-feed it to my son. I know nothing about medicine, but I came out of this encounter feeling that the doctor was incompetent. I did not trust his advice.

Almost Done

At this point you have your asset allocation, your money managers, and you know why you are investing. Endowments take it one step further by putting everything in writing. The next chapter will focus on how you can create your own Investment Policy Statement like the endowments do.

21

Putting It in Writing

THE INVESTMENT POLICY STATEMENT

As mentioned in previous chapters, an endowment is required to have an Investment Policy Statement (IPS). An IPS lays out in writing your investment goals; your investment strategy; and how investments will be chosen, sold, and monitored. Having a well-thought-out IPS keeps you from making the mistakes that most investors make, because all investment decisions are made based on your IPS and not based on what the talking heads on CNBC are saying. There are five steps you need to take to develop your IPS:

1. Determine your goals
2. Determine your risk tolerance
3. Determine your investment objectives
4. Decide if you want any restrictions on your investments—socially responsible, environmentally friendly, and so on
5. Develop your investment methodology

Here is a sample IPS that has been replicated from Tuttle Wealth Management, LLC. (Please note that my comments are in *italics*.) The sections include:

I. Investment Policy Summary
II. Asset Allocation
III. Review Frequency
IV. Investment Philosophy

I. Investment Policy Summary

Investor	Sample Client (Investor)
Type of Assets	Trust Assets
Current Assets	Approximately $3,500,000
Investment Time Horizon	Greater Than 10 years
Return Objective	6% over CPI
Risk Tolerance	Moderate

II. Asset Allocation

Asset Class	Target	Range	Benchmark
Absolute Return	25%	20 to 50	HFRI Fund of Funds
Equity	30%	5 to 40	S&P 500
Fixed Income	15%	0 to 20	Lehman Brothers Aggregate
Energy & Natural Resources	25%	5 to 30	Dow Jones AIG
Real Estate	3%	3 to 30	Wilshire REIT
Cash	3%		
	100%		

The information above states the asset classes you will use, your initial allocation, the range that your allocation can move within, and what you will benchmark your asset classes against. The range determines when you will need to rebalance. If your objectives change and require you to allocate to an asset class outside of the range, then you will need to change your IPS. Please make sure that you are doing this because your circumstances have changed and not because we are in a bubble for some type of investment and you want to get in on it.

Once you determine your IPS, you should sign it even if you are not working with an advisor as it signifies that you are serious about following it. How often will you review your IPS and your investments? I recommend quarterly. Below is a sample of what you would sign.

III. Review Frequency

The Portfolio will be reviewed quarterly or sooner if major events require it.

> I have reviewed my investment policy and understand the risk and return parameters of the proposed investment strategy. I also recognize that this policy assumes at least a 5-year investment horizon. I will notify Tuttle Wealth Management, LLC (Advisor) if my circumstances change.
>
> Accepted _____ Date _____
>
> Accepted _____ Date _____

IV. Investment Philosophy

Our investment policy is structured using a combination of academic theory and informed market judgment. The six asset classes we use are defined by their expected response to economic conditions, such as price inflation, changes in interest rates, and are weighted in the portfolio by considering risk-adjusted returns and correlations.

Asset Classes

What is your asset allocation policy, and why? You should list the asset classes you are going to use and why you are going to use them. Below is a list of the asset classes you can use.

> *Absolute Return:* Absolute return managers seek to produce positive returns regardless of the direction of the stock market. They do this by employing market neutral strategies, merger arbitrage strategies, convertible arbitrage strategies, event-driven strategies, distressed debt strategies, long/short strategies, and so on.

Opportunistic Equity: Portfolio theory suggests that equities will produce higher long-term rates of return than less risky assets such as bonds and cash. The equity part of the allocation consists of managers who have the flexibility to invest across the style and market capitalization spectrum. We believe that this flexibility gives the equity portion of the portfolio the potential for higher returns with less risk. There can be no guarantee that this objective will be met.

Enhanced Fixed Income: Traditionally, fixed-income assets provide a stable return with little correlation to stocks. We are not particularly attracted to traditional fixed-income managers as we do not believe that they offer attractive risk/return characteristics versus our other asset classes. The enhanced fixed-income class is used for exposure to fixed-income sectors that exhibit value, currency diversification, and managers who have wide latitude.

Energy & Natural Resources: Energy and natural resources historically have provided attractive return prospects, excellent diversification, and a hedge against inflation.

Real Estate: Like energy and natural resources, real estate has also historically provided attractive return prospects, excellent diversification, and a hedge against inflation. Currently, our real estate portfolio consists entirely of investments overseas since that is where we see the most value.

We believe in maintaining a strategic asset allocation and reviewing the allocation quarterly. Changes are made based on our estimation of the future risk/return characteristics of various asset classes. We believe in rebalancing to the strategic asset allocation annually. However, the influence of taxes and transaction costs leads us to conclude that rebalancing with fairly wide bands of latitude is the most appropriate solution.

V. Introduction

Many of the illustrations in this plan involve the use of numbers because they are the most effective means of presenting a financial picture. These figures can lend an aura of false precision. Sets of numbers dealing with financial issues five years (and longer) down the road are not intended to be viewed as predictive but rather represent projections, based on a certain set of assumptions. While real-life events can rarely be predicted with accuracy, these projections are useful in comparing the likely results of different approaches and plans of action. If, upon reviewing this plan, you have any questions regarding the data or assumptions, please bring them to our attention.

The Role of the Investment Advisor

Our role at Tuttle Wealth Management, LLC (Advisor) is that of advisor and counselor. We have prepared an investment policy which, when followed consistently, will assist you in attempting to achieve your financial goals. The policy is based on your objectives and on generally accepted financial principles. Its implementation will increase the probability of attaining your goals while minimizing the volatility of your portfolio. The Advisor is a Registered Investment Advisor and shall act as the investment advisor and fiduciary to the Investor until the Investor decides otherwise. Advisor shall be responsible for:

1. Designing and implementing an appropriate asset allocation plan consistent with the investment objectives, time horizon, risk profile, guidelines and constraints outlined in this statement.
2. Recommending an appropriate custodian to safeguard the Investor's assets.
3. Advising the Investor about the selection of and the allocation of asset categories.
4. Identifying specific assets and investment managers within each asset category.
5. Monitoring the performance of all selected assets.
6. Recommending changes to this investment policy statement.
7. Being available to meet with the Investor within reason at the Investor's request.
8. Preparing and presenting appropriate reports.

Discretion and Title

The Advisor will not take title to any assets. Investor does grant Advisor discretionary authority for purchases and sales of Investor's securities. Advisor shall have no authority to withdraw funds from Investor's accounts, except to cover payment of previously agreed to fees or at Investor's specific direction.

Proxy Voting

The Investor is responsible for proxy voting.

All of this stuff only applies if you are working with an advisor. If you are working with an advisor you will want to know what their responsibility is and what yours is. You will also want to know if they take discretion, meaning they can make trades on your behalf. We prefer to take discretion as we want to make moves when we deem them necessary and don't want to have to track down clients on vacation in the Caribbean. Be careful if you grant discretion to a commission-based advisor as this gives them carte blanche to churn your account and earn lots of commissions. It is also important to find out if your advisor takes title to your assets or they stay in your name. Obviously, you want your assets to stay in your name.

VI. Investment Management

Overview

In designing your personal investment strategy, we began by reviewing your objectives and constraints. We then developed recommendations appropriate for you.

Investment Objectives

Your investment objectives have been established based on an understanding of your current and projected financial requirements. These investment objectives are to:

- Maintain your current lifestyle during your retirement years. We understand this to mean approximately $XX,XXX after tax annually in today's dollars.
- Develop specific guidelines and limitations for you to ensure that assets are being managed in accordance with your goals and objectives.
- Preserve principal. Reasonable efforts should be made to preserve principal, but preservation of principal shall not be imposed on each individual investment.
- Maintain flexibility in setting future strategic allocations.

- Achieve a favorable long-term, real rate of return in order to build your investment portfolio to provide for future financial needs.
- Reduce risk by diversifying markets, managers, and maturity dates.

What are your goals and objectives? These are the reasons you are investing the way you are investing. It helps to have goals in writing. A study was once done at an Ivy League college in the 1950s (Harvard or Yale, I don't remember which one). They asked the graduating class how many of them had written goals: It was only 3% of the class. They went back and surveyed the surviving members of the class years later and found that the 3% with written goals had amassed a net worth in excess of the other 97% combined.

VII. Guidelines and Investment Policy

Time Horizon

The investment guidelines are based upon a time horizon greater than five years, so that interim fluctuations should be viewed with appropriate perspective. Similarly, your Investment Policy is based on this long-term horizon.

Time horizon is not necessarily when you will start needing money from your investments. While you might be 2 years away from retirement, you might live another 40 years in retirement, so in my mind you still have a long-term time horizon. I have never been a fan of investment strategies that get you more conservative as you move closer to retirement because of the fact that you could live for so much longer and those types of strategies put you at risk for running out of money. I would much prefer to have to delay retirement a few years because of losses than run out of money at age 80 and try to find a job.

Risk Tolerances

You recognize the difficulty of achieving any specific investment objectives in light of the uncertainties and complexities of contemporary investment markets. You also recognize that some risk, primarily in the form of principal volatility, must be accepted in order to achieve your long-term investment objectives.

In establishing your risk tolerance, we have considered your ability to withstand short- and intermediate-term volatility. Based on our discussions and the composition of your current portfolio, we understand that you can accept, in the intermediate term, a high-volatility portfolio.

Your desire to plan for a standard of living of approximately $XX,XXX, after tax, per year, in today's dollars, requires that you adopt a long-term investment perspective.

In summary, your current financial condition, prospects for the future, and your personal attitudes suggest collectively that you are prepared to, and in fact need to, tolerate this intermediate-term fluctuation in your portfolio market value and rates of return in order to achieve your long-term objectives.

Your risk tolerance is going to be very important. If your investments are too risky for you, it will cause you personal pain and anguish and you will eventually panic and sell.

VIII. Guidelines and Investment Policy

Performance Expectations

Our recommended portfolio allocation is for an absolute return portfolio. A reasonable expectation for the long-term rate of return of the recommended portfolio is 6% greater than the rate of inflation as measured by the Consumer Price Index (CPI). This expectation is based on the assumption that future real rates of return will approximate the historic, long-term real rates of return experienced for each asset class in your Investment Policy. You realize that market performance fluctuates and that a 6% rate of return may not be meaningful during some periods.

What are your performance expectations? We find it is best to state this as a spread over inflation since it is the real return that matters. If inflation is 20% and you are up 15%, it might sound nice but in real terms you are losing money.

Rebalancing

On a yearly basis, the account shall be reviewed to determine if the portfolio composition is consistent with the asset allocation variance within the limits established. If not, it is rebalanced to maintain the risk/reward relationship implied by the stated long-term objectives. This process may result in withdrawing assets from the investment managers who have performed well, or adding assets to managers who have lagged in the most recent period. This policy may necessitate the purchase and/or sales of securities, which might create additional transaction costs to the account and the recognition of capital gains and/or losses.

How often will you rebalance?

In summary, the most essential aspect of developing an investment policy that addresses more than just your immediate concerns is determining how your assets should be allocated among major asset classes. By diversifying appropriately, you take advantage of the current and expected economic climate, while ensuring that you will generally have some assets that perform well regardless of changes in economic conditions.

IX. Portfolio Review and Analysis

Proposed Portfolio

Commentary: The proposed portfolio is designed to produce absolute returns that are not correlated with the stock market.

Asset Class	Allocation
Absolute Return	25%
Equity	30%
Fixed Income	15%
Energy & Natural Resources	24%
Real Estate	3%
Cash	3%
	100%

Manager Security Guidelines

Money managers will be given wide latitude within their chosen style; however, we will look for the following:

- Managers shall have the discretion to invest a portion of the assets in cash reserves when they deem appropriate. However, the managers should, in accordance with Association for Investment Management and Research (AIMR) standards, be evaluated against their benchmark based on the performance of the total funds under their direct management.
- Managers should generally have long-term positive alphas and favorable Sharpe ratios as compared to comparable style managers.

- Managers should generally have at least a three-year operating history within their fund or managing a similar style.

This lists your guidelines for selecting money managers; this can also be for individual stocks and bonds.

Selection of Money Managers: The Tuttle Wealth Management, LLC Portfolio Investment Process

Step 1 →	Step 2 →	Step 3
Asset Allocation	Manager Selection	Risk Management
▶ Macro and market analysis ▶ Global theme development ▶ Target strategy allocation ▶ Overweight and underweight classes and sectors	▶ Extensive due diligence qualitative and quantitative ▶ Maintain bench team of future managers	▶ Identify risks affecting managers and markets ▶ Monitor, measure, and understand portfolio risks ▶ Determine portfolio's strengths and needs ▶ Take action and prevent surprises

Evaluating the Managers

The following items should be available for manager evaluation:

- A clearly articulated investment philosophy and process and documentation that the philosophy has been successfully adhered to over time
- Detailed information on the history of the firm, the fund, and key personnel
- History of asset growth, volatility, style, and expenses
- Historical monthly performance figures
- Performance evaluation reports prepared by an objective third party that illustrate the risk/return profile of the manager relative to other managers of like investment style

This is the process you will go through in selecting money managers. Again, this could be for individual stocks and bonds.

X. Monitoring of Money Managers

Review of Money Managers

On a timely basis, but no less than quarterly, the following will be reviewed:

- Managers' adherence to their stated and implied investment style
- Material changes in the manager's organization, investment philosophy, and/or personnel
- Comparisons of the manager's results to appropriate indices

Absolute Return	HFRI Fund of Funds
Domestic equity managers:	S&P 500 Index, Russell 2000, NASDAQ, Morningstar
Fixed income:	One- and Two-Year Treasuries, Lehman 1- to 3-Year Govt., Lehman Aggregate, Lehman Municipal
International equity:	MSCI EMF ID, MSCI EAFE ND
Real assets:	GSCI, Dow Jones-AIG, Wilshire REIT

Guidelines for Corrective Action

Corrective action should be taken as a result of an ongoing investment manager review process. The following are instances where corrective action or termination may be in order:

1. Major organizational changes in the firm, including any changes in portfolio managers
2. Style drift
3. Overall restructuring
4. Long-term underperformance
5. Other events or circumstances that are deemed in the best interest of the client

This states how you will monitor money managers and when you will take corrective action.

XI. Monitoring of Portfolio

Reports

The investment custodian shall provide monthly statements for each account held. Such reports will show values for each asset and all transactions affecting assets within the portfolio, including additions and withdrawals.

Advisor will provide quarterly reports showing portfolio performance over the past quarter, year to date, and since inception.

Meetings and Communications

As a matter of course, the Advisor shall keep the Investor apprised of any material changes in the Advisor's outlook, recommended investment policy, and tactics. The Advisor will be available to meet with the Investor within reason. Investor will have the opportunity to meet or schedule a conference call to discuss quarterly reports.

This stuff only matters if you are working with an advisor. It is important to know what kind of reports you will get and how often you will communicate with your advisor. Some advisors set up quarterly meetings; others might prefer to meet as often as you need, with a minimum of at least one meeting/year.

Your IPS will serve as a guide for all of your investment decisions. If you come across a new opportunity and it doesn't fit in with your IPS, then you won't do it. For example, someone called me with a great investment opportunity after seeing me on TV. He needed $2 million for a membership service he was creating which was sure to generate lots of money. In my experience, if an investment is really good I would be begging to get in on it, not the other way around. Since it didn't fit into my IPS, I had to take a pass.

If you are retired, you will also have to come up with a spending policy.

Spending Policy

If you are retired you will likely need to be taking withdrawals from your accounts every month to supplement your income (Social Security, pensions, etc.). Endowments are like retirees in that they also must have a spending policy that keeps the principal intact while still able to spend what they need to meet their mandate.

Today's retiree faces five key risks in planning for lifetime income: longevity risk, inflation risk, investment risk, health-care cost risk, and withdrawal risk.

Longevity Risk

Since 1900, medical science has extended the average life span by 31 years! According to the Society of Actuaries, a 65-year-old male now has a 50% chance of living to age 85 and a 25% chance of living to age 92. A 65-year-old female has a 50% chance of living to age 88 and 25% chance of living to age 94. A 65-year-old couple has a 50% chance that one of them will live to age 92. This means that a person retiring at 65 might live 30 years or more with no salary coming in—a scary thought, isn't it? When planning your lifetime income needs, you need to plan as if you will be around for a long time.

Inflation Risk

Conventional advice used to be to place all of your money in fixed-income investments and live off the interest. You know how I feel about fixed income from earlier parts of the book. Because people are living longer, they will have to deal with inflation. For example, let's assume you are a retiree in 2006 who is living on $72,058 a year. At a 3% inflation rate, your income need 25 years from now will be $150,873, more than double what it is today. Just think what would happen if you put all of your money into fixed-income investments that generated $72,000 a year. In 25 years, they would still be generating that same $72,000. What would you do then? The bad news is that 3% may not even be that realistic. A study done by Families USA found that between 1994 and 1999, prices for the 50 most commonly prescribed drugs for older Americans rose 25.2%—nearly twice the overall inflation rate for the same five-year period. Also, when the news talks about inflation numbers, they like to strip out food and energy, but last time I looked that's what I spend the majority of my money on.

Investment Risk

Anyone who had his or her money invested in the stock market from 2000 to 2002 understands what I am talking about here. The value of the stock market went down more than 40%. Because of longevity and inflation, most retirees cannot afford to absorb the kind of market losses we saw during those years. According to a study commissioned by the AARP, among investors age 50 to 70 who lost money in stocks, 76% modified their current lifestyle or expectations of their retirement lifestyle. Of those who are not yet retired, one in five has postponed retirement. Of those who are retired, one in ten has returned to work.

This data might suggest that you adopt an ultraconservative strategy such as investing in CDs or AAA bonds, but don't forget longevity and inflation risk. This strategy won't keep up with inflation and won't work if you live a long time.

Let's assume we have three investors. Investor number 1 has a portfolio 100% in money market accounts; investor number 2 has a conservative portfolio of 20% stocks, 50% bonds, and 30% in money market accounts; and investor number 3 has a portfolio of 50% stocks, 40% bonds, and 10% in money market accounts. Using historical returns on these assets from 1926 to 2002 and assuming each investor is taking 5% (inflation adjusted) of his portfolio out every year for expenses, here is what happens after 25 years. Investor number 1 has a 100% chance of running out of money. Investor number 2 has a 60% chance of running out of money. Investor number 3 has only a 20% chance of running out of money.

Health-Care Cost Risk

A 2002 study by the Fidelity Employer Services Company estimates that a married couple retiring today at age 65 will need current savings of $160,000 to supplement Medicare and cover out-of-pocket health-care costs in retirement, unless they have an employer-funded retirement health plan. Unfortunately, these plans are evaporating fast. In the years from 1995 to 2001, the percentage that offered retiree health benefits fell from 35% to just 23% for companies employing more than 500 workers.

None of these estimates include long-term care expenses, which could run over $100,000 a year.

Withdrawal Risk

This is the risk of taking too much money out of your portfolio every year. The actual amount you should be withdrawing depends on your age, your health, your needs, and your desire to leave a legacy. During the late 1990s, I often met people who had been advised to withdraw 10% of their portfolio every year. After all, stocks were increasing by 30% a year, so why not?

Generally, I recommend that clients withdraw 4% to 5% per year from a diversified portfolio. Endowments typically fall into this range also. Whatever withdrawal rate you choose can have a significant impact on your net worth. Here is an example: Suppose you have a portfolio of 50% stocks, 40% bonds, and 10% money markets. The table that follows shows how long your portfolio would last using withdrawal rates from 4% to 10% and using historical returns from 1926 to 2002.

Withdrawal Rate	Projected Life of Portfolio (Years)
10%	11
9%	13
8%	15
7%	18
6%	21
5%	27
4%	33

Source: Fidelity Investments.

So, for example, if you had $100,000 and took out 4% per year, that would equate to $4,000. A 4% withdrawal rate does not offer guaranteed retirement security, but it is clear that rates much above that increase the risk that you will outlive your assets.

We don't want to forget about inflation, and we also understand that your account values can fluctuate from year to year, which can impact spending. Because of that we recommend using spending rules like most endowments use to smooth things out. Instead of just taking your withdrawal percentage and multiplying it by the account value each year, we recommend a more complicated approach that results in a more even yearly withdrawal. In the first year we just multiply the withdrawal amount that we choose by the account value. In the second year we apply the following formula and steps:

1. We take the prior year's withdrawal and increase it by inflation, as measured by the CPI; we weight this 70%.
2. We then take our withdrawal percentage and multiply it by the year-end account value; we weight that 30%.

Once we have these two numbers, we add them together and that is that year's withdrawal amount.

So here is an example of what your spending might look like under this policy.

Year 1 Spending Policy

January 1 Account balance	$1,000,000
Spending rate:	4.5%
Year 1 Spending:	$45,000 ($1 million × 4.5%)

Year 2 Spending Policy

CPI	3%
December 31 Account balance	$1,200,000
Year 1 Spending adjusted for inflation:	$46,350 ($45,000 × 1.03 to increase for inflation) 70% weight
December 31 Account balance × 4.5% spending rate	$54,000 30% weight

Year 2 Spending = $48,645 (30% × $54,000) + (70% × $46,350)

With our spending policy, you would take less out of your account when it appreciates than you would if you just applied the 4.5% spending rate to the year-end account value.

Below is another example of what would happen if your account went down in value.

Year 1 Spending Policy

January 1 Account balance	$1,000,000
Spending rate:	4.5%
Year 1 Spending:	$45,000 ($1 million × 4.5%)

Year 2 Spending Policy

CPI	3%
December 31 Account balance	$850,000
Year 1 Spending adjusted for inflation:	$46,350 ($45,000 × 1.03 to increase for inflation) 70% weight
December 31 Account balance × 4.5% spending rate	$38,250 30% weight

Year 2 Spending = $43,920 (30% × $38,250) + (70% × $46,350)

With our spending policy, you would take more out when the account declines than if you had just applied the 4.5% spending rate to the year-end account value.

Using this smoothing method will smooth out the withdrawals.

Your spending policy becomes part of your IPS.

Final Thoughts

Years ago, Harvard, Yale, and other large college endowments took a risk by thinking outside the box about how a portfolio should be managed. The result has been year after year of outperforming the market with less risk. As an individual investor, some of the strategies and money managers these endowments use are out of your reach, but the ideas and the philosophies are not. I challenge you to also think outside the box when it relates to your investments. The investment industry is slowly moving toward an endowment, absolute return approach. More and more mutual funds get introduced each day that have an absolute return focus. Hedge funds are increasingly becoming a more important force in the marketplace. With all of these new products, structuring an endowment type of portfolio will only become easier.

Appendix

KEY TERMS

Below are some helpful definitions of some of the terms I used throughout this book. Investing is complicated and terms that might be very familiar to me might sound like a foreign language to you. I hope this is helpful.

accredited investor According to the SEC, an accredited investor is at least one of the following:

1. A bank, insurance company, registered investment company, business development company, or small business investment company

2. An employee benefit plan, within the meaning of the Employee Retirement Income Security Act, if a bank, insurance company, or registered investment advisor makes the investment decisions, or if the plan has total assets in excess of $5 million

3. A charitable organization, corporation, or partnership with assets exceeding $5 million

4. A director, executive officer, or general partner of the company selling the securities

5. A business in which all the equity owners are accredited investors

6. A natural person who has individual net worth, or joint net worth with the person's spouse, that exceeds $1 million at the time of the purchase

7. A natural person with income exceeding $200,000 in each of the two most recent years or joint income with a spouse exceeding $300,000 for those years and a reasonable expectation of the same income level in the current year

8. A trust with assets in excess of $5 million, not formed to acquire the securities offered, whose purchases a sophisticated person makes

Hedge funds, hedge fund of funds, and private equity funds are only available to accredited investors.

alpha Alpha is a measure of excess return. In a perfect world if money managers took as much risk as the market, they would have the same return. If they took less risk, they would have less return, and more risk would mean more return. A positive alpha shows that a money manager is providing more return than expected given how much risk it is taking. For example, the Vanguard 500 Index Fund tracks the S&P 500 without deviation. The only difference between it and the index is that it charges a fee. According to Morningstar, as of 5/31/08 it had an alpha of –.12. It takes the same risk as the market but because of its fee it slightly underperforms. On the other hand, the Fidelity Contrafund beats the market pretty consistently. It takes a little more risk than the market (S&P 500) but has almost doubled the return over the past three years. According to Morningstar, as of 5/31/08 its alpha was 5.74.

Investors need to be careful with alpha in that they cannot compare apples to oranges. For example, comparing the alpha of a stock fund and a bond fund would not be very useful. Alpha is best used as a way to compare like funds. Alpha can also be used to compare different portfolios.

beta The measure of an asset's risk relative to the market. An asset with a beta of 1 should move up and down as much as the market. An asset with a beta of 1.5 will move 1.5 times more up and down. An asset with a beta of .5 will move half as much up and down. (More precisely beta refers to excess return, not actual return. For our purposes, the higher the beta the higher the risk.)

Alpha and beta are very important concepts throughout this book. Traditional money managers get most of their return from beta whereas the money managers that endowments use get most of their return from alpha.

Black Swan The term *black swan* comes from the book *The Black Swan: The Impact of the Highly Improbable* by Nassim Nicholas Taleb. For centuries, Europeans believed that black swans didn't exist because nobody had ever seen one. Then one day someone discovered a black swan. Wall Street works the same way; they assume that if they haven't seen something happen it won't ever happen—until it actually does. Black swan events happen quite often like the 1987 stock market crash, the 1998 Asian Contagion, the 2000 bursting of the technology bubble, and the current subprime credit crisis. These types of happenings are also referred to as fat tail events. The standard deviation of an investment tells us the range where 95% of returns for that investment should fall. *Should* is the key word here. The 5% not predicted by standard deviation are the tails of the distribution of returns. Unfortunately, investments have a nasty habit of falling outside of their predicted range, usually to the downside, more than 5% of the time. This is a fat tail event.

correlation Correlation is a measure of how assets move or don't move together at the same time. A positive correlation of 1 means that assets move in exactly the same direction. When one goes up so does the other. A negative correlation of 1 means that assets move in exactly the opposite direction—when one goes up the other goes down. A correlation of 0 means that assets have no direct relationship at all. In order to have a diversified portfolio, it is essential to add assets that have a very low or negative correlation.

emerging markets' stocks and bonds Stocks and bonds issued by developing countries.

fundamental analysis Fundamental analysis involves analyzing data about a company or market to make investment decisions. For example, when a fundamental analyst looks at a stock he or she might look at earnings, debt, projected earnings, etc.

international stocks Stocks of companies that are based in other countries.

large-cap growth stock A stock of a large company that is expected to grow in the future. These are usually technology stocks, biotechnology stocks, and so on.

large-cap value stock A stock of a large company that is deemed to be undervalued. These are usually financial stocks, industrial stocks, and so on.

long When you buy something hoping it will rise in value. For example, if I buy 100 shares of Microsoft, I am long 100 shares.

maximum drawdown This is the worst loss, peak to trough, that a money manager can suffer. This gives you a good idea of the risk of an investment because if it can go down a certain amount in the past, it can also go down the same amount or more in the future.

mid-cap growth stock Stocks of medium-sized companies that are expected to grow.

mid-cap value stock Stocks of medium-sized companies that are undervalued.

net asset value (NAV) The value of all the assets of a mutual fund divided by the shares outstanding. When you see mutual funds quoted in the newspaper or on the Internet, they are quoted NAV. For example, if a fund has $1,000 in total assets and has 1,000 shares outstanding, the NAV will be 1 (1,000 ÷ 1,000). No-load funds are purchased at NAV whereas load funds might have a front end or back end sales charge.

qualified purchaser According to the SEC, a qualified purchaser is at least one of the following:

1. Individuals who own $5 million in investments, which include securities, financial contracts entered into for investment purposes, cash, cash equivalents held for investment purposes, real estate held for investment purposes, CDs, bankers acceptances and other similar bank instruments held for investment purposes. Investments do not include real estate held for personal purposes, jewelry, art, antiques, and other collectibles. Debt used to acquire the investments is excluded from the value of the investments

2. Institutional investors who own $25 million in investments

3. A family-owned company that owns $5 million in investments

4. For trusts with less than $25 million, a trust where the trustee and each person who contributes assets to the trust is a Qualified Purchaser

5. A "Qualified Institutional Buyer" under Rule 144A of the Securities Act of 1933, except that "dealers" under Rule 144 must meet the $25 million standard of the 1940 Act, rather than the $10 million standard of Rule 144A. Rule 144A generally defines a "Qualified Institutional Buyer" as institutions, including registered Investment Companies, that own and invest on a discretionary basis $100 million of securities that are affiliated with the institution, banks

that own and invest on a discretionary basis $100 million in QIB securities and have an audited net worth of $25 million, and certain registered dealers

6. A company owned beneficially only by Qualified Purchasers; however, a company will not be deemed to be a qualified purchaser if it was formed for the specific purposes of acquiring the securities offered by a 3(c)(7) fund

Some hedge funds, fund of funds, and private equity investments are only available to qualified purchasers.

real returns Real returns are your returns after inflation. For example, if you have an investment that went up 7% while inflation was up 3%, then your real return was 4% (7% – 4%). It is important to think about returns in real terms. You might have an investment that goes up 50% but if inflation is up 60%, then in real terms you actually have less money than you started with because even though your actual money went up by 50%, it is not worth as much as it was because inflation went up even more.

Sharpe ratio A risk-adjusted return measure developed by William F. Sharpe, calculated using standard deviation and the return over and above a risk-free rate such as T-bills. The higher the Sharpe ratio for an investment, the better the risk-adjusted return.

short When you sell something you don't own, hoping it will go down in value so you can buy it back at a lower price. For example, XYZ stock is currently trading at $100/share, and I think it is going lower. I borrow 100 shares from my broker and sell them, netting $10,000 ($100/share × 100 shares). Later, when the shares are trading at $50/share, I buy the 100 shares back for $5,000 ($50/share × 100 shares) and return them to my broker, and I make $5,000 (my $10,000 from selling the stock short minus the $5,000 it cost to buy it back).

small-cap growth stock Stocks of small companies that are expected to grow.

small-cap value stock Stocks of small companies that are undervalued.

standard deviation Standard deviation is a measure of risk. It shows how much an investment moves around its average return. The higher the number, the higher the risk will be. For example, if a mutual fund averaged 10%/year over a five-year period and every year it was up 10%, it would have a standard deviation of 0. The more an investment moves from year to year, the higher the standard deviation. Table A.1 shows a few examples of investments that average 10% but have different standard deviations. Just looking at average annual return is not enough; all other things being equal, you would think that Investment A is superior to Investment B and Investment C.

Statistically speaking, an investment would be expected to differ from its average annual return by no more than plus or minus the standard deviation approximately 68% of the time. Approximately 95% of the time the investment's return should be within a range of plus or minus 2 standard deviations, and 99.7% of the time it should move no more than 3 standard deviations. So investment B should fall between −16.22% and 36.22% 68% of the time, between −42.44% and 62.44% 95% of the time, and between −68.66% and 88.66% 99.7% of the time.

Standard deviation is extremely important when looking at an investment. Most investors just focus on average return. This reminds me of the story of the statistician who drowned in a lake where the water averaged 12 inches deep! He just looked at the average, not the standard deviation which would have told him that there were places in the lake that were 10 feet deep. Investors need to look at average returns *and* standard deviation when looking at investments.

Table A.1   Standard Deviation

	Investment A	Investment B	Investment C
Year 1	10%	5%	5%
Year 2	10%	20%	15%
Year 3	10%	−10%	5%
Year 4	10%	50%	15%
Year 5	10%	−15%	10%
Average annual return	10%	10%	10%
Standard deviation	0.00	26.22	5.00

stop order A stop is an order placed below the current price if you are long or above the current price if you are short. For example, a futures trader might buy gold today at $906/oz and to protect him- or herself might place a stop order at $900/oz. If gold went down to $900/oz then his or her position would automatically be sold.

style box A term used to describe what types of investments a money manager makes, that is, a money manager who buys large-cap growth stocks would fall into the large-cap growth style box.

technical analysis A technical analyst believes that everything known about a stock or a market is already reflected in its price. Therefore, technical analysts use all sorts of tools to predict whether a price will go up or down based on its current and past activity.

About the Author

Matthew Tuttle is a nationally renowned money manager and SEC Registered Investment Advisor who specializes in absolute return investment strategies. He is a frequent guest on Fox Business News, CNBC, BusinessWeek TV, CNN, and Yahoo Finance. He is frequently quoted in the *Wall Street Journal,* the *New York Times,* CNBC.com, *Forbes, SmartMoney, Kiplinger's Personal Finance,* the *Christian Science Monitor, USA Today, Greenwich Time, Journal of Financial Planning,* and many other publications.

Matthew is the author of *Financial Secrets of My Wealthy Grandparents.* He has also written two chapters for the *Life Insurance Answer Book* and contributed to *The Wealth Management Manual* and *Sid Kess' Practical Alternatives to Commonly Misused and Abused Small Business Tax Strategies.*

Matthew is President of Tuttle Wealth Management, LLC, and a partner in the Private Client Group, LLC, where he oversees investment services. He is a Certified Financial Planner™ Professional and has an MBA in Finance.

Matthew lives in Greenwich Connecticut, with his wife, Jarah; daughter, Cameron; and sons, Jared and Braden.

Tuttle Wealth Management, LLC
1 Stamford Plaza, 263 Tresser Blvd. 9th Floor
Stamford, CT 06901
203-564-1956
800-462-1655
matthew@matthewtuttle.com
www.matthewtuttle.com

Certified Financial Planner Board of Standards, Inc. owns the certification marks CFP®, Certified Financial Planner™ and federally registered CFP (with flame logo) in the U.S., which it awards to individuals who successfully complete CFP Board's initial and ongoing certification requirements.

Index